SHOCKTOBER

SHOCKTOBER

The BIGGEST UPSETS *in* WORLD SERIES HISTORY

JONATHAN WEEKS

LYONS
PRESS

Essex, Connecticut

An imprint of The Globe Pequot Publishing Group, Inc.
64 South Main Street
Essex, CT 06426
www.globepequot.com

Distributed by NATIONAL BOOK NETWORK

British Library Cataloguing in Publication Information available

Library of Congress Cataloging-in-Publication Data available

ISBN 978-1-4930-8703-7 (paperback)
ISBN 978-1-4930-8704-4 (e-book)

∞™ The paper used in this publication meets the minimum requirements of American National Standard for Information Sciences—Permanence of Paper for Printed Library Materials, ANSI/ NISO Z39.48-1992.

Contents

CONTENTS

INTRODUCTION

Although the first official World Series took place in 1903, there were earlier tournaments held to crown the champions of baseball. Beginning in 1884 and continuing for several years, National League pennant winners squared off against rival American Association teams. There were no set rules determining the format and the matchups (often referred to as the "World's Championship Series") varied from three to 15 games.

At the end of the 1891 campaign, the NL merged with the American Association, forming a single 12-team circuit. A split-season format was adopted followed by a championship playoff. The 1892 showdown matched the Boston club (popularly known as the "Beaneaters") against the Cleveland Spiders. In spite of excellent attendance figures, league executives opted to abandon the arrangement and shorten the schedule the following year.

The idea of a postseason tournament was revived in 1894, when Pirates' executive William Chase Temple furnished the NL with an ornate silver trophy to be awarded annually to the league champions. The Temple Cup Series, which pitted the top two National League squads against one another in a best-of-seven showdown, continued uninterrupted for four years. But trouble arose during the inaugural playoff when members of the Giants allegedly cheated various Orioles players out of their postseason shares. The second-place teams won three of the four matchups, prompting fans and players to question the validity of the event. Enthusiasm wavered among both, and the series was discontinued after the 1897 campaign.

Postseason baseball returned in 1900, when a local Pittsburgh newspaper sponsored a best-of-five playoff between the first- and second-place NL teams. The Chronicle-Telegraph Cup—a one-and-done affair—pitted the runner-up Pirates against the pennant-winning Brooklyn Superbas. Brooklyn won handily and there were no championship series for the next two years.

The founding of the American League (AL) led to an ugly clash between the two rival circuits. Aptly describing the chicanery that took place in the early days, researcher Eric Enders wrote, "It all started with a war. For two years after the American League declared itself a major league in 1901, it fought a bitter battle with the National League for supremacy of the United States. Contracts were broken, lawsuits were filed, and the two sides bickered at each other in the press. The American League, in its quest for legitimacy, staged a full-frontal assault on the National, signing away many of its best players."

For a brief period, the balance of power shifted in favor of the AL as junior circuit clubs began outdrawing their National League counterparts. In 1903, representatives from both leagues finally agreed to put an end to the roster raids that had been plaguing the sport. Near the end of the 1903 campaign, Pirates owner Barney Dreyfuss sent a letter to Boston Americans owner Henry J. Killilea, challenging his club to a postseason showdown. Killilea consulted with AL president Ban Johnson, who jumped at the opportunity to prove the superiority of his circuit. "Play them and beat them," Johnson said gravely. "You *must* beat them."

The two executives agreed to a best-of-nine format with games taking place at Boston's Huntington Avenue Grounds and Pittsburgh's Exposition Park. The Pirates jumped out to a three-to-one Series lead before suffering four consecutive defeats at the hands of the Americans. With the exception of 1904 (owners' dispute) and 1994 (players' strike), the World Series has remained an unbroken annual tradition ever since.

Baseball's October showcase has provided some high drama over the years. Willie Mays's spectacular catch in 1954, Bill Mazeroski's walk-off homer in 1960, and Kirk Gibson's pinch-hit blast in 1988 are just a few of the memorable moments that have dominated highlight reels. The outcome of the Series has not always been terribly surprising—especially during the late 1940s and early 1950s when the Yankees captured five consecutive championships, breaking their previous record of four straight titles from 1936 to 1939. But in spite of its predictability at times, the Fall Classic has taken many unexpected turns. The 1906 Cubs lost to the weak-hitting White Sox after establishing a new regular-season record for wins. The 1955 Dodgers avenged seven prior October failures with an improbable victory over the seemingly invincible Yankees. And in 1969, the Mets finally shed their image as "loveable losers," dethroning the powerful Orioles. In more than a century of World Series play, a number of similar scenarios have emerged. Those stories are told on the pages ahead.

CHAPTER I

White Sox vs. Cubs 1906

AMONG THE FIERCEST COMPETITORS OF ALL TIME, TY COBB ONCE described baseball in the early twentieth century as follows: "It's no pink tea and the mollycoddles had better stay out. It's a struggle for supremacy, a survival of the fittest." Few who played the game during the Deadball Era challenged Cobb's point of view.

Although existing rules prohibited the defacing of baseballs, monetary fines were light and seldom enforced. Pitchers routinely scuffed balls or moistened them with sweat, tobacco juice, and slippery elm bark. Umpires made things even more difficult for batters by keeping balls in play until they were misshapen and spongy. Fans were actually encouraged to return fouls hit into the stands (sometimes under threat of arrest). As a direct result, home runs were scarce. Dramatically illustrating the point, Cobb won the American League home run crown in 1909 without lifting a single fair ball over the outfield wall. All of his nine homers that year were of the inside-the-park variety.

With pitchers enjoying a number of unfair advantages, runs were manufactured one base at a time. Managers resorted to "small ball" strategies, moving players around the basepaths by bunting, stealing, and sacrificing. Most hitters chopped down on the ball or "slapped" pitches into the outfield gaps. Ballparks typically had short foul lines and cavernous alleys. To keep batters on their heels, pitchers deliberately threw at them to move them off the plate. Infielder Hughie Jennings, who appeared in more than 1,200 games between 1891 and 1903, was beaned 287 times—a painful record that is likely to stand forever.

The life of a pitcher was no picnic either. There was no such thing as a "reliever" in the game's early days. Hurlers frequently worked on short rest and were expected to go the distance. Through the entire 1904 campaign, Boston manager Jimmy Collins pulled his starters just nine times. Most teams used a bullpen-by-committee format, and it wasn't until the late 1940s that moundsmen came to be groomed exclusively for relief.

After capturing a pennant in 1904, Giants owner John T. Brush refused to participate in the World Series, claiming that it would tarnish the reputation of the National League to face an inferior opponent. He altered his stance during the offseason, drafting a set of guidelines regulating October play. The "Brush Rules" were officially adopted by major-league executives and the 1905 Fall Classic went off without a hitch. Christy Mathewson delivered one of the most masterful performances in postseason history, shutting out the Philadelphia Athletics three times as Brush's Giants captured their first official World Series title.

Although the Giants and A's were favored to repeat as league champions, the White Sox entered the 1906 campaign with high hopes. Compensating for an anemic offense that produced one of the worst collective batting averages in the majors, Chicago's dynamic pitching staff kept the club in contention throughout the 1905 slate. Frank Owen and Nick Altrock formed a potent one-two punch at the front end of the rotation, combining for 44 wins and a 1.99 ERA. Doc White—a hard-throwing southpaw who set a long-standing major-league record in 1904 with five consecutive shutouts—added 17 victories of his own as the Sox finished just two games behind the A's. The addition of Ed Walsh as a full-time starter in 1906 strengthened the team considerably.

A fiery right-hander with an elusive spitball, Walsh averaged more than 360 innings of work in a seven-year span. The result was a lame arm that kept him on the bench during the latter stages of his career. His 1.82 lifetime ERA—the lowest in major-league history—ensured his election to Cooperstown. Describing the movement on Walsh's pitches, Detroit Tigers great Sam Crawford remarked, "I think that ball disintegrated on the way to the plate and the catcher put it back together again. I swear when it went past the plate, it was just the spit that went by."

Figure 1.1 Ed Walsh's 1.82 lifetime ERA is the lowest of all time. He won two games for the White Sox in the 1906 World Series.
PHOTO COURTESY OF THE LIBRARY OF CONGRESS.

In the absence of strong pitching, the Sox would likely have been perennial non-contenders. They hit .242 as a collective unit from 1903 through 1905. Their .230 team batting average in 1906—worst among any pennant-winning squad in history—earned them the dubious nickname the "Hitless Wonders." But player/manager Fielder Jones knew how to make the most of his club's limited opportunities. A clever strategist, he encouraged his men to exercise patience at the plate and use their speed to an advantage. It paid great dividends as Chicago placed no lower than third during Jones's four full seasons at the helm.

The most accomplished hitter on the club was shortstop George Davis. Known to many as "Gorgeous George" for his handsome features and smooth defensive play, he kept his batting average above the .300 mark for nine consecutive campaigns. A reliable clean-up man, he paced the Sox in doubles and RBIs in 1906. He also finished among the AL leaders in multiple defensive categories. His career achievements went largely unrecognized until 1998, when the Veterans Committee posthumously voted him into the Hall of Fame.

Nicknamed the "Bald Eagle" on account of his vanishing hairline, Frank Isbell was one of the most versatile players in the majors. By the time he completed his nine-year stint with the White Sox, he had appeared at every position on the diamond—an extraordinary feat for a player of any era. Isbell had excellent speed and a knack for finding the outfield gaps. He put forth one of his finest offensive efforts in 1906, leading the team with 11 triples and 37 steals.

The 1906 campaign held few surprises in the first half as the A's hovered near the top of the standings through the end of July. The ChiSox caught fire in August, assembling an incredible 19-game winning streak. Their 21–4 record during the month gave them a precarious lead. As the Athletics fell into a prolonged slump, the New York Highlanders made a serious bid, trading places with Chicago multiple times in September. A strong late-season run allowed the Sox to clinch the pennant with three games remaining.

The National League race was not as hotly contested. Playing as the Colts and later as Orphans, the other Chicago club finished in fourth place or lower for 11 straight seasons. But a steady incursion of talent at the turn of the century brought them to the brink of a dynasty. By 1906, the Cubs (renamed for their youth and vast potential) were arguably the strongest team in the majors.

In addition to Johnny Kling—one of the premier defensive catchers of the era—the Cubs had a trio of Hall of Famers anchoring their infield. Double play partners Frank Chance, Johnny Evers, and Joe Tinker worked so efficiently together that they became the subject of a famous poem penned by *New York Evening Mail* columnist Franklin Pierce Adams. In the enduring composition (titled "Baseball's Sad Lexicon"), Adams complained that Chicago's "trio of bear cubs" had killed far too many New York Giant rallies with their defensive skills. "These are the saddest of possible words," Adams asserted, "Tinker, to Evers, to Chance."

Evers was regarded as one of the smartest players of his time. According to multiple sources, he spent several hours every night reading the rulebook in bed while binging on candy bars. His intricate knowledge of the sport paid off in 1908, when he single-handedly changed the course of the season by lodging a successful appeal to umpire Hank O'Day after Giants infielder Fred Merkle failed to touch second base on what should have been a game-winning hit. The contest was declared a tie, necessitating a winner-take-all playoff between the Cubs and Giants at season's end. A slick-fielding second baseman with a keen batting eye, Evers compiled the best strikeout-to-walk ratio of the Deadball Era. An incorrigible motormouth, he got into dozens of fights over the years. At 5-foot-9, 125 pounds, he rarely got the best of his opponents. "I wish he had been an outfielder so I wouldn't have to listen to him," Chance once joked.

A daring base runner and all-around tough competitor, Chance took over managerial responsibilities in 1905, guiding the club to four pennants and a pair of championships. The World Series was often his finest hour as he compiled a lifetime on-base percentage of .402 in postseason play. He led the National League with 57 stolen bases and 103 runs scored in 1906. He also finished among the league leaders in multiple defensive categories at first base.

Tinker was the least celebrated of Chicago's Hall of Fame infield trio, but by no means the least talented. His middling .262 lifetime batting average was not an accurate measure of his prowess at the plate. Giants pitching legend Christy Mathewson cited Tinker as one of the toughest batters he ever faced. And *Baseball Magazine* ranked him as the second-best shortstop in the National League behind Honus Wagner. With four fielding titles at his position, it's likely that Tinker would have captured several Gold Gloves had the award existed then.

Complementing a potent offense that paced the NL in runs, hits, and total bases, the Cubs' pitching staff was virtually unhittable in 1906, tossing 28 complete game shutouts. The most reliable hurler by far was Mordecai Brown—a 20-game winner in six consecutive seasons. A pair of childhood misadventures had left him with a permanently disfigured hand that produced dramatic movement on his pitches. Describing his durability and coolness under fire, Evers once remarked: "[Brown] had plenty of nerve, ability, and willingness to work at all times under any conditions. Crowds never bothered him." The right-handed curveballer enjoyed one of his greatest seasons in 1906, winning 26 games while posting a 1.04 earned run average—the second-lowest mark of the Dead-ball Era among pitchers with at least 200 innings of work.

The Giants got off to a hot start, compiling a 12–3 record in April. But they had difficulty keeping pace with the Cubs, who set the all-time standard for wins in a season with 116. Incredibly, the New Yorkers finished 20 games behind Chicago in spite of their 96 victories, which exceeded the total of every pennant-winning AL squad of the decade to that point.

Entering the postseason, the Cubs had won 50 of their last 57 games, making them an obvious favorite among sportswriters and odds makers. Evaluating the showdown in later years, one researcher remarked: "It was a classic matchup of heavyweight vs. featherweight." Writers of the era repeatedly drew comparisons to David and Goliath. Making a Cubs' victory seem even more inevitable from the onset, ChiSox slugger George Davis fell ill at season's end and was unavailable for the Series opener.

Chicago was seized by baseball fever. A number of hotels were filled to capacity as people came from faraway places to witness the first intracity battle of the twentieth century. The opener took place at West Side Grounds—home of the Cubs. A chilly day with scattered flurries prompted fans to don their winter garb. Although the stadium was capable of holding 16,000, the inhospitable weather kept many fans away. The pitching matchup featured Altrock (owner of a 20–13 record during the regular season) against Brown. The two hurlers matched zeros until the fifth inning, when Sox third baseman George Rohe led off with a triple and scored on a rare error by Kling. The ChiSox added another run in the sixth on an RBI single by Isbell. Cutting the lead in half, the Cubs broke through with a run in the bottom of the frame. It was Altrock's only hiccup of the afternoon as he came out on the winning end of a 2–1 decision.

Figure 1.2 Mordecai "Three Finger" Brown (pictured here on a tobacco card) was a 20-game winner in six straight seasons for the Cubs.
PHOTO COURTESY OF THE LIBRARY OF CONGRESS.

Since the two stadiums were located in close proximity, games were played on consecutive days at alternating sites. The second meeting was held at South Side Park, which had a seating capacity of around 13,000. Brisk temperatures inspired many fans to stay away, and White Sox executives began to worry about meager financial returns. The game was a bust for the home team as right-hander Ed Reulbach, who had led the National League with a .826 winning percentage, tossed a one-hitter. Tinker scored three runs as the Cubs breezed to a 7–1 win.

Attendance was below capacity again for Game 3—a Thursday matinee at West Side Grounds. Shortly before the first pitch, a mischievous fan set a chicken loose on the field. Clad in a pair of white socks, it strutted around the outfield throughout the game, occasionally dodging projectiles hurled by disgruntled Cubs fans. Walsh was dominant for the Sox, allowing just two hits and one walk all afternoon while piling up 12 strikeouts. The big blow for the visitors came in the top of the sixth, when Rohe—a .333 hitter during the Series—delivered a bases-loaded triple off of southpaw Jack Pfiester. There was a scary moment just moments before then. With nobody out and a pair of runners aboard, right fielder Ed Hahn was hit directly in the face with a pitch. He collapsed to the ground with blood streaming from a broken nose. Although he was removed from the game, he returned to play in each of the remaining contests, gathering four hits in the finale.

An overflow crowd saw the Cubs get back on track at South Side Park the following day. Brown delivered the finest postseason performance of his career (a two-hit shutout), striking out five and walking a pair of batters. Runs were scarce against Altrock as well, but one proved to be enough as the Cubs evened the Series at two games apiece with a nail-biting victory.

The next meeting brought about something entirely unexpected—an offensive explosion. Isbell led the way for the visitors, pounding four doubles as three Cubs pitchers yielded a total of eight runs. The Sox had a few troubles of their own, committing six costly errors that led to five unearned runs and an early exit for Walsh, who was pitching for the second time in three days. The 8–6 White Sox victory stunned members of the Cubs, who suddenly found themselves on the brink of elimination.

Game 6 began on a sour note for the National Leaguers when Cap Anson, who had managed the Cubs to their last pennant in 1886, was asked to leave the visitor's dugout. Anson hadn't played or managed in nearly a decade, prompting umpire Silk O'Loughlin to enforce a seldom-invoked rule that allowed only active players on the bench. The Cubs drew first blood on an RBI double by outfielder Frank "Wildfire" Schulte. But manager Frank Chance made a glaring miscalculation when he sent Brown back to the hill on short rest. By the end of the second inning, the so-called Hitless Wonders had tagged the Cubs' exhausted staff ace for seven earned runs.

On the heels of a convincing 8–3 Series-clinching victory, Sox fans set bonfires in the streets and gathered around Fielder Jones's home to serenade him. An all-night celebration took place at the White City Amusement Park on Chicago's South Side. In an uncharacteristic display of frivolity, White Sox owner Charles Comiskey donated $15,000 of his own funds to enhance his players' postseason shares.

The Cubs recovered from the shocking loss, capturing three pennants and two World Series titles over the next four seasons. The White Sox went in a completely different direction, placing no higher than third for the rest of the decade. By 1910, only a handful of players from the over-achieving championship squad remained.

CHAPTER 2

Athletics vs. Braves 1914

AMERICAN AND NATIONAL LEAGUE EXECUTIVES FOUND THEMSELVES with unexpected competition in 1914 when the Federal League opened for business as a self-declared major league. The circuit had come together under the guidance of baseball promoter John T. Powers in 1913. Originally a minor league, the first season was played with six teams. Before the 1914 campaign, manufacturing mogul James A. Gilmore assembled a group of investors and restructured the circuit, expanding it to eight clubs—each stationed in a major city. Since Federal League teams operated outside of organized baseball's National Agreement (a set of contractual rules binding players to the organizations they signed with), Gilmore's "outlaw" league was able to lure a number of talented individuals away from established ballclubs. Hall of Famers Joe Tinker and Mordecai Brown were among the players to make the jump. The 1914 season opened with twenty-four top-level teams in three leagues spread from Massachusetts to Missouri.

In the AL, the Athletics were still the team to beat. Having won three World Series in a four-year span, they owed a great deal of their success to manager Connie Mack. The "Tall Tactitian" (as he came to be known) had started out as a catcher. He was noted for his innovative play, becoming one of the first backstops to position himself directly behind the batter. Before rules prohibiting the practice came into existence, he made a habit of deliberately dropping pop-ups to turn easy double plays. He was also known to tip the bats of opponents with his glove.

As a manager, Mack had a marvelous eye for talent and was willing to gamble on untested players—often signing them straight off of college campuses. His *New York Times* obituary declared that "No other manager in the history of the game handled more young players and brought more of them to stardom and fortune." Mack ran a tight ship but was not an autocrat. He never chastised his men in front of peers and avoided the use of profanity. He allowed players to make their own decisions on the field until it became detrimental to the team. Even then, he found a way to offer constructive criticism.

Universally admired by peers, Mack presided over two dynasties, guiding the A's to five pennants and three World Series titles between 1905 and 1914. He later steered the club to three consecutive AL championships in the late 1920s and early 1930s. By the time he retired, he had spent a total of 50 years at the Philly helm. Adhering to the old maxim, "If it isn't broke, don't fix it," Mack made few changes to the A's lineup in 1914.

In sharp contrast, the Braves were a team that had a long history of losing. Aside from one distant third-place finish in 1902, they had languished near the bottom of the standings throughout the twentieth century. This included four consecutive last-place finishes from 1909 through 1912. The club changed names multiple times in that span, playing as the Doves and (unofficially) the Rustlers before adopting the moniker they would carry into the next millennium. Improvement was evident in 1913, when the team climbed into fifth place under manager George Stallings.

Stallings was the polar opposite of Mack. Politely described by one researcher as "a frank person who freely spoke his mind without inhibition," the excitable Georgia native played in four games with the Brooklyn Bridegrooms in 1890. He inserted himself into three more games while managing the Phillies a few years later. His tactless interpersonal skills led to an open revolt among players that cost him his job in Philadelphia. Summarizing his character, a biographer from *TOTAL Baseball* wrote, "Stallings was a cultured southern gentleman off the field, but an unspeakable, profane monomaniac in the dugout. Some considered his use of vicious invective more devastating than John McGraw [one of the most abusive managers in baseball history]."

Highly superstitious, Stallings hated the color yellow. All yellow ball-park signs had to be painted over. He also loathed discarded peanut shells and scraps of paper. When Stallings's teams were doing well in a game, he would freeze like a statue, believing that the practice would prolong his good fortune. He did this even if it meant holding an uncomfortable pose.

Stallings was not opposed to cheating in order to secure victory for his clubs. While managing the New York Highlanders in 1909, he rented an apartment across the street from Hilltop Park with an unobstructed view of home plate. He then planted a spotter in the apartment equipped with binoculars. The spotter would watch the opposing catcher's signs and relay them to batters using a hand mirror. Since this only worked on sunny days, Stallings moved his sign-stealing operation beyond the outfield fence. The spotters utilized a crossbar apparatus located within an advertising sign on the outfield wall. A black crossbar signaled a fastball while a white bar indicated an impending breaking ball. The Highlanders were formally accused of cheating in a September 1909 issue of *Sporting Life*. The operation was shut down shortly afterward by Detroit manager Hughie Jennings, who sent his team trainer out to investigate. The crossbar device was promptly dismantled.

Referring to the 1914 Braves, Stallings described the roster as "one .300-hitter, the worst outfield that ever flirted with sudden death, three pitchers, and a good working tandem around second base."

The .300 hitter was left fielder Joe Connolly, whose brief major league career lasted from 1913 through 1916. He started out as a pitcher in the minors but was assigned to the outfield when he proved to be formidable with a bat. In his rookie season with the Braves, he led the team in runs, triples, and RBIs while hitting .281. He reached his peak in 1914 with a career-best .306 batting average. Hitting third in the Boston order, he finished among the league leaders in a number of offensive categories. A mediocre year in 1916 led to a dramatic salary cut. He refused to sign and was sold to a minor league affiliate.

Stallings's "good working tandem around second base" was comprised of Hall of Famers Johnny Evers and Rabbit Maranville. Playing in his thirteenth major league season, the 32-year-old Evers was the elder statesman of Boston's positional players. Awarded the honorary title of captain, he set a good example for his teammates with a club-best 87 walks and 81 runs scored. He also appeared among the league leaders in putouts, double plays, and assists. Hitting mostly out of the second slot in the order, his efforts ultimately led to the only MVP Award of his career (known then as "Chalmers Award"—named for the automobile manufacturer that sponsored it).

A fun-loving jokester, Maranville was one of the most colorful characters of the era. He once dove into a hotel fountain while intoxicated and emerged with a goldfish in his mouth. During a brief managerial stint with the Cubs in 1925, he paraded through a train car, dumping water on the heads of his sleeping ballplayers. Hall of Fame manager Joe McCarthy once said, "When I heard about [Maranville], about all the stuff he pulled, I said to myself for a fellow to do all those crazy things and still keep his job, he had to be a darned good ballplayer."

He was. And he kept his job as a player until the age of 43, when he finally retired.

Maranville picked up the nickname "Rabbit" on account of his diminutive size and darting speed on the basepaths. Primarily a singles hitter, his average typically hovered in the .250 range. He was more renowned for his glovework, leading the league in putouts seven times and fielding percentage on three occasions. Often used as a clean-up hitter in 1914 (a practice that seems questionable on the surface), he reached a career-high of 78 RBIs. He finished second to Evers in MVP voting.

Stallings has been credited as the first manager to use a platoon system. His maligned outfield was a combination of 11 different players who appeared in at least 14 games apiece. They weren't as bad as advertised. Although center fielder Les Mann and right fielder Larry Gilbert combined for 17 errors, they hit at a fairly respectable .254 clip, which was slightly above the league average. Mann's 11 triples were fifth in the National League.

It was Stallings's "three pitchers" who almost single-handedly carried the team to a pennant. Dick Rudolph, Bill James, and Lefty Tyler made 107 starts and accounted for more than 70 percent of the club's total win share in 1914. After that, they faded into obscurity.

A right-hander, the under-sized Rudolph (who stood 5-foot-9 and weighed 160 pounds) had three dominant seasons in the majors before succumbing to arm problems. From 1914 through 1916, he tossed 300 innings every year and won no fewer than 19 games. He had good speed and an excellent curve. He also toyed around with an occasional spitball.

James carried the nickname "Seattle Bill" to distinguish him from another deadball pitcher of the same name. After going 26–7 during the Braves pennant-winning effort of 1914, arm fatigue limited him to 13 appearances the following year. He never recovered. In the wake of multiple operations and comeback attempts, he retired with just 84 games to his credit.

Tyler posted double-digit win totals in seven consecutive seasons and played for two pennant-winning squads (the Braves in 1914 and Cubs in 1918). But he never emerged as a staff ace. Using a crossfire overhand delivery, he was known for his slow-moving changeup. His unorthodox style threw hitters off balance, enhancing the effectiveness of his fastball and sweeping curve. By the time he retired after his 12th season, he had gathered 127 wins.

While Stallings's starting rotation was a truncated combination of overachieving no-names, Mack had three Hall of Famers on his pitching staff. A Native American with Chippewa roots, Charles Bender picked up the politically incorrect nickname "Chief." He recalled being teased by children and teammates, who mocked him with native war cries. "I do not want my name to be presented in public as an Indian," he once told a reporter, "but as a pitcher." On the mound, he had superior control and an elusive curve. He threw from a variety of arm angles, including sidearm. He went 17–3 in 1914—the highest winning percentage in the majors.

Southpaw Eddie Plank arrived in Philadelphia without a shred of minor league experience. Using a fastball, change, curveball combination, he assembled an impressive lifetime total of 326 wins. A notoriously slow worker, he was once referred to as the "King of the Fidgets." He took his time between pitches, tugging at his belt, adjusting his cap, and moving his feet about listlessly. One biographer claimed that Plank's stalling tactics actually impacted attendance because fans coming from across town knew they would be late for their regular trains. The crafty left-hander was 38 years old in 1914, but still managed to pick up 15 wins in spite of his advancing age.

The third Hall of Famer on Mack's staff was a 20-year-old lefty named Herb Pennock. Used only sporadically in his first two seasons, Pennock saw action in 28 games during the 1914 slate, posting a handsome 11–4 record. His best years would come with the Red Sox and Yankees during the 1920s. Mack later admitted that he missed the boat when he traded Pennock. "That was my biggest blunder," Mack said. "I got the impression that [he] was nonchalant, that he lacked ambition. . . . [He] made me rue the day."

During the height of the A's dynasty, Mack remarked to a sportswriter that he wouldn't trade any of his infielders for $100,000 (a stratospheric figure in those days). The quote became a catchphrase that stuck. Mack's so-called $100,000 Infield consisted of Stuffy McInnis at first base, Eddie Collins at second, Frank Baker at third, and Jack Barry at shortstop.

Collins was the most accomplished of the bunch. Among the second basemen currently enshrined at Cooperstown, he ranks first in hits, runs, and stolen bases. He is also baseball's all-time leader in sacrifices. But numbers alone don't accurately reflect his impact on the clubs he played for. When his days with the A's were finished, he helped the White Sox to a pair of pennants in 1917 and 1919. Singing his praises, Giants' manager John McGraw once said: "He is the most perfect and most resourceful player in the world. He did more to beat the Giants out of two world championships than any other member of Connie Mack's squad."

Among the most renowned sluggers of the Deadball Era, Frank "Home Run" Baker retired with 99 lifetime homers (including the postseason). The two he hit in consecutive games of the 1911 World Series earned him his famous nickname. Baker swung with a violent snapping motion and was said to use heavy bats weighing up to 52 ounces. When it was suggested in later years that his teammates deserved most of the credit for his accomplishments at the plate, Collins rushed to his defense. "When it came to hitting, Baker needed help like Andrew Carnegie needed money." The pressure of the World Series didn't rattle Baker at all as he compiled a .363 lifetime batting average in baseball's October Showcase. Described by many as "awkward" at third base, he was known for his extensive range. The Veterans Committee deemed him Hall of Fame worthy in 1955.

The remaining members of Mack's "$100,000 Infield" kept a fairly low profile. McInnis played in portions of 19 major league seasons, compiling a lifetime .307 batting average. A right-handed line-drive hitter, he produced mostly singles. In the field, he had sure hands and quick reflexes. He was also an accomplished sign-stealer. Barry was a typical deadball shortstop—"all field, no bat." Though he never gathered more than 126 hits in a season, he was a tough out in clutch situations. Tiger manager Hughie Jennings once remarked, "In a pinch, [Barry] hits better than anybody in our league outside of Cobb." Although this was a bit of an exaggeration, it would not be stretching the truth to rank Barry alongside the best defensive shortstops of the era.

In spite of their star-studded roster, the A's got off to a relatively slow start in 1914. By the fourth week of May, they were trailing Detroit and Washington in the standings. Leaning heavily on pitching legend Walter Johnson (who made 51 appearances that year), the Nationals (often referred to as the Senators) remained legitimate contenders until late July. The Tigers faded around the same time, but the Red Sox made things interesting down the stretch, posting a 21–9 record in September. In the end, the A's held their ground, finishing eight and a half games in front of the surging BoSox.

The National League pennant race was far more surprising. Through the first two months of the season, the Braves were mired in last place with a dreadful 10–22 record. When the summer months arrived, they began to show signs of life. A series sweep over Cincinnati in mid-July moved them out of the NL basement for good. It was a gradual climb to the top from there. At the end of play on August 30, they were a mere half-game behind the Giants in the standings. Completing their astounding worst-to-first journey, they took two of three games from New York in early September, breaking a first-place tie. McGraw's squad—heavily favored to claim their fourth straight pennant—played mediocre ball in the second half, allowing the upstart Braves to overtake them and build a sufficient lead. By the time the two teams met for a six-game series beginning on September 30, Boston was on the verge of clinching.

The Braves' "feel-good" story was a welcome distraction from troubling world events. On June 28, Archduke Franz Ferdinand (heir to the Austrian throne) was assassinated, setting off a chain of developments that led to the start of World War I. By early August, the major countries of Europe were embroiled in conflict. The United States declared neutrality but would ultimately be pulled into the fray.

Prior to the 1914 World Series, umpire Hank O'Day, who had taken over as manager of the Cubs, went on record saying: "The Boston club won't win a game and I don't care if you quote me." The loquacious Johnny Evers begged to differ, remarking, "I am perfectly confident that the A's are destined to receive the one big surprise of their lives." Evers was on-point with that statement.

Enhancing their status as underdogs, the Braves had no distinct home field advantage. In August, they had abandoned their archaic home of more than 40 years and taken up temporary residence in Fenway Park while their new home—a 40,000-seat "super-stadium"—was being built. Another factor working against the NL champs: American League clubs had won each of the previous four World Series. No one was more aware of this than Bender of the A's. Near the end of the season, Mack gave his staff ace a week off to scout the Braves. Bender reportedly went on vacation instead, commenting that it was pointless to waste his time watching a bunch of "bush league" hitters.

The Series opened at Shibe Park in Philadelphia. Bender received a hard lesson in humility as the Braves tagged him for six runs on eight hits. Much of the damage was administered by catcher Hank Gowdy. Playing in his first season as a full-timer, the lanky backstop fell one hit short of the cycle, going 3-for-3 with a single, double, and triple. He scored twice and drove in a run. Maranville added a pair of RBI singles as Bender was chased from the mound in the sixth inning. Rudolph was brilliant for the Braves, scattering five hits and striking out eight in the 7–1 Boston win.

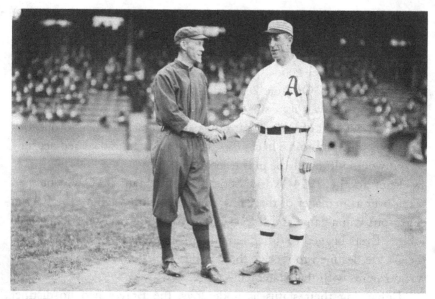

Figure 2.1 Braves team captain Johnny Evers poses with A's hurler Eddie Plank before the start of the 1914 World Series.
PHOTO COURTESY OF THE LIBRARY OF CONGRESS.

Game 2 was a pitching duel between James and Plank. Through eight innings, the game remained scoreless. The Braves, who had failed to move a runner beyond second base to that point, finally broke through in the ninth as infielder Charlie Deal hit a one-out double and stole third. Mann put Boston on the board with an RBI single to right field. In the bottom of the ninth, a tiring James walked a pair of batters but preserved his two-hit shutout by inducing a game-ending double play off the bat of outfielder Eddie Murphy.

Game 3—the pivotal match—was a heartbreaker for 21-year-old right-hander "Bullet Joe" Bush. The game remained knotted at two until the top of the 10th, when Baker delivered a clutch two-run single for the A's. Not to be outdone, the Braves came storming back with a solo homer off the bat of Gowdy and an RBI sacrifice by Connolly. Mack allowed Bush to go the distance, but Stallings exercised a bit more caution, summoning James to close out the game. James held the A's scoreless for two frames while Bush—obviously tiring—served up a leadoff double to

Gowdy in the bottom of the 12th. Pinch-hitter Larry Gilbert was intentionally walked to set up a double play. Herbie Moran followed with a bunt back to the mound. Bush fielded it cleanly and fired to third for the force, but his throw sailed wide of the bag. Mann—pinch-running for Gowdy—scampered home with the winning Boston run.

Capturing the moment in dramatic detail, the *New York Times* reported:

"The crowd went wild. All the feeling and enthusiasm that had been bottled up as the game see-sawed one way and then the other burst forth with unrestrained fury. . . . A heart-broken youth, his eyes blurred with tears, slunk away under the big stands as the paeans of victory rang in his ears. His had been a great responsibility. His teammates, the fading world champions, had played masterful ball behind him and they were all fighting shoulder to shoulder to try to stem the onslaught of an all-powerful enemy. Then, by one tragic throw, he had knocked the foundation out from under the Mackian machine and it came tumbling down in ruins. There was no comfort for Bush."

After the game, Evers went on record saying: "Tomorrow we will have Dick Rudolph in the box and he knows the Athletic hitters down to hairlines when it comes to their likes and dislikes at the plate as he showed in his first game, which was really the toughest of the Series to pitch because the first one always puts everyone under the big strain. Rudolph should be as good tomorrow as he was last Friday."

Boston's "Royal Rooters," a Red Sox fan club assembled in 1901, turned out in full force to lend their support to the Braves in Game 4. Dramatically illustrating their loyalty, some wore feathers and war paint. The game was scoreless until the bottom of the fourth, when the Braves pushed a run across using "small ball" tactics. A's starter Bob Shawkey helped his own cause in the top of the fifth with an RBI double but couldn't subdue the Braves' attack in the bottom of the frame. Rudolph singled, Moran doubled, and Evers followed with a two-run single, giving Boston a 3–1 lead. Rudolph closed out a spectacular afternoon on the mound with his second win of the Series. Interviewed after the game, he paid the A's little respect. "I'd rather pitch against the Athletics than the worst teams in the National and American Leagues, and

I know my average would be far better. They swung at anything I sent up to them, whether low, high, or wide. They did not show any batting judgment at all."

Thousands of fans swarmed the Boston dugout, prompting Stallings to deliver a speech. Maranville was pulled half-dressed from the showers and compelled to address fans from the dugout roof. The "Royal Rooters" led a parade of 5,000 fans through the Fens and down Huntington Avenue. Several Braves players—including the fun-loving Maranville—joined the procession.

In the wake of the sweep, Stallings's blue-collar crew was referred to as the "Miracle Braves." A writer from *Sporting Life* declared that the Series "was the most amazing feat of the age and the most stunning surprise ever dealt in the baseball world." Interestingly, the Indianapolis Hoosiers—champions of the Federal League—challenged Boston to a playoff, but the invitation was declined.

Stallings hung around Boston for six more seasons, never recapturing the magic of 1914. The Braves slipped to second place the following year, and by the end of the decade, they had become a sub-.500 team. Beantown fans would wait until 1948 for another NL pennant.

Meanwhile, in Philadelphia, a disgruntled Mack began selling off his best players. This included members of his coveted "$100,000 Infield." Bender and Plank defected to the Federal League. Collins joined the White Sox. Baker boycotted the 1915 major league slate when his salary demands were not met. Mack's rebuilding project went on for many years as the A's wound up in last place for seven consecutive seasons.

CHAPTER 3

White Sox vs. Reds 1919

THE 1919 WORLD SERIES SHOOK THE FOUNDATIONS OF BASEBALL AND set in motion a sequence of sweeping changes that forever altered the complexion of the sport. Although the White Sox were universally regarded as the better team, the affair was undermined by corruption and greed. No one will ever know which club would have won in a fair fight.

When details of the 1919 Series scandal were made public, the reaction among the masses was a combination of shock and outrage. Distressing as the news was, it should really have come as no surprise. Gambling and cheating had been present in the sport for a very long time. In 1882, National League umpire Dick Higham was accused of deliberately making calls against the Detroit Wolverines to pad the pockets of gamblers. In 1910, members of the St. Louis Browns plotted to rob the universally unpopular Ty Cobb of a batting crown. And in September of 1919 (just weeks before Chicago's infamous clash with Cincinnati), Hal Chase of the Giants was suspended under suspicion of fixing games.

To understand why members of the White Sox conspired with gamblers to throw the 1919 World Series, one must take into account the financial climate of baseball in the early twentieth century. Players weren't paid exceptionally well (at least in comparison to today). Before the advent of free agency, owners held most of the advantages when it came to negotiating contracts. Players were more or less stuck with the clubs they had signed with until team executives decided it was time to get rid of them. Typical deadball stars were minimally educated and rough around the edges. In their free time, many gravitated to bars and pool halls, where men of questionable integrity could be found. Some players developed relationships with members of the underworld—especially bookmakers who were willing to tamper with the outcome of games in order to turn a profit.

Ty Cobb, one of the biggest names of the era, was paid $20,000 in 1919—equivalent to about $370,000 today. No one else was making that much at the time—not even Babe Ruth. Pitcher Eddie Cicotte, at a little over $9,000, was the highest paid member of the Chicago conspirators. The others were earning significantly less.

A common misconception among contemporary fans is the idea that Chicago team owner Charles Comiskey was a nefarious miser who drove his men to commit the crime of the century. Multiple myths have persisted regarding Comiskey's penny-pinching ways—the most salacious being the story about how he delivered a case of flat champagne to his players as a World Series bonus in 1917. Other fallacies have been handed down over the years.

In reality, Comiskey was prone to acts of generosity. He allowed a number of Chicago organizations to use his ballpark for free and gave out complimentary grandstand tickets to school children. During World War I, he donated a significant portion of his annual income to the Red Cross. While it's true that he could also be frugal, charging players for laundry fees, he actually paid his men pretty well. The White Sox Opening Day payroll in 1919 was among the highest in baseball.

While the specific motivations of each conspirator have been endlessly debated, it's safe to assume that the primary incentive was financial gain. By his own account, it was first baseman Chick Gandil who approached gamblers with the idea of a fix. At the time, the club was divided into two social cliques with tension existing between the two. The educated players fell under the influence of Ivy League graduate Eddie Collins. The rest of the joiners cast their lot with Gandil—a former boxer with an attitude toward authority. Shortstop Swede Risberg played a major role in the fix as well, helping Gandil lure other players (ones who could be trusted to keep their mouths shut) into the fold. Boston-based bookmaker Joseph "Sport" Sullivan convinced New York underworld kingpin Arnold Rothstein to bankroll the plot. Others involved included

"Sleepy Bill" Burns (a former pitcher) and Abe Attell (a former feather-weight boxing champion). Both were associates of Rothstein's.

Risberg made a colossal error in judgment when he advised his pal Joe Gedeon (an infielder for the St. Louis Browns) to bet heavily on the Reds. When foul play later became evident to authorities, Comis-key offered a hefty reward for information. Gedeon—looking for a big payday—turned on Risberg. In addition to the ringleaders, six others were implicated in the scheme, including third baseman Buck Weaver, outfielder Happy Felsch, and pitcher Lefty Williams. All were perma-nently banished from baseball. Perhaps the most unfortunate among the condemned—"Shoeless" Joe Jackson—hit .375 in the Series with 6 RBIs. According to multiple sources, he refused to accept any money and even tried to tell Comiskey about the plot. But the Sox owner allegedly refused to meet with him. The other conspirators later admitted that Jackson did not attend any of the secret meetings that were held before the Series began.

Had all of Gandil's cohorts given their best efforts, it would likely have ended with a Chicago victory. There are many who believe that Jackson—32 years old and very much in his prime—was destined for Cooperstown before he got tangled up in the scandal. A semi-literate small-town boy from South Carolina, he started out with the A's in 1908. Upon arriving in the big city, he was ridiculed by teammates for his ignorance and backward social skills. He failed to maximize his potential and wound up in Cleveland, where he became a superstar, exceeding the .400 mark at the plate in 1911. Although he never won a batting title, his .356 lifetime average (compiled over portions of 13 major-league seasons) is among the highest in history.

Cicotte's name has also surfaced in Hall of Fame discussions. Although he didn't invent the knuckleball, he was among the first to effectively control it. He came up through the Tiger system and caught on with the Red Sox in 1908. In four seasons as a full-timer with Bos-ton, he lost almost as many games as he won. Accused of being apathetic by owner Jon I. Taylor, he was suspended multiple times and eventu-ally traded. He built an extensive array of pitches over time, employ-ing a slider, emery ball, and rising fastball in addition to his signature

Figure 3.1 Pictured here during his days with Washington, Chick Gandil was the self-proclaimed ringleader of the 1919 World Series fix.
PHOTO COURTESY OF THE LIBRARY OF CONGRESS.

offering—the knuckler—which he used about three-quarters of the time. During the White Sox World Series year of 1917, Cicotte narrowly missed a Triple Crown, finishing second to Walter Johnson in strikeouts. His 28 wins and 1.53 ERA were tops in the American League. During the 1919 campaign, he paced the circuit again with 29 victories and 30 complete games. He entered the ill-fated World Series with a lifetime 1.57 earned run average in postseason play.

Cicotte wasn't the only talented hurler on the Chicago pitching staff. Spit-baller Red Faber won 254 games during his career and wound up in the Hall of Fame. But 1919 was not his finest year. The United States was embroiled in World War I from April of 1917 to November of 1918. Many soldiers serving overseas fell ill with the H1N1 virus, which eventually spread worldwide, resulting in millions of deaths. Faber was among those who were sickened during the pandemic. While struggling with the flu, he also suffered from ankle and arm injuries in 1919. He compiled an 11–9 record, nonetheless. Out of action through most of the second half, he managed to avoid involvement in the fix.

The Sox were solid at every infield station. Collins was the most highly regarded second baseman in the game. Gandil was known for his sure hands at first and Weaver, described by one researcher as a "territorial animal . . . who guarded the spiked sand around third like his life," was coming into his own both offensively and defensively. Among the most popular players of the era, the perpetually grinning Weaver attended meetings regarding the fix, but chose not to roll over. He hit .324 in the Series and played errorless ball. In spite of his minimal involvement, he was deemed guilty by association.

Rounding out Chicago's stellar cast, Ray Schalk was a steady presence behind the plate. He led AL backstops in putouts every year from 1913 through 1920. And his lifetime caught stealing percentage (51.6) is among the top 10 marks of all time. When Cicotte and Williams refused to follow his signals during the 1919 Series, he realized there was a plot afoot. He fought hard to undermine the conspirators, hitting .304 and guiding Dickey Kerr—an honest member of the Chicago rotation—to a pair of wins.

Since the Series was not on the level, very little has been made of the Cincinnati lineup. Near the end of the 1918 campaign, manager Christy Mathewson left his managerial post to serve overseas in a chemical unit of the US Army. He was accidentally exposed to poison gas during a training exercise and fell seriously ill as a result. While recuperating, he was replaced by Pat Moran. Moran had served primarily as a catcher during his 14-year playing career. In 1915, he managed the long-suffering Phillies to the first World Series appearance in franchise history. When he turned the same trick in Cincinnati, he cemented his status as a man who could alter the fortunes of under-performing ball clubs. Moran excelled at spotting young talent. Dave Bancroft, Eppa Rixey, and Edd Roush all forged paths to Cooperstown on his watch.

An interesting character, Roush didn't have a middle name—just an initial ("J") that had been given to him to avoid offending his grandfathers, Joseph and Jerry. Although he played left-handed, he was ambidextrous. Appearing briefly with the Giants at the start of his career, he was traded to the Reds after clashing with prickly manager John McGraw. Roush used a heavy bat with a thick handle and claimed that he never broke it. As the story goes, the cumbersome piece of lumber allowed him to make contact with pitchouts, which he slapped into left field for hits. He didn't believe in risking injury during spring training, so he held out almost every year until the regular season was about to start. In later years, he defended the Reds' championship effort, claiming that the Chicago conspirators resorted to fair play after they failed to receive payment for throwing the first game (an erroneous assertion).

Third baseman Heinie Groh was another productive member of the Cincinnati lineup. From 1916 through 1919, he forged a .300 batting average while leading the league in multiple offensive categories. Using an oddly shaped "bottle bat" (which had contours similar to a boat oar), he adopted a typical deadball approach to hitting. "You couldn't hold that bottle bat down at the knob end because the way the weight was distributed, the ball would knock it right out of your hands," he explained. "But I always choked up and chopped down on the ball." Although his performance has been largely discounted, Groh tied with Roush for most runs scored in the 1919 Series.

The Reds were competently served at other infield stations as well. A line-drive hitter with a slashing-style swing, Jake Daubert captured back-to-back batting crowns with the Brooklyn Dodgers before a trade landed him in Cincinnati. Defensively, he was considered to be among the best first basemen of the era, posting the highest fielding percentage at his position on three occasions. Behind the plate, the Reds employed a tandem of Bill Rariden and Ivey Wingo. Rariden was an excellent gloveman with a knack for handling pitchers. Wingo was a far better hitter, driving in runs and demonstrating occasional power. In 1919, he had more extra-base hits than any catcher in the league.

Pennants have always been built around exceptional pitching and the Reds were particularly strong in that department. Starters Slim

Sallee, Hod Eller, and Dutch Ruether combined for a 59–22 record in 1919. Utilizing a crossfire delivery, a high leg-kick, and an assortment of arm angles, Sallee won a career-high total of 21 games while posting a miserly 2.06 ERA. Eller, a short-lived phenom with a sidearm motion, learned how to get dramatic movement on his pitches by polishing one side of the ball and rubbing the other with dirt (an offering that came to be known as the "shine ball"). He won 48 games in a three-year span using the quirky pitch. Ruether—a sturdy southpaw with a sneaky delivery—enjoyed a breakout season in 1919, leading the NL with a .760 winning percentage.

The 1919 pennant race wasn't terribly close. The Reds spent a majority of the first half in second place as the Giants got off to a typical hot start. But no one could keep up with Cincinnati's 44–14 record through July and August. The Reds took over the NL lead on July 31 and never let go. By season's end, they had left the two most dominant teams of the decade (New York and Chicago) far behind.

Gandil's swindlers could not have picked a worse time to sully the reputation of America's favorite sport. The 1918 campaign had been shortened by World War I and the flu pandemic had caused more than 300,000 American deaths. Longing for a return to normalcy, fans flocked to stadiums throughout the 1919 season. Cashing in on the high demand for baseball, executives agreed to a best-of-nine World Series format, which hadn't been used since 1903.

Describing the manipulations that took place behind the scenes, one writer remarked that "the plot was a chaotic disaster from day one as gamblers double-crossed other gamblers, gamblers double-crossed players, players double-crossed gamblers, and players double-crossed players. It seemed as if everybody knew about the fix as the opening game approached. . . . But nobody wanted to be the first to speak up."

Although the White Sox were initially listed as favorites, swirling rumors shifted the odds in Cincinnati's favor. It seems very likely that Chicago manager Kid Gleason became aware of the scheme at some point. What remains uncertain is whether or not he actually chose to do anything about it. There is some evidence that he may have confronted players while the Series was underway, although no record of the incident

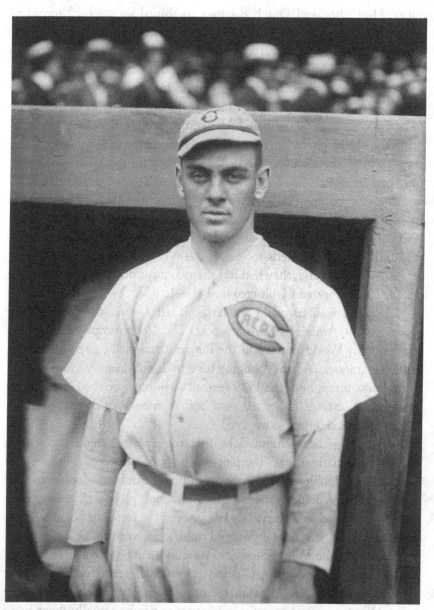

Figure 3.2   Right-hander Hod Eller won 19 regular season games for the Reds in 1919. He added a pair of wins in the World Series.

PHOTO COURTESY OF THE LIBRARY OF CONGRESS.

formally exists. He did tell a reporter later: "Something was wrong. I didn't like the betting odds. I wish no one had ever bet a dollar on the team."

Game 1 was held at Redland Field in Cincinnati. Cicotte took the mound for the White Sox while Ruether got the start for the Reds. The venue was filled beyond capacity and scalpers outside the stadium profited greatly. Cicotte, who had received a partial payoff the night before, hit leadoff batter Morrie Rath—a signal to gamblers that the fix was on. He made a show of it until the fourth inning, when he allowed five consecutive batters to reach base, staking the Reds to a 6–1 lead. Ruether turned in one of the finest performances of his career, allowing just one unearned run on six hits. He also went 3-for-3 at the plate with 3 RBIs.

According to multiple sources, Cicotte was the only conspirator who had been paid prior to Game 2. The others were willing to do their part regardless. Gandil, Risberg, and Felsch combined for an anemic 2-for-10 showing at the plate. Williams had a fourth inning meltdown, issuing three walks and a pair of hits. Counteracting the fix, Schalk thwarted two stolen base attempts and scored a run in the 4–2 Chicago loss. Pleased with the outcome, the gamblers coughed up a sizeable deposit and gave it to Gandil, who divided it among his collaborators.

There was dissention in the ranks before Game 3, which took place at Comiskey Park. Gandil's clan had originally agreed to lose, but ultimately decided against it. Kerr—playing in his rookie season—worked brilliantly with Schalk, tossing a three-hit shutout. Gandil drove in a pair of runs. Risberg tripled and scored, aiding Chicago to a 3–0 victory.

Cicotte was all business at the start of Game 4, tossing four scoreless frames before resorting to chicanery. With one out in the top of the fifth, he threw wildly to first on a slow roller by Pat Duncan, who wound up at second base. After giving up a single to Larry Kopf, Cicotte cut off Jackson's throw to the plate and bobbled the ball, allowing Duncan to score. The crowd of 34,000-plus issued a collective groan at the unforgiveable gaffe. Putting the finishing touches on his sham performance, Cicotte yielded an RBI double to Greasy Neale. The two runs were all Cincinnati needed as right-hander Jimmy Ring held the ChiSox to three hits on the afternoon. After the game, the conspirators received another good faith deposit from gamblers, which was divvied up evenly among Risberg, Felsch, and Williams.

The fifth game was delayed by a day due to rain. Williams saved his obligatory collapse for the sixth inning, when he coughed up four runs. Most of the scoring could be attributed to poor fielding on the part of Felsch, who allowed a pair of catchable balls to drop and made a wild throw. Eller struck out nine Chicago batters and scattered three hits in a lopsided Cincinnati win.

With the Reds on the verge of clinching, Gandil and his cohorts expended their best efforts. Game 6 was the closest of the Series as the Sox erased a four-run deficit, storming back for a dramatic 10-inning victory. Cicotte was on-point in Game 7, yielding just one run on seven hits as the Reds dropped their second straight at home.

Members of the gambling syndicate were alarmed by the sudden shift in momentum. Looking to stave off a possible rebellion, Sullivan dispatched one of his henchmen to speak to Williams, who was scheduled to pitch the following day. The message was quite clear: lose the game or suffer dire consequences.

There was unrest in the Cincinnati clubhouse as well. Responding to whispers of a fix, Roush voiced concerns to Moran that gamblers may have attempted to bribe assorted members of the Reds. Moran confronted Eller—the projected starter for Game 8. Asked if he had been propositioned, the hurler responded openly: "After breakfast this morning, a guy got on the elevator with me and got off on the same floor I did. He showed me five $1,000 bills and said they were mine if I'd lose the game today."

"What did you say?" Moran countered.

"I said if he didn't get damn far away from me real quick, he wouldn't know what hit him. And the same went if I ever saw him again."

Satisfied with that answer, Moran sent Eller to the mound in what would prove to be the deciding contest. Shaken by Sullivan's threats, Williams served up lollipops to Cincinnati batters from the onset. He was pulled in the first inning with one out and three runs in. The Chicago bullpen wasn't much better, allowing the Reds to build an impregnable 10–1 lead. The ChiSox fought back in the bottom of the eighth, tagging

Eller for four runs, but it was as close as they would get. A writer from the *Chicago Herald Examiner* proposed afterward that the 1919 Series should be the last one ever played.

The conspirators escaped punishment until September of 1920, when a Cook County jury was assembled to evaluate claims that the Cubs had thrown a three-game Series with the Phillies. When the probe was extended to include the 1919 World Series, the ugly truth was exposed. Cicotte acknowledged his role and implicated several teammates. Comiskey promptly suspended each of the involved parties—a decision that cost the White Sox the 1920 pennant. Baseball disbanded its National Commission, a three-man governing body, and installed Judge Kenesaw Mountain Landis as the first commissioner. He was given absolute power.

Eight members of the 1919 White Sox were indicted for conspiracy to defraud the public. No charges were imposed upon Rothstein, but Sullivan fled the country to avoid standing trial for multiple counts of conspiracy. Surprisingly, all of the players were acquitted. They were not allowed to walk away scot-free, however, as Landis banned them from baseball for life. Joe Gedeon—Risberg's pal—was also banned by Landis for having knowledge of the plot. After rendering his decision, the commissioner issued the following declaration: "Regardless of the verdict of juries, no player that throws a ball game, no player that undertakes a promise to throw a ball game, no player that sits in a conference with a bunch of crooked players and gamblers where the ways and means of throwing games are discussed, and does not promptly tell his club about it, will ever play professional baseball."

Although the sport had been dealt a devastating blow, recovery was imminent as Landis remained dedicated to cleaning up baseball. With an emphasis on fair play, spitballs and other trick pitches were officially declared illegal along with deceptive deliveries. Umpires were encouraged to put fresh balls into play more often. The result was an unparalleled offensive explosion that drew fans to ballparks in record numbers.

CHAPTER 4

Yankees vs. Giants 1923

MANY CASUAL FANS ARE UNDER THE MISTAKEN IMPRESSION THAT THE New York Yankees have always been a dominant club. While it's true that they have captured more championships than any other team by far, they actually came from humble beginnings. They were formed from the remnants of the Baltimore Orioles, who finished dead last in 1902 after their roster had been plundered by National League rivals. During the offseason, AL president Ban Johnson decided it would be best to dissolve the Orioles and place a team in New York. Though the fledgling club had no formal nickname during the 1903 campaign, sportswriters and fans took to calling them the "Highlanders" in reference to their home stadium, which was located in one of Upper Manhattan's highest elevations. During their first ten years of existence, the Highlanders finished in fourth place or lower seven times.

The team nickname was officially changed in 1913, but it had little effect on the club's performance. The "Yankees" were non-contenders until 1919, when an ongoing series of revitalizing transactions with the Red Sox began. Boston owner Harry Frazee, who was juggling a number of business interests, gradually dismantled his lineup, sending most of his best players to New York. In December of 1918, he traded left fielder Duffy Lewis to the Yankees along with pitchers Ernie Shore and Dutch Leonard. In July of 1919, he added Carl Mays—another talented hurler—to the New York staff. Babe Ruth—the most celebrated slugger in baseball history—followed before the 1920 campaign. A number of additional blockbuster deals led to an eventual dynasty.

In 1921, the Yankees captured their first pennant, squaring off against the Giants, who were making their sixth postseason appearance of the twentieth century. The Yankees had been renting the Polo Grounds from their opponents since 1913 and it was the first World Series to take place at a single site. It was the last to employ a best-of-nine format due to a significant decline in attendance. Ruth—the driving force of the Yankee offense—sustained an injury and played a limited role in the last few games. The team crumbled without him, scoring just one run in a span of 25 innings. It was the Giants' first championship since 1905.

In 1922, Ruth was suspended multiple times due to various misbehaviors. He played in just 110 games and failed to lead the league in any major statistical category (aside from slugging percentage). The Yankees clinched the pennant again in spite of the Babe's transgressions, but the World Series—a rematch from the previous year—was a virtual disaster. Realizing that Ruth was highly sensitive to insults, the Giants' bench jockeys harassed him mercilessly. At one point, the hot-tempered outfielder stormed into the Giants' clubhouse to confront his tormentors. He hit .118 in the Series as the Yankees lost four of five games (one of which ended in a controversial tie). AL president Ban Johnson later remarked: "I have never seen a team representing our organization in the World Series play worse than the Yankees. The Giants have humiliated the American League in a way that cannot be forgotten."

As Ruth proceeded to shatter all existing home run records, the Yankees began to draw larger crowds than their co-inhabitants of the Polo Grounds. This provoked resentment from Giants' management—especially John McGraw, who talked owner Charles Stoneham into terminating the Yankee lease. Under pressure from Ban Johnson and other AL executives, Stoneham retracted the eviction. Yankee owners Jacob Ruppert and Cap Huston offered to buy a half-share of the 155th Street venue, but when their proposal was rejected, they began looking for a suitable location to build their own ballpark. They settled on a large plot located across the Harlem River in the Bronx. In the spring of 1921, construction of Yankee Stadium got underway with a budget of over $2 million.

When the 58,000-seat stadium opened in 1923, it was considered a modern marvel. A writer from *Baseball Magazine* compared it to the pyramids of Egypt. The facility, itself, was not the only impressive feature. The Yankee roster was top-heavy with talent by then.

Before the ascension of Lou Gehrig to full-time status in 1925, Ruth hit behind Bob Meusel in the lineup. A lanky outfielder with a rifle-arm and flat affect, Meusel was misunderstood by many sportswriters, who perceived him to be lazy and antisocial. In spite of the negative stigma that followed him, he was a consistent performer. Essentially, he and Ruth were the first true slugging tandem in the American League, combining for at least 50 homers every year from 1920 through 1924 (although Ruth did most of the heavy hitting). After Gehrig assumed the clean-up role, Meusel was moved further down in the batting order.

The Yankees continued to reap the benefits of Frazee's fire sale, adding Waite Hoyt and Wally Schang to their ranks in 1921. Everett Scott, Bullet Joe Bush, and Sam Jones joined the exodus out of Boston before the 1922 campaign. Herb Pennock changed uniforms the following year. The net result was disastrous for the Red Sox as they finished in fifth place or lower for 15 consecutive seasons.

Labeled as a "Schoolboy Wonder," Hoyt's Hall of Fame career began when he signed with the Giants as a teenager. He made his big-league debut in 1918, but McGraw sent him back to the minors, insisting that he wasn't ready yet. Sparsely used in two seasons with Boston, Hoyt became a star in New York, winning 19 games for the Yankees in 1921. He matched that total the following year. In addition to a standard fastball/curve/change-up combo, Hoyt later added a slider to his arsenal. He appeared very relaxed on the mound, rarely showing any signs of fatigue or pressure.

A member of the dominant A's teams of the early 1910s, the switch-hitting Schang was the first player to homer from both sides of the plate in a game. When the Lively Ball Era arrived, he established himself as one of the best offensive catchers in the majors, posting a .297 batting average from 1920 through 1929. His strong, accurate arm allowed him to regularly finish among the league leaders in runners caught stealing.

Small in stature at 5-foot-8, 148 pounds, Everett Scott was one of the smartest shortstops in the game. He knew precisely where to play opponents and could produce accurate throws from anywhere on the diamond. By the time he was traded to the Nationals in 1925, he was baseball's reigning "Iron Man," having played in 1,307 consecutive games (a record later eclipsed by Gehrig).

After breaking up the A's dynasty in 1914, Connie Mack hung onto pitcher Joe Bush for three more seasons. The team finished dead last every year, but the hard throwing right-hander still managed to win 31 games in that span. A serious arm injury in 1919 prompted Bush to develop a forkball, which revived his career. He reached his peak with the Yankees, compiling a 62–38 record from 1922 through 1924.

Sam Jones was a 20-game winner for the Red Sox during a season in which the team finished below .500 (a relatively uncommon feat). A *New York Herald Tribune* writer saddled him with the nickname "Sad Sam" because he often looked dejected on the field. A right-hander with a sharp-breaking curve, he had the unusual distinction of rarely throwing to first base to keep runners in check. His crowning achievement came in September of 1923, when he no-hit the A's without recording a single strikeout. He was the winningest pitcher on the Yankee staff that year.

Lefty-slinging Hall of Famer Herb Pennock had a smooth, effortless delivery that made it appear as if he were just warming up on the mound. This led opponents and managers to misjudge his talents. Underappreciated with the A's and Red Sox, he became a major contributor in New York, averaging 19 victories per year between 1923 and 1928.

With a roster full of stars, the Yankees got very little resistance from opponents in 1923. They spent 162 days in first place and finished 16 games ahead of their closest rivals—the Tigers. It was a monster year for Ruth, who flirted with the .400 mark at the plate and belted a league-leading 41 homers. Even so, the team's abominable performance against the Giants in 1922 made them heavy underdogs heading into the postseason.

The Giants had a virtual all-star team of their own. Five of the players who regularly appeared in the lineup were later enshrined at

Cooperstown. This put manager John McGraw (a Hall of Famer himself) in a convenient spot.

First baseman George Kelly went hitless in his first 21 major-league plate appearances and carried a .139 batting average into his fourth season. Believing he was worth the wait, McGraw worked tirelessly to build Kelly's confidence and improve his swing. It paid off as the resilient San Francisco native (nicknamed "High Pockets" for his tall, lean frame) remained one of McGraw's top RBI men for nearly a decade.

Second baseman Frankie Frisch had a mediocre debut with the Giants in 1919, but quickly developed into one of the most dynamic players in baseball. Nicknamed the "Fordham Flash," he was among the stolen base leaders during 15 seasons. He also hit for high averages, retiring with a .316 lifetime mark. McGraw appointed him team captain, but later embarrassed him in front of teammates with a stream of verbal abuse. This prompted Frisch to depart for St. Louis, where he made four more World Series appearances.

Shortstop Dave Bancroft was nicknamed "Beauty" for his sparkling glovework. He was the first at his position to turn 100 double plays in a season and is still among the all-time leaders in multiple defensive categories. After spending portions of six campaigns with the Phillies, he reached his offensive peak in New York, exceeding the .300 mark at the plate in three straight seasons. During the 1923 slate, he struggled with various health issues. At one point, he wound up in the hospital with pneumonia. His absence created a golden opportunity for Travis Jackson.

The heir to Bancroft at shortstop, Jackson played multiple positions in 1923 (which was his rookie year) and proved to be more than competent at all of them. He eventually earned the nickname "Stonewall" for his phenomenal defensive play. He also fared pretty well with a bat, cracking the .300 mark six times during his 11 seasons as a full-time player.

Ross Youngs was the heart and soul of the Giants lineup. He was known for his aggressive base running, often throwing full-body blocks on opposing infielders to break up double plays. Impressed with his grit and hustle, McGraw nicknamed him "Pep." Sadly, his career was cut short by a kidney disease for which there was no effective treatment at the time. He lost more than 60 pounds before he died at the age of 30. A memorial plaque was installed at the Polo Grounds, honoring him as "a brave untrammeled spirit of the diamond, who brought glory to himself and to his team."

Prior to the opening game of the 1923 Series, McGraw exuded supreme confidence. The caustic Giants skipper had disliked Ruth from his days as a pitcher, predicting that the Babe would hit into 100 double plays per year if he was converted to an everyday player. The statistic was not officially tracked until the 1930s, but McGraw was way off the mark. The popular Yankee idol actually ran pretty well in spite of his bulky frame. Based on his previous performances against the Giants, however, McGraw didn't see Ruth as a threat. "I believe the same system that nullified [Ruth's] presence in the batting order in 1921 and 1922 will suffice," he boasted to reporters. Again, he was wrong in his assessment.

The Series opened at Yankee Stadium to much hype and fanfare. The game drew more than 55,000 spectators—many of them hoping to see Ruth smash the first postseason homer in the stadium's history. They would have to wait as the Babe had a relatively quiet day at the plate, going 1-for-4 with a triple and a run scored. Oddly enough, it was another future Yankee icon who stole Ruth's thunder. With the game tied at four in the top of the ninth, Giants center fielder Casey Stengel—nearing the end of his career as a player—lined a Joe Bush pitch into the left-center field gap. The ball rolled all the way to the wall, allowing a less than nimble Stengel to circle the bases with the deciding run. He later reported that his shoe came loose and almost fell off while he was completing the circuit.

Ruth reclaimed the spotlight in Game 2 at the Polo Grounds, blasting a pair of solo homers. The first one sailed all the way to the right field roof, breaking a 1–1 tie. The second one, a screaming line drive that landed just inside the right field foul pole, extended the Yankees' lead to 4–1. Commenting on the Babe's raw power after the game, sportswriter John Kieran quipped, "Ruth is not only original, he is sometimes positively aboriginal." Pennock delivered a solid performance for the Yanks, limiting the Giants to a pair of runs on nine hits. It was the first World Series victory of his career.

Figure 4.1   Giants manager John McGraw poses with Babe Ruth before an exhibition game. McGraw believed that his pitchers could contain Ruth in the 1923 World Series, but he was mistaken as Ruth belted three homers.
PHOTO COURTESY OF THE LIBRARY OF CONGRESS.

McGraw took Ruth a bit more seriously in Game 3, ordering starter Art Nehf to feed the Yankee slugger a steady diet of curveballs outside the strike zone. The result was a harmless single and a pair of walks for the Babe. The rest of the Yankee regulars were stifled by Nehf's offerings all afternoon. Again, it was Stengel (a .339 hitter in limited duty during the regular season) who emerged as a hero, lifting a Sam Jones pitch into the right field bleachers. It was the only run of the game.

Entering the fourth meeting, the Yankees had won just four of 16 postseason games against the Giants. But their luck was about to change. Facing right-hander Jack Scott, the Yanks batted around in the second inning, jumping out to a 6–0 lead. It was all the offense they would need in a dominant 8–4 victory. It was more of the same in Game 5 as the Yankees scored early and often, assaulting Giants pitchers with a 14-hit barrage. Third baseman Joe Dugan had three singles and a homer—the big blow coming in the second inning with a pair of runners aboard. Bush was brilliant on the mound, allowing just five batters to reach base. The 8–1 win brought the Yankees one step closer to redemption.

A capacity crowd at the Polo Grounds saw Ruth set a new precedent in the first inning of Game 6. The Babe's third home run of the Series (a short-lived record he would break three years later) landed in the upper deck just barely fair. For the next few innings, most of the cheering was done by Giants fans as they built a 4–1 lead. Refusing to accept defeat, the Yankees staged a remarkable rally in the top of the eighth, sending nine men to the plate. Nehf allowed three straight batters to reach safely before issuing a bases loaded walk. Rosy Ryan—summoned from the bullpen with one out—promptly yielded a free pass, forcing in another run. Thousands of Giants fans breathed a sigh of relief when Ruth went down swinging. But Ryan was not out of the woods yet as Meusel poked a single through the hole between shortstop and second base. Center fielder Bill Cunningham delivered an errant throw that cleared the bases and gave the Yankees a 6–4 lead. Taking over for Pennock, Sam Jones closed out the game with two scoreless frames. The Yankees had finally done what many thought was impossible, stealing the Series from their powerful intracity rivals.

The *New York Times* reported after the game: "The Giants had finally been beaten. In three years of championship play, they had never before met their match. With uncanny, almost superhuman ability, they had risen to meet every crisis fairly and they could make the boast of every champion that they had never felt defeat. This series put before them their hardest test. Could they break all baseball tradition and win three World Series in a row? They could not, and so yesterday a great team finally went down."

The Yankees would continue to import a steady stream of marquee players to the Bronx throughout the twentieth century, becoming the winningest team in baseball history. The Giants, on the other hand, distinguished themselves as one of the most star-crossed October franchises, losing a total of 11 Fall Classics before the new millennium arrived. As of 2024, the Giants' eight World Series titles ranked fourth among major-league teams behind the Yankees (27), Cardinals (11), A's (9), and Red Sox (9).

CHAPTER 5

Nationals vs. Giants 1924

SOME TEAMS SEEM DESTINED TO LOSE. THE CHICAGO CUBS WENT without a championship for over a century. The Red Sox experienced a drought of more than 80 years. And the Cleveland Guardians (formerly known as the Indians), are currently in the midst of an extensive dry spell. Among the original members of the American League, the Washington Nationals (known to many as the "Senators") set the standard for futility, finishing in fifth place or lower dozens of times between 1901 and 1960. Their abysmal performances in the early years prompted sportswriter Charley Dryden to famously quip: "Washington—first in war, first in peace, and last in the American League."

After another sub-.500 finish in 1923, few believed that the Nationals were capable of staging a pennant run. But a number of important changes prior to the 1924 slate altered the team's fortunes overnight. The most notable development was the dismissal of manager Donie Bush. Although Bush had upgraded the Senators from sixth place in 1922 to fourth place the following year, owner Clark Griffith chose not to retain his services. His replacement—27-year-old infielder Bucky Harris— forged a Hall of Fame career at the helm of five different clubs.

As a player, Harris was a steady hitter and highly capable second baseman. As a manager, he had a knack for recognizing and strengthening the weaknesses of his teams. Instead of taking a domineering approach in 1924, he openly admitted to players that he was inexperienced and asked for their help. They responded well to his humility, rallying around him all year. By the end of the season, sportswriters were referring to Harris as the "Boy Wonder."

The Lively Ball Era was in full swing during the 1924 campaign. With fewer pitchers resorting to deception on the mound and umpires supplying a steady stream of fresh baseballs, collective batting averages were on the rise. Home runs had become a common occurrence as well. Babe Ruth was light years ahead of the curve, resetting the single-season record for long balls three times between 1920 and 1927. After clubbing his 60th blast in the latter campaign, he allegedly boasted: "60—Count 'em, 60!! Let's see some other son of a bitch match that!"

Over the course of the 1923 slate, Donie Bush noted that most of his starters were losing their effectiveness in the late innings of ballgames. Addressing the issue, he assigned relief duties to more than a dozen different pitchers. Allen Russell (who was allowed to continue throwing spitballs due to a grandfather clause) was the busiest of the bunch, making 47 appearances out of the bullpen. Following Bush's lead, Harris assembled a smaller platoon of relief men in 1924. Russell got into 37 games without making a single start. Byron Speece—a right-handed curveballer with a submarine delivery—was handed 20 relief assignments. And Firpo Marberry became the most celebrated fireman of the era.

"Marberry" (whose birth name was Frederick) received his nickname on account of the striking resemblance he bore to Luis Firpo—a heavyweight boxer who once knocked Jack Dempsey out of the ring. A right-hander, Marberry intimidated opponents by stomping around the mound and leering angrily at them. He had a lively fastball but tended to lose velocity the longer he pitched. Serving as a swingman for most of his big-league tenure, he was used exclusively out of the bullpen from September of 1924 to July of 1926. He was the first player to record 100 saves (although the save was not an official statistic at the time) and his career-high mark of 22 was a single-season record that stood until the 1940s.

With a competent cast of relievers at his disposal, Harris was able to get by with a four-man rotation. He employed a variety of starters on the fourth day, including Marberry, who won several decisions in that role. The workhorse of the staff was Cooperstown great Walter Johnson.

A solidly built right-hander with a windmill windup and sidearm delivery, Johnson (known to many as the "Big Train") established himself as baseball's all-time shutouts leader, blanking opponents 110 times. He was pretty handy with a bat as well, gathering 159 extra-base hits, including 24 homers. Praising his extraordinary abilities, journalist Shirley Povich once wrote, "Let there be no misunderstanding, no delusion that Walter Johnson is or was a baseball legend. Not only inaccurate is that description, it demeans him." Although Johnson was 36 years old at the start of the 1924 campaign, he still had plenty left to offer, claiming his fifth ERA title and third Triple Crown.

The deep, uniform dimensions of Griffith Stadium were not ideal for home runs and the Nationals finished dead-last in that category during the 1924 slate. They didn't need homers to get the job done, however, as they averaged close to five runs per game. The lineup was bolstered significantly by the return of Joe Judge and Ossie Bluege, both of whom missed significant portions of time due to injuries the previous year.

Small for his position at 5-foot-8, Judge was described by many as "agile" around first base. Among the most popular players in Washington, he maintained his status as a first-stringer from 1916 through 1930. He fashioned a commendable .298 batting average during his long career, peaking at .333 in 1920. He gathered no fewer than 63 RBIs in 10 consecutive seasons.

Bluege was a defensively gifted third baseman with a strong arm. Highly impressed by his extensive range and quick reflexes, catcher Luke Sewell claimed that Bluege was "two of the greatest infielders who ever played. . . . He played third and short at the same time. And nobody could come up with a bunt and snap it to first base as fast as Bluege." Holding his own at the plate, Bluege's batting averages typically hovered in the mid-.270 range. He seldom struck out, averaging just one per every 14 plate appearances.

The bulk of the heavy hitting in Washington rested on the shoulders of Hall of Famers Sam Rice and Goose Goslin. A late bloomer, Rice waited until he was 25 years old to make his major-league debut. He played 19 seasons with Washington before ending his career in Cleveland. Among the finest defensive outfielders of the era, he led players at

Figure 5.1   Walter Johnson (on the right) is baseball's all-time shutouts leader with 110. He is pictured here with his frequent battery mate, catcher Muddy Ruel.
PHOTO COURTESY OF THE LIBRARY OF CONGRESS.

his position in putouts and double plays four times apiece. He accrued a handsome .322 lifetime batting average, falling just short of 3,000 hits—a mark he would surely have surpassed had he arrived in "the Show" sooner. His 216 base hits in 1924 were tops in the American League.

According to a widely distributed tale, outfielder Leon Goslin picked up the nickname "Goose" because he flapped his arms while chasing fly balls. Other sources have maintained that his protruding nose and long neck were the inspiration for the moniker. One thing that has never been disputed is Goslin's ability to hit. Supremely confident, the New Jersey native claimed he was a natural. "Never had to practice a lot," he said in later years. "Good eyes, quick reflexes, strong arms—Oh, did I ever love to get up there and hit .... I never could wait for spring to come so I could get out there and swat those baseballs." Goslin's massive swing often sent him crashing to the dirt when he missed. He didn't miss many opportunities to drive in runs, reaching the century mark in RBIs 11 times and finishing on the cusp twice. If he had one major weakness it was his defense. His lifetime error total in left field is second only to Hall of Famer Zack Wheat.

The key to winning an American League pennant during the 1920s was to conquer the New York Yankees. In order to accomplish that feat, pitchers had to tame Babe Ruth. The Babe was an aggressive hitter who tended to be impatient at the plate, but he never struck out more than 93 times in a single season. And so, for some hurlers, the best approach was to take the bat out of his hands. Walking Ruth forced pitchers to deal with Bob Meusel, who (at the very least) was not a looming home run threat. Washington pitchers did a fair job of curtailing Meusel's production in 1924, limiting him to 15 RBIs in 20 games. They were even better at suppressing baseball's reigning home run king, holding Ruth to 10 extra-base hits and seven ribbies in 96 plate appearances.

The Nationals played .500 ball through mid-June before assembling a 10-game winning streak that lifted them into first place. Their reign at the top was interrupted by a major slump in early August, but a 13–4 run later in the month put them back in front. Yankee Stadium was like a home away from home for the Nats as they forged a 9–2 record there. Nullifying early predictions of an all–New York World Series, Washington clinched the first pennant in franchise history with a 4–2 win over the Red Sox on September 29. This prompted rumblings in the Bronx about restructuring the Yankees' aging pitching staff.

Meanwhile, on the other side of the Harlem River, the reigning National League champions were fixing to capture an unprecedented fourth consecutive pennant. Minor changes to the lineup had made the Giants even more formidable. Prior to the 1924 campaign, 33-year-old shortstop Dave Bancroft was traded to the Braves along with Casey Stengel. Bancroft's departure left a full-time opening for the much younger and equally gifted Travis Jackson. Jackson's induction to the Hall of Fame in 1982 ended a long-standing bias against shortstops, opening the door for other all-time greats such as Phil Rizzuto, Pee Wee Reese, and Luis Aparicio.

The New York outfield was still solid in 1924 with Ross Youngs and Irish Meusel occupying the corner positions. Meusel—whose brother Bob spent 10 years with the Yankees—was a dominant hitter in the early

1920s, gathering no fewer than 100 RBIs in four consecutive seasons. He was productive on the October stage as well, scoring 10 runs and gathering 17 ribbies in World Series play.

Remembered more for his peak years with the Cubs, center fielder Lewis Wilson made his full-time debut with the Giants in 1924. Short and barrel-chested with broad shoulders and powerful arms, he picked up the nickname of "Hack" on account of his resemblance to professional wrestler George Hackenschmidt. Although he performed quite well in his rookie campaign, he ended up being traded to the Cubs after developing a puzzling inability to handle curveballs. The condition was only temporary as he went on to lead the NL in homers four times. In 1930, he elevated the single-season RBI record to 191—a mark that still stands.

The Giants were well stocked with capable hurlers in 1924. Southpaw Art Nehf remained one of the club's most reliable starters, compiling a .778 winning percentage. A bit on the small side at 5-foot-9, the college-educated Nehf could have worked as an electrical engineer. But he chose a career on the diamond instead, signing with the Braves in 1915. The Giants thought so highly of him that they were willing to part with four players and a large sum of cash to acquire his services in August of 1919. On the mound, Nehf was highly resourceful, using a variety of arm angles to fool hitters. To offset his fastball/curve combination, he added a "floater" (a kind of changeup that behaved like a knuckleball) to his arsenal in later years. He continued to pitch in spite of a neurological condition that made it difficult for him to grip the ball. The affliction grew worse over time, forcing him out of the majors prematurely.

Other returning starters in 1924 included Jack Bentley, Hugh McQuillan, and Virgil Barnes, who collectively added 46 wins to the Giants' cause. None of them went on to highly remarkable careers in the majors although Bentley established himself as a decent two-way player, fashioning a .291 lifetime batting average as a pinch-hitter and first baseman.

John McGraw missed a significant chunk of time in 1924 due to illness—a development that likely pleased more than one Giants player. In his absence, the eminently likeable Hughie Jennings took over. Jennings, a cheerful and enthusiastic Hall of Famer, joined the New York coaching staff in 1921 after spending 14 years as a manager in Detroit. He was called upon numerous times to sub for McGraw, who suffered from a variety of ailments. Jennings spent more than a month in charge of the Giants in 1924, guiding the club to a 32–12 record.

The pennant race was not an easy ride as the Giants encountered stiff resistance from Brooklyn and Pittsburgh. After several years of development, the Pirates were on the cusp of greatness, carrying four Hall of Famers on their roster (Pie Traynor, Kiki Cuyler, Max Carey, and Rabbit Maranville). The Robins had three—two of which were the backbone of their pitching corps. Flamethrower Dazzy Vance captured a Triple Crown and spitballer Burleigh Grimes piled up 22 wins for Brooklyn, but it wasn't enough as the Giants clinched with one game still remaining.

In 2020, a writer from ESPN ranked the 1924 World Series as the third greatest of all time. Four of the seven games were decided by a single run and two required extra innings to determine the outcome. Including the managers, a total of 13 Hall of Famers played a significant role in developments on the field.

Although most sportswriters expected the Giants to win handily on account of their experience and depth, the betting odds slightly favored Washington. The opener was held in DC, where President Calvin Coolidge was on-hand to throw out the first pitch. Hometown fans honored Walter Johnson with a new car before game time. The Big Train was conspicuously nervous. "I am doggone fidgety about my job this afternoon," he admitted. "Every last soul in the ballpark expects me to win, including the President of the United States."

He didn't win, but he came very close.

Fittingly, Johnson squared off against Nehf—McGraw's favorite October hurler. The Giants opened the scoring in the second inning with a solo homer by George Kelly. They tacked on another run with a shot off the bat of Bill Terry in the fourth. The Nationals bounced back in the sixth inning, when Sam Rice delivered an RBI groundout. Shortstop Roger Peckinpaugh tied the score in the bottom of the ninth with a clutch double, sending the game into extra innings. Both managers allowed their starters to go the distance. The Giants took advantage of a tiring Johnson in the 12th, putting their first three batters on base. Frankie Frisch grounded into a force at home, but Youngs followed with an RBI single, and Kelly provided an insurance run on a sacrifice fly. With the Nats trailing 4–2, Mule Shirley led off for Washington with a catchable popup that was dropped by Travis Jackson (a highly unusual event). Hustling all the way, Shirley ended up at second base. Earl McNeely flied out and Bucky Harris followed with a run-scoring single. Fans cheered wildly as Washington's best hitters took their turns at-bat. With one out, Rice singled to center field. Harris moved to third, but Rice was thrown out trying to advance to second. In spite of the thunderous crowd noise and unimaginable pressure, Nehf composed himself, inducing a harmless grounder off the bat of Goslin. The Giants walked away with an anxiety-inducing 4–3 win.

Game 2 was decided in the final at-bat. Goslin put the Nationals up 2–0 in the first with a long homer off of Giants starter Jack Bentley. Harris padded the lead with a fifth inning solo shot. The Giants clawed their way back with a run in the seventh and another pair in the top of the ninth, but once again, Peckinpaugh was the man of the hour, pounding a game-winning double. He strained a thigh muscle running it out and was benched for most of the remaining games.

Harris's decision to start Marberry in Game 3 at the Polo Grounds proved to be a mistake as the hurler wasn't up to the task, tossing three shaky innings. Washington's precocious player/manager dropped a catchable relay from Bluege on a second inning double play attempt. It led to a pair of critical runs in a 6–4 Washington loss.

The Nationals evened the Series with a breezy 7–4 victory in Game 4. But their confidence was shattered the following day when Walter Johnson faltered on the mound. Feeling the strain of advancing age and an unwieldy workload, the legendary hurler allowed six runs (two of them unearned) on 13 hits. The 6–2 defeat put Washington on the brink of elimination and prompted speculation that Johnson might be nearing the end of his career after 18 brilliant seasons.

Showing the resiliency that had characterized them all year, the Nationals fought back in Game 6. Rice made three spectacular catches in right field and Tom Zachary—a 15-game winner during the regular season—effectively stifled the Giants offense, allowing just one run on seven hits. Harris's two-out single in the bottom of the fifth accounted for both of Washington's runs as the Nats forced a pivotal Game 7.

Asked about it years later, Giants pitcher Jack Bentley said that the 1924 Series finale was one of the "weirdest" games he ever played in. ESPN correspondent Sam Miller referred to it as one of the greatest in baseball history. It began with a savvy bit of strategy on the part of Harris, who selected seldom-used right-hander Curly Ogden to start. Ogden—claimed off of waivers in May—was just a decoy. McGraw adjusted his lineup accordingly and Harris pulled Ogden after two batters, sending lefty George Mogridge to the mound. The subterfuge worked well for several innings as the Nationals carried a 1–0 lead into the top of the sixth. It was then that things began to fall apart for Washington.

Mogridge yielded a leadoff walk to Youngs and a single to Kelly. Harris turned to Marberry, who became a victim of sloppy defense. Errors by Judge and Bluege (who was subbing at shortstop for the injured Peckinpaugh) allowed the Giants to open a 3–1 lead. In the bottom of the eighth, Harris came through yet again with a bad-hop single that eluded rookie third baseman Freddie Lindstrom. For the second time in the span of a week, a Giants–Nationals matchup dragged on for 12 innings.

Proving that rumors of his demise were greatly exaggerated, Johnson redeemed himself with four scoreless innings in relief. The game was tied at three in the bottom of the 12th when things took a peculiar turn. Nationals catcher Muddy Ruel hit a popup near home plate that was dropped by opposing backstop Hank Gowdy, who tripped over his own mask while chasing after it. Given new life, Ruel doubled to left field. Washington caught another break when Jackson committed his second error of the game on a ground ball by Johnson. With runners at first and second and one out, Earl McNeely hit what should have been a playable grounder to third. But the ball hit a pebble or a clod of dirt and hopped right over the head of Lindstrom. Ruel crossed the plate with the winning run, giving the Nats their first and only World Series title while stationed in Washington. Owner Clark Griffith believed that it was divine intervention. "God was on our side in that one," he said years later. "[Or] else how did those pebbles get in front of Lindstrom, not once, but twice?"

It was the last World Series appearance for McGraw, who handed the reins to Bill Terry in 1932 and walked away with more than 100 games still remaining in the season. The Giants rose to prominence under Terry, winning a World Series in 1933 and capturing two more pennants before the end of the decade. The Nationals returned to the Fall Classic in 1925 and 1933, losing both times. It was a gradual descent into mediocrity from there. After nearly three decades without a pennant, the team moved to Minnesota and became the Twins. A new club officially known as the Senators became the running joke of the American League.

CHAPTER 6

Yankees vs. Cardinals 1926

THE 1925 CAMPAIGN WAS DISAPPOINTING FOR THE YANKEES. AFTER narrowly missing a pennant the previous year, they were expected by many to finish on top. Unfortunately, Babe Ruth's insatiable appetite for food, alcohol, and women led to a serious illness that kept him off the field until June. In his absence, outfielder Bob Meusel picked up some of the slack, leading the American League in homers and RBIs. But the pitching staff underperformed all year. By the time the season ended, the club was sitting in seventh place with a sub-.500 record.

There were a few bright spots for the Yankees in 1925. Hall of Famer Earle Combs (whose big-league debut had been cut short in 1924 due to an injury) nailed down the starting job in center field with a .342 showing at the plate. Lou Gehrig—just 22 years old and playing in his first full season—gathered 53 extra-base hits. And in August, scout Bill Essick convinced Yankee GM Ed Barrow to purchase the contract of Pacific Coast League prospect Tony Lazzeri, who set a PCL record with 60 home runs. Other teams had approached the slugger with caution on account of his epileptic condition. But Barrow's gamble paid off as Lazzeri forged a Hall of Fame career at second base.

The Yankees carried three marquee pitchers on their roster in 1926. Herb Pennock emerged as the staff ace with a career-high of 23 victories. Urban Shocker gathered 19 wins while posting a handsome 3.38 earned run average. And Waite Hoyt proved to be highly versatile, making 28 starts and 12 relief appearances. He ended up with 16 wins and four saves.

With so many talented players at his disposal, Yankee manager Miller Huggins often failed to receive due credit for the team's success. But A's manager Connie Mack knew how irreplaceable Huggins was. "There seemed to be an impression here and there that anybody could manage so great a team. That's wrong," Mack once asserted. "It took Huggins to make those fellows fight and hustle." Huggins made a bold statement in 1925 when he suspended Ruth for insubordination and training violations. The Babe threatened to quit, but Huggins stood his ground, demanding an apology. The penitent outfielder eventually came to his senses, humbling himself in front of the entire team. Determined to prove that he was still baseball's premier slugger, Ruth went off on a tear in 1926, finishing just six points behind Heinie Manush of the Tigers for the batting title. Had he come up with just a few more hits (a difficult task considering that pitchers were walking him at a rate of once per every 4.5 plate appearances), he would have captured a Triple Crown.

Aided tremendously by the Babe's prodigious efforts, the Yankees took up permanent residence in first place on May 10. A 16-game winning streak immediately followed. In spite of a rough patch in late September, the Bombers finished three games in front of Cleveland.

No one could have predicted the outcome of the National League pennant race in 1926. Absent from postseason play for nearly four decades, the Cardinals finally rose to prominence under player/manager Rogers Hornsby. Commenting on his penchant for insulting the people around him, sportswriter Lee Allen remarked that Hornsby was "frank to the point of being cruel and as subtle as a belch." Even mild-mannered (and deeply religious) GM Branch Rickey took a swing at Hornsby after a game one day. But in spite of his deficient interpersonal skills, "the Rajah" turned out to be a capable leader.

Peak performances from ordinary players were the key to St. Louis's success in 1926. Catcher Bob O'Farrell—dumped by the Cubs for a pair of utility players in May of 1925—captured the NL MVP Award. Les Bell—a defensive liability at third base—put up career-high numbers in almost every major offensive category. And right-hander Flint Rhem—remembered more for his drinking problems off the field—tied for the league lead with 20 victories. The Cardinals also got help from a pair of aging Hall of Fame pitchers, one of whom was well past his prime.

Grover Alexander was forced to deal with a number of health issues during his career. While playing in the minors, he was hit in the head by a throw and rendered unconscious for more than 24 hours. He suffered from double vision for the rest of the season and later ended up with epilepsy. While serving on the front line with the US Army in WWI, the star-crossed hurler caught shrapnel in his right ear and was left with muscle damage from the repetitive motion of firing a howitzer. Additionally, the relentless shelling cost him the hearing in his left ear. Upon returning to the United States, a severe case of "shell shock" (known today as PTSD) drove him to alcoholism.

None of these afflictions stopped Alexander from capturing multiple Triple Crowns and piling up more than 370 wins. However, his incessant drinking began to hamper his performance in 1926. Believing that he was hurting the team, Cubs manager Joe McCarthy placed Alexander on waivers. Hornsby felt that the fading moundsman was a worthy investment, rescuing him from the scrap heap in late June. Over the next several months, Alexander won nine games and picked up a pair of saves while keeping his ERA below the 3.00 mark. His performance in the 1926 World Series has become legendary.

A right-hander with outstanding control, Jesse Haines entered the majors with a fastball/curve combination. When those offerings became ineffective, he added a knuckleball to his arsenal. Since the quirky pitch put minimal strain on his arm, Haines remained active beyond the age of 43. He picked up the nickname "Pop" because of the positive influence he had on younger teammates. Plagued by inconsistency in 1924 and 1925, he got himself straightened out during the Cardinals' pennant run, posting a 13–4 record with a 3.25 ERA. Interestingly, Haines's election to the Hall of Fame via the Veterans Committee in 1970 generated controversy. The committee included some of the hurler's former teammates and, since his period of dominance was relatively brief, his enshrinement led to accusations of cronyism. Bill James—the father of Sabermetrics—agreed with that assessment, citing Haines as one of several players who should not be in the Hall of Fame.

Figure 6.1 Pete Alexander won three consecutive Triple Crowns beginning in 1915. Although he was past his prime in 1926, he held the Yankees to just three earned runs in more than 20 innings during the World Series that year.
PHOTO COURTESY OF THE LIBRARY OF CONGRESS.

Also included on James's list, Cooperstown inductee Jim Bottomley had an excellent offensive year for the Cardinals in 1926, leading the league with 40 doubles and 120 RBIs. He was not as adept with a glove, pacing the circuit in errors at first base. A happy-go-lucky sort who was quick to console teammates when they made mistakes, Bottomley was nicknamed "Sunny Jim" for his cheerful temperament. Similar to Haines, his peak years were somewhat abbreviated.

Another player of questionable Cooperstown merit, outfielder Chick Hafey was in his third season with the Cardinals in 1926. A line-drive hitter with deceptive power, Hafey suffered from sinus problems and poor eyesight. He was eventually forced to wear glasses, which was highly unusual for a player of the era. In spite of his maladies, he won a batting title in 1931 and retired with a .317 lifetime average. His election to the Hall of Fame has drawn criticism, however, given the fact that he missed close to 600 games during his 12 full seasons in the majors. Hafey played in 78 regular season games during the 1926 campaign, managing a modest .271 batting average.

The National League pennant race was a three-way dogfight between the Reds, Pirates, and Cardinals. St. Louis got off to a shaky start, posting a sub-.500 record through the month of May, but a 16–6 effort in June put them back in contention. By the first of September, the Redbirds were sitting on top of the standings with a slender lead over their rivals. The Pirates and Reds both crumbled down the stretch, combining for a 6–13–1 showing in their last 10 games. This allowed the Cardinals to capture their first pennant since 1888, when they had played under a different name in the American Association.

The Cards entered the October showcase as heavy underdogs. Overmatched but unintimidated, Hornsby boldly declared that St. Louis was the better team. Huggins begged to differ, telling reporters that the Bombers would slug their way to victory. The Series—another seven-game classic—ended with a questionable gambit on the basepaths.

A crowd of nearly 62,000 turned out at Yankee Stadium for the opener. A large throng of fans without tickets assembled outside of City Hall in Manhattan, where two large scoreboards had been set up to track the events on the field. The pitching matchup featured Pennock against Bill Sherdel—a left-hander who had compiled a 16–12 record during the regular season. Dignitaries in attendance at the game included New York Supreme Court judge Robert F. Wagner, Commissioner Kenesaw Mountain Landis, and heavyweight boxing champion Jack Dempsey.

Pennock got off to a rocky start when outfielder Taylor Douthit smashed a leadoff double and moved to third on a slow grounder to second base. With two outs, Bottomley delivered a bloop single that gave the Cardinals a 1–0 lead. It was the only run they would score all afternoon as Pennock allowed just one hit and three walks the rest of the way. The Yankees tied the score in the bottom of the first on an RBI groundout by Gehrig. Ruth provided a moment of comic relief in the bottom of the third when he split his pants sliding into second. But the sixth inning was no laughing matter for the Cardinals as Gehrig picked up his second

RBI of the game, driving Ruth home with a single. It proved to be the deciding run in a 2–1 Yankee win.

Alexander was on-point in the second meeting, scattering four hits and striking out 10. Combs was the only starting member of the New York lineup who was not a strikeout victim. After falling behind 2–0, the Cardinals tied the score in the third on a key single by Bottomley. Right fielder Billy Southworth broke the game open for St. Louis with a three-run homer in the seventh. Enshrined at Cooperstown as a manager years later, Southworth had a phenomenal Series with 10 hits and six runs scored.

St. Louis mayor Victor J. Miller officially ended the workday early on October 4 to allow Cardinals fans time to assemble at Union Station to welcome their team home. Thousands of St. Louis fans jammed the streets, treating players to a rousing ovation. A crowd in excess of 37,000 at Sportsman's Park saw Haines pitch a masterful five-hit shutout the following day, giving the Cardinals a 2–1 Series edge.

Game 4 enhanced the rapidly expanding legend of Ruth. The Babe hit three home runs—a World Series record that has been tied, but never broken. One of those shots fulfilled a promise to a sick kid named Johnny Sylvester, who had been badly injured in a fall from a horse. Upon hearing that the 11-year-old New Jersey boy was in grave condition, Ruth sent him an autographed ball inscribed with the message: "I'll knock a homer for you Wednesday." On the heels of the Bambino's landmark performance, Sylvester's physical condition was said to have miraculously improved. Although the inscribed baseball has been authenticated, the rest of the story was likely embellished to some extent.

The fifth game was among the most exciting of the Series as Pennock and Sherdel battled to a 2–2 tie through nine innings. In the top of the 10th, the veteran St. Louis hurler began to show signs of fatigue. Shortstop Mark Koenig led off with a single and moved to second on a wild pitch. After a walk to Ruth, Meusel moved the runners up with a groundout. Taking no chances with the dangerous Gehrig, Sherdel intentionally loaded the bases. Lazzeri followed with an RBI sacrifice, giving the Yankees a 3–2 Series advantage.

The Cardinals pushed back hard in Game 6. Again, it was Alexander who captured the spotlight, holding Ruth, Gehrig, and Lazzeri to a combined 1-for-11 showing at the plate. Les Bell came up huge for the Redbirds, driving in four runs. Hornsby added three more RBIs as St. Louis forced a pivotal seventh game with a 10–2 rout.

The finale was played in damp conditions at Yankee Stadium. Well rested after his sparkling Game 3 performance, Haines returned to the mound for the Cardinals. Huggins countered with Game 4 winner Waite Hoyt. Ruth opened the scoring for the Yankees in the bottom of the third with his fourth home run of the Series (a new record), but the 1–0 lead quickly evaporated as Koenig botched what could have been an inning-ending double play in the top of the fourth. Meusel followed with a costly error in the outfield, enabling a three-run outburst by St. Louis. Trailing 3–1, the Bombers inched closer in the sixth on an RBI double by catcher Hank Severeid. The drama that unfolded in the next inning has attained almost mythical status.

Combs led off the seventh with a line-drive single and moved to second on a sacrifice by Koenig. After a one-out intentional walk to Ruth, Meusel reached on a fielder's choice. Gehrig followed with another walk, bringing Lazzeri to the plate with the bases loaded and two outs. This prompted a mound visit from Hornsby. At some point during the game, Haines had developed a blister on his pitching hand, and it was actively bleeding.

"Can you throw it anymore?" Hornsby asked, referring to Haines's signature knuckleball.

"No. I can throw the fastball, but not the knuckler," Haines replied.

"Well," said Hornsby, "we don't want any fastballs to this guy."

Taking a major risk, Hornsby called upon Alexander to rescue the Cardinals from peril.

"I can still see him yet, to this day, walking in from the left field bullpen through the gray mist," Les Bell recalled years later. "The Yankee fans recognized him right off, of course, but you didn't hear a sound from anywhere in that stadium." Rumors have persisted that Alexander had been drinking the night before and was still intoxicated when he entered the game, but the hurler vehemently denied those claims. Whatever state he was in, there was no margin for error against a rookie slugger who had gathered 117 RBIs during the regular season.

Details of the encounter vary from source to source. Some say that Alexander went right to work without any warm-up tosses in order to preserve his arm. Others claim that he made a few half-hearted practice throws. With the count at 1-and-1, Lazzeri smashed a long drive down the left field line that hooked foul at the last second. By some reports, he missed a home run by inches and by others it was several feet. Alexander, himself, remarked: "Less than a foot made the difference between a hero and a bum." After a brief mound conference, the veteran hurler went back to work, striking out Lazzeri on the next pitch (a fastball or breaking ball depending on who is telling the story).

Inning over. Threat extinguished.

Securing his status as a World Series hero, Alexander retired the Yankees in order in the bottom of the eighth then returned to close out the game. With two outs, he walked Ruth on a borderline pitch, bringing Meusel to the plate. Meusel had raked Alexander for a double and a triple in Game 6. With Gehrig on-deck, the last thing anyone expected was for Ruth to attempt a steal of second base. But that's exactly what happened. Unfortunately for the Yankees, he didn't get a good jump. St. Louis Catcher Bob O'Farrell's throw arrived well ahead of the slugger, who was tagged out by Hornsby to end the Series. After the game, Huggins defended Ruth's actions, commenting: "We needed an unexpected move. Had Ruth made the steal, it would have been declared the smartest piece of baseball in the history of World Series play."

The two teams squared off again in the 1928 Series with different results. Both enjoyed long periods of success during the 1930s and early 1940s. By the end of the twentieth century, they were the winningest clubs in major-league history.

CHAPTER 7

Yankees vs. Cardinals 1942

As the world began drifting toward war in the 1930s, Congress passed a series of neutrality acts aimed at preventing US involvement in foreign conflicts. On December 7, 1941, the Imperial Japanese Navy Air Service brought war to America's doorstep with a surprise military strike on the US Naval base at Pearl Harbor. Japanese forces attacked with more than 300 aircraft, inflicting massive damage on the unsuspecting US fleet. There were more than 2,000 American casualties reported. Shortly afterward, President Franklin Delano Roosevelt officially declared war on Japan.

There was talk of shutting down baseball in the wake of the catastrophe, but on January 15, 1942, FDR drafted a letter to Commissioner Landis urging major-league executives to keep the sport active. "I honestly feel that it would be best for the country to keep baseball going," the president wrote. "There will be fewer people unemployed, and everybody will work longer hours and harder than ever before. And that means they ought to have a chance for recreation and for taking their minds off of their work even more than before." Following the president's suggestion, baseball continued undaunted throughout World War II. As the fighting intensified overseas, the face of the game underwent a dramatic transformation.

In the years immediately following the attack on Pearl Harbor, more than 400 ballplayers traded their major-league uniforms for military attire. The A's, Phillies, and Dodgers were hit the hardest as each franchise lost more than 30 players to the armed forces by 1945. The Yankee lineup became virtually unrecognizable with the gradual departure of the entire Hall of Fame corps. But in 1942, the Bombers were still one of the most powerful clubs in the majors.

Looking to expand the team's talent base, Yankee owner Jacob Ruppert purchased the Newark Bears of the International League. During the late 1930s and early 1940s, the Bears supplied the Yankees with a steady influx of top-tier players. This included corner outfielders Tommy Henrich and Charlie Keller, who combined for more than 350 homers and 1,500 RBIs in spite of extensive military absences. Second baseman Joe Gordon—whose slick glove and powerful bat landed him in the Hall of Fame—was also a Newark alumnus.

Yankee interests were not limited to International League prospects. Joe DiMaggio and Lefty Gomez were both discovered in the Pacific Coast League. Phil Rizzuto spent a majority of his minor-league days in the American Association. Although Gomez's best years were behind him by 1942, DiMaggio and Rizzuto were very much in their prime.

Nicknamed "Scooter" for the way he ran the bases, Rizzuto was a staple in the Yankee lineup for 12 full seasons. A five-time All-Star, he was once described by a teammate as the glue that held the club together. Although his statistics appear somewhat ordinary on the surface, he possessed many intangible qualities that prompted frequent comparisons to the best shortstops of the era.

DiMaggio is still widely regarded as one of the greatest all-around players in baseball history. Describing his defensive abilities, Yankee manager Joe McCarthy once said, "You never saw him fall down or go diving for a ball. He didn't have to. He just knew where the ball was hit and he went and got it." Explaining the effect he had on the American public, author Ernest Hemingway remarked, "There was a majesty in his swing and a self-assured confidence of style that was uniquely Joe DiMaggio's. In the eye of his public, he was more than a sports hero. He was among the most cherished icons of popular culture."

Rounding out a stellar supporting cast, the Yankees got a number of outstanding pitching performances in 1942. Spud Chandler, a gritty right-hander who intimidated batters with his high intensity, won 16 of 21 decisions while posting a sterling 2.38 ERA. Ernie Bonham, jokingly

Figure 7.1 After Lou Gehrig's abrupt departure in 1939, Joe DiMaggio became the face of the Yankees. This photo was taken during his 56-game hitting streak in 1941.

nicknamed "Tiny" on account of his beefy frame, led the American League with six shutouts and an .808 winning percentage. Rookie right-hander Hank Borowy—another Newark product—posted a handsome 15–4 record. And Red Ruffing, who was nearing the end of his Hall of Fame career, added 14 victories to the Yankee effort.

The AL pennant race provided little excitement for fans outside the Bronx. By the time the All-Star break arrived, the Bombers had climbed to the top and built a sturdy lead. A pair of nine-game winning streaks kept the Red Sox hopes alive until late August. But in spite of a strong finish, they fell nine games behind New York. It was the Yankees' sixth AL championship in a seven-year span.

In almost any other season, the Brooklyn Dodgers would have run away with the National League pennant. Their 104 victories in 1942 were a franchise record that stood for a decade. But the St. Louis Cardinals remained a step ahead throughout the second half.

Playing in his first full major-league season, rookie outfielder Stan Musial endeared himself to Cardinal fans with a .315 batting average—the second highest mark on the club behind Enos Slaughter. Slaughter—known for his aggressive style of play—turned in one of his finest offensive efforts, leading the National League in hits, triples, and total bases. Although both men were later elected to the Hall of Fame, Musial's lifetime numbers were far greater. Over the course of 21 full seasons, "Stan the Man" captured seven batting titles and three MVP Awards while earning 24 All-Star selections. Cheerful and approachable off the field, it was once said that he retired with more friends than any player before him. He became a beloved figure in St. Louis, where the Cardinals honored him with a pair of statues outside their ballpark. In 2011, Musial received the ultimate civilian honor—the Presidential Medal of Freedom.

With Musial and Slaughter anchoring the offense, the Cardinals relied heavily upon Mort Cooper and Johnny Beazley for pitching support. Among the most successful wartime hurlers, Cooper paced the circuit with 22 wins, 10 shutouts, and a 1.78 ERA. He logged three consecutive 20-win campaigns before arm troubles drove him out of the majors for good in 1949. Beazley—another short-lived phenom—gathered 21 wins in 1942 while posting the second-best ERA in the league at 2.13. A right-hander with three effective pitches in his arsenal, Beazley injured his arm in exhibition games with the Army Air Force. Like Cooper, he was washed up by the end of the decade.

The St. Louis pitching staff was skillfully handled by catcher Walker Cooper—Mort's younger brother. At 6-foot-3, 210 pounds, Cooper was a commanding presence behind the plate. His lively arm and pinpoint control allowed him to stop 45 percent of all attempted steals during his career. He was also adept with a bat, putting up double-digit home run totals in seven seasons while forging a .285 lifetime batting average.

Few teams have ever gotten far in the absence of solid defensive work. The Cardinals had one of the best glovemen in the majors stationed at shortstop. Describing Marty Marion's style of play, former teammate Joe DeMaestri commented: "Marty was a different kind of shortstop. He was about 6-foot-3 with long, long arms, and he played the position like a spider, drifting from side to side." Others likened Marion to a cephalopod, nicknaming him "Octopus" because it often appeared as if he had extra arms. An eight-time All-Star, Marion posted the highest fielding percentage at his position on three occasions. He was more than competent at the plate—especially in 1942 when he led the league with a career-high 38 doubles.

The Cardinals were relatively slow out of the gate, compiling an 18–15 record through the third week of May. But they caught fire in the second half, posting a .768 winning percentage. Their 106 victories are a team record that has survived into the twenty-first century.

Dating back to the "Murderer's Row" year of 1927, the Yankees had compiled a 32–4 overall record in postseason play. They entered the 1942 Series as heavy favorites. Most insiders picked them to clinch in five or six games—even without slugger Tommy Henrich, who was lost to military duty in early September. Interestingly, the Bombers would have lost Rizzuto as well had the affair stretched beyond five games.

Yankee pundits vastly underestimated the Cardinals' youth and speed, which proved to be a critical factor. With an average age of 26, the dynamic Redbirds ranked fourth in the majors in stolen bases during the regular season. Describing what happened during the Series, one reporter bluntly observed that the Cardinals "just ran the hell out of the Yankees on the bases." Braves manager Casey Stengel quipped, "It isn't a ballclub, it's a track team."

Game 1 opened at Sportsman's Park in St. Louis. Yankees skipper Joe McCarthy surprised many when he passed over staff ace Tiny Bonham for veteran Red Ruffing. Ruffing made the most of the opportunity, carrying a no-hitter into the eighth. The Yankees led 7–0 with two outs in the ninth before Ruffing inexplicably fell apart. The Cardinals chased him from the game with a four-run outburst and brought the winning run to the plate in the form of Stan Musial. Buddy Hassett handled Musial's hard grounder to first for the final out, but the course of the Series had been permanently altered. "[We] showed we could throw a scare into the Yankees," pitcher Max Lanier later recalled. "And then we did more than scare them."

Bonham took his turn on the mound in Game 2 and got off to a wobbly start, yielding a two-run double to Walker Cooper in the first. The Cards expanded the lead with another run in the seventh. Beazley was brilliant for St. Louis until the top of the eighth, when DiMaggio delivered an RBI single, and Charlie Keller followed with a two-run homer to deep right field. Unfazed, St. Louis pushed the deciding run across in the bottom of the frame as Slaughter doubled and Musial drove him home. It was Slaughter who saved the game for the Cardinals in the ninth, making a fine throw to third base to nail pinch-runner Tuck Stainback, who was trying to take an extra base on a single by Hassett. Had Stainback reached safely, he would likely have scored on a fly ball out by pinch-hitter Red Ruffing. The 4–3 St. Louis win evened the Series at a game apiece.

The third meeting was a tight pitching duel between southpaw Ernie White (who had been plagued by shoulder issues earlier in the year) and Chandler. The Cardinals manufactured a run in the third using "small ball" tactics then relied on strong pitching and defense to carry them the rest of the way. Musial, Slaughter, and Terry Moore all made sensational plays in the outfield. Frustrated by White's offerings all afternoon, the Yankees lost their composure. McCarthy lodged a number of petty protests. And infielder Frankie Crosetti threw a massive tantrum after a close call at third base went against New York. Crosetti—a Yankee lifer who won a total of 17 championships as a player and coach—slammed the ball on the ground and shoved umpire Bill Summers, who promptly returned the favor. The Cardinals added a run in the ninth on a timely single by Slaughter. Sportswriter John Drebinger reported that the 2–0 loss sent the Yankees "stumbling to their locker room stunned and bewildered."

Game 4 was a heartbreaker for New York. With close to 70,000 fans in attendance at Yankee Stadium, Hank Borowy failed to retire any of the batters he faced in the fourth inning, leaving the game with runners on the corners and four runs on the board. Reliever Atley Donald did him no favors, allowing both of the inherited runners to score. Things looked bleak for the Bombers until the sixth, when they rallied to tie the score. The big blow came off the bat of Keller—a three-run homer that knocked Mort Cooper out of the game. Just minutes after the Yankee rally brought the crowd to its feet, Donald walked two batters and coughed up an RBI single to Walker Cooper. Summoned from the bullpen, Bonham was victimized for another run on a sacrifice fly by Marty Marion. The final score was 9–6 in favor of St. Louis.

Trailing three games to one, the Bombers' fate rested on the shoulders of Ruffing, who knew a thing or two about overcoming adversity. While working in a coal mine as a teenager, his left foot got caught between a pair of coal cars, costing him several of his toes. Formerly an outfielder, he switched to pitching full-time and adjusted his follow-through to compensate for the handicap. He won 273 major-league games in spite of incessant pain in his foot. The future Cooperstown incumbent put forth another valiant effort in Game 5, holding the Cardinals to two runs on seven hits through eight innings. With the score tied in the top of the ninth, he surrendered a two-run homer to third baseman Whitey Kurowski. It proved to be the coup de grace as the Bombers failed to score in their last at-bat of the Series.

Summarizing the Yankees' humbling defeat, Dick McCann of the *New York Daily News* reported: "It was the first time the Yanks had lost a Series since another audacious gang of Cardinals whipped them four games-to-three in 1926. . . . For eight innings of the first game, the experts were right. The Yankees swaggered, the Cards staggered, and it looked like the National League was again going to be humiliated in short and shameful style. But the Cards rallied in the ninth inning of the opener, almost pulled it out of the fire and were in command of the Series practically every sizzling second since."

St. Louis manager Billy Southworth was elated with his team's performance. "We took 'em and took 'em good, in clean, honest fashion," he bragged to reporters. "It's an honor to beat a team like the Yankees. If ever a bunch of fellows was typical of American youth this bunch of mine is."

Frustrated with the outcome, McCarthy snarled at the press corps: "What's the matter—What do we have to do, win all the time?" Composing himself, he added "They're a good ballclub and they beat a good ballclub. They deserve all credit, but my boys weren't disgraced."

Over the next four seasons, the Cardinals emerged as the winningest team of the war era, capturing three pennants and two World Series. Their only October failure in that span came at the hands of the Yankees in 1943. The convincing New York victory (four games to one) was accomplished without the services of Ruffing, Rizzuto, DiMaggio, and Henrich—all of whom were serving in the military. The Cardinals entered the 1943 Series without Beazley, Slaughter, and Terry Moore. In all, close to 50 players from both clubs joined the armed forces during World War II.

CHAPTER 8

Indians vs. Giants 1954

HISTORY HAS NOT ALWAYS BEEN KIND TO THE WINNINGEST TEAMS. THE 1906 Cubs lost the World Series after collecting 116 victories during the regular season. The 2001 Mariners failed to advance beyond the American League Championship Series after matching Chicago's record-setting total. Following a similar path, the 1954 Indians set the twentieth-century standard for wins by an AL club in a 154-game season before collapsing on the October stage.

Entering the 1954 campaign, the Indians were among the unluckiest franchises in baseball, having captured just two pennants in more than 50 years of play. Competing with the Yankees, who had won 20 AL titles to that point, certainly didn't work to Cleveland's advantage. During the Bombers' historic run of five straight championships (which began in 1949), the Indians finished second on multiple occasions.

On paper, the Indians didn't look like world-beaters in 1954. Three of their regular players hit in the low .200 range. But the pitching staff was formidable. Hall of Famer George Kell recalled: "[Bob] Feller, [Bob] Lemon, [Mike] Garcia, [Early] Wynn—all threw bullets. When you went into Cleveland for a four-game weekend series, if you didn't manage your times at bat well, you'd come out of there 0-for-15. You had to plan on getting your hits. There was no letting up."

A fierce competitor, Early Wynn made a habit of throwing inside on batters. The slightest perceived transgression against him almost always led to a knock-down in a later at-bat. He was familiar with the weaknesses of opponents and knew how to exploit them, feeding hitters a steady diet of whatever pitches they couldn't handle. The 1954 campaign was among his greatest statistical years as he led the league with 23 wins and 36 starts—his highest marks to that point

Bob Lemon—a durable right-hander with a fastball/curve/slider combination—began his professional career as an infielder. During a three-year stint in the Navy, he was used as a pitcher in military games. It became his permanent job when he returned to action in 1946. He fared exceptionally well in the role, gathering no fewer than 20 victories during seven seasons. His 23 wins and 21 complete games landed him among the MVP candidates during the 1954 slate. He was enshrined at Cooperstown in 1976.

Nearing the end of his career in 1954, Bob Feller had lost some velocity on his celebrated fastball. Manager Al Lopez considered releasing the aging flamethrower during spring training, but GM Hank Greenberg decided to keep him around to prevent a public outcry among the Cleveland fan base. It proved to be a wise move as Feller posted a sterling 13–3 record and 3.09 ERA. It was the last great season of his Hall of Fame career.

Although he failed to join his former staff mates in Cooperstown, Mike Garcia was one of the most successful pitchers in the American League during the early 1950s. Equipped with a blazing fastball and effective curve, he captured a pair of ERA titles before mechanical problems and injuries set in. He won 19 games in 1954 while tossing a league-high five shutouts.

The pitching staff was handled efficiently by catcher Jim Hegan. A five-time All-Star, Hegan posted the highest caught-stealing percentage during three campaigns. His ability to work in sync with even the most temperamental hurlers drew high praise from Yankee manager Casey Stengel. Asked which member of the Indians' starting rotation was superior, the veteran skipper replied, "Give me that fellow behind the plate. He's what makes them."

The Cleveland offense was driven by Al Rosen and Larry Doby. Rosen—a multidimensional third baseman—reached the century mark in RBIs in five consecutive seasons. Following up his MVP year of 1953, he posted the highest on-base percentage among Cleveland regulars at .404. His sensational fielding would likely have netted him multiple Gold Gloves had the award existed during his relatively brief career. Doby—the first Black player to appear in the American League—had a spectacular year in 1954, pacing the circuit with 32 homers and 126 ribbies. The performance earned him the sixth of seven consecutive All-Star selections. He finished second in MVP voting to Yogi Berra that year.

Doby and Rosen weren't the only Cleveland players capable of producing runs. A legend in the Mexican League, Bobby Avila became an inspiration to his fellow countrymen when he ascended to the majors in 1949. A slick-fielding second baseman, he regularly finished among the league leaders in putouts, assists, and double plays. Hitting primarily out of the second slot in the batting order, he enjoyed his finest season in 1954, capturing a batting title with a .341 mark.

Always looking to bolster his team's pennant chances, Greenberg traded for slugger Vic Wertz in June of 1954. Wertz, who got off to a tepid start with the Orioles that year, had averaged more than 100 RBIs per season with the Tigers and Browns from 1949 through 1952. Upon arriving in Cleveland, he promptly returned to his old form, finishing the second half of the season with 14 homers and 48 RBIs.

The Indians were like a runaway train in 1954, compiling two individual winning streaks of 11 games. Although they had difficulty shaking the Yankees, they blew away the rest of the competition, finishing 17 games ahead of Chicago and 42 games in front of Boston. The hapless Philadelphia A's wound up 60 games out of the running.

When the curtain opened on the 1954 campaign, the Giants hadn't hoisted a world championship banner in over 20 years. Their last three trips to the World Series had been fruitless ventures. But a new crop of talented players had begun to turn things around.

Whenever discussions were raised in the 1950s regarding the greatest center fielders in the game, Willie Mays's name was invariably mentioned—especially in New York where there were three prime candidates. Sportswriter Red Smith once commented: "[Duke] Snider, [Mickey] Mantle, and [Willie] Mays. You could get a fat lip in any saloon by starting an argument as to which was best. One point was beyond argument, though. Willie was by all odds the most exciting." A five-tool player,

Mays combined awesome power with lightning speed and defensive excellence. Fifty years after he logged his last at-bat, he still ranked among the top ten of all time in total bases, home runs, and extra-base hits. After spending portions of two seasons in the army, he returned to capture the 1954 batting crown. He also clubbed 41 homers while leading the NL with 13 triples.

Nicknamed "Mandrake the Magician" for his ability to find holes in the opposing defensive alignment, right fielder Don Mueller had his finest offensive year in 1954, finishing second to Mays with a .342 batting average. Not only could he deliver the hits, but he came up with them in tight spots, compiling a .387 mark in "late and close" situations (defined as plate appearances in the seventh inning or later with the Giants tied or leading by one or with the tying run on deck). During New York's September stretch run, Mueller hit safely in all but two games.

The first Black player to make appearances for the Giants and St. Louis Browns, third baseman Hank Thompson led the Kansas City Monarchs to a pennant in 1946. In 1948, he paced the Negro American League in runs scored and stolen bases while hitting .337. Although he never led the National League in any major statistical category, he hit for moderate power and drove in plenty of runs for the Giants. In 1954, he slugged a career-high total of 26 homers while drawing 90 walks—more than any player on the club.

Outfielder Monte Irvin spent some of his greatest seasons in the Negro National League, winning three batting titles and fashioning a lifetime .337 average. There's no telling what he could have done for the Giants had he arrived in New York sooner. Newark Eagles owner Effa Manley said, "Monte was the choice of all Negro National and American League club owners to serve as the number-one player to join a white major-league team. We all agreed in a meeting that he was the best qualified by temperament, character, ability, sense of loyalty, morals, age, experience, and physique to represent us. . . . Of course, Branch Rickey lifted Jackie Robinson out of negro ball and made him the first, and it turned out just fine." Appearing most often in the middle-third of the batting order, the 35-year-old Irvin accumulated 64 RBIs in 1954 and scored 62 runs.

The Giants' pitching staff posted the lowest earned run average in the National League during the 1954 pennant run. The ace of the staff was Johnny Antonelli, a left-handed curveball specialist who had failed to maximize his abilities with the Braves. Recognizing his untapped potential, GM Chub Feeney brought him to New York in a trade involving slugger Bobby Thomson. Antonelli enjoyed a breakout year, leading the NL with six shutouts and a 2.30 ERA. The Cy Young Award didn't exist then, but he would have been among the top contenders.

Antonelli's efforts were strongly supported by Sal Maglie and Ruben Gomez. Maglie—nicknamed "the Barber" because he often threw high and tight—was a sinister presence on the mound, scowling at batters with contempt. Using a fastball and hard curve, he won 14 of 20 decisions while finishing among the NL ERA leaders. Gomez, who was among the first pitchers from Puerto Rico to reach the majors, had a handful of decent seasons with the Giants before fading into relative obscurity. He posted a 17–9 record in 1954 with a handsome 2.88 earned run average.

In the bullpen, the Giants had Hoyt Wilhelm—a durable knuckleballer who later became the first reliever enshrined at Cooperstown. The right-handed flutterball specialist appeared in 57 games in 1954, compiling a 12–4 record while holding opponents to a frail .195 batting average.

It took the Giants awhile to get their footing. After a 9–11 start, they caught fire in June, taking over first place with a 24–4 run. They were never completely secure in the months that followed. Although they led by seven games on July 21, they lost seven of the next eight and found themselves fending off the Dodgers throughout the month of August. In a critical three-game series at Brooklyn during late September, Maglie and Gomez were brilliant in consecutive starts, allowing the Giants to clinch.

With their dominant pitching staff and record-setting 111 victories, the Indians were heavy favorites to win the Series. But the experts didn't count on the contributions of surprise star Dusty Rhodes, who put on a display of pinch-hitting never before equaled in postseason play. A lefty-swinging outfielder, Rhodes gained a reputation as a fun-loving jokester and late-night carouser. He was under no illusions about his abilities, bluntly telling one writer: "I ain't much of a fielder and I got a lousy arm, but I sure do love to whack that ball." Whack it he did, accruing a .667 batting average in the Series while delivering clutch hits in three of the Giants' four wins.

Giants skipper Leo Durocher sent Maglie to the mound in Game 1, as Al Lopez—Cleveland's Hall of Fame manager—countered with Bob Lemon. Lemon was effective through nine innings, holding the New Yorkers to a pair of runs on eight hits. But Lopez's decision to leave Lemon on the mound after the game moved into extra innings proved to be a mistake. Most of the scoring took place early. Maglie got off to a wobbly start, hitting leadoff batter Al Smith and yielding a single to Avila before serving up a hittable pitch to Vic Wertz, who sent both runners home with a triple. The Giants answered with a pair in the bottom of the third as Mueller and Thompson each drove in a run. The score remained tied until the tenth frame.

The game is best remembered for a remarkable defensive play made by Mays in the top of the eighth. After a leadoff walk to Doby, Rosen singled, chasing Maglie from the game. With left-handed curveballer Don Liddle on the mound, Wertz drove a pitch to the deep recesses of the Polo Grounds. The stadium's most striking feature was its elongated shape, which resembled a bathtub or a bowling alley from above. The right field foul pole was only 258 feet from home plate while the left field corner was a meager 280-foot stretch. The power alleys were monstrous in comparison at 450 feet while the wall in dead-center field was a 480-foot expanse. Mays—with his incredible speed and rifle arm—was uniquely suited to patrol the perimeter. Sportswriter Donald Honig once quipped that "putting Mays in a small ballpark would have been like trimming a masterpiece to fit a frame."

Mays knew that batters tended to hit grounders off of Liddle, so he was playing shallow in the hope of cutting down a runner at the plate in the event of a single. With Mays in hot pursuit of Wertz's drive, Irvin rushed over from left field to play the carom off the wall. There would be no carom, however, as Willie made a stupendous grab. Without missing a beat, he spun and threw the ball back to the infield to hold both of the runners on base. Describing the play in his column, Arthur Daley of the *New York Times* reported, "This was akin to an optical illusion.

Figure 8.1 Sadly, little remains of the Polo Grounds today. Pictured here in a state of disrepair is the John T. Brush Stairway, which led to the stadium on Coogan's Bluff in Upper Manhattan. The stairway was fully restored in 2011.
PHOTO COURTESY OF H.L.I.T. ON VISUAL HUNT.

. . . Catching the ball appeared a sheer impossibility. But Willie, running like a frightened gazelle for the bleacher wall and with his back to the plate, speared it over the shoulder with a gloved hand. It was one of the great catches in World Series history." Asked if it was the best play of his career after the game, Mays said, "I don't know whether I made a greater catch any time. I just try to get a jump on the ball and go get it. I thought I had that one all the way."

In the bottom of the tenth, Mays drew a one-out walk and stole second. Thompson was intentionally walked to face Rhodes, who was inserted in place of Irvin. Rising to the occasion, Rhodes thrilled the 52,000-plus fans in attendance with a walk-off homer to deep right field.

Game 2 was a Thursday matinee that attracted a slightly smaller crowd. Wynn was Lopez's choice to start as Durocher handed the ball to Antonelli. For the second day in a row, the Indians got on the board first with a leadoff homer by Al Smith. Halfway through the game, it looked as if Cleveland's slender lead might hold up. After retiring the first 12 batters he faced, Wynn surrendered a leadoff walk and a single to open the fifth. Durocher—playing a hunch—substituted Rhodes for Irvin again.

It proved to be a savvy move as Rhodes delivered an RBI single, tying the game. Antonelli later helped his own cause with an RBI groundout, putting the Giants ahead, 2–1. After Rhodes had padded New York's lead with a solo shot in the seventh, the Indians nearly recovered. There were two runners aboard and two outs in the ninth when Wertz drilled a ball to deep left field. Rhodes, never known for his glovework, made the grab to preserve a 3–1 New York win.

It was Garcia's turn to face the red-hot Giants in Game 3. Gomez took the mound for New York. Cleveland Stadium was jam-packed with over 71,000 fans—most of them hoping to see the Indians get back on track. It didn't happen. In fact, the game went off the rails early. With one out and a runner on first in the opening frame, Mueller hit a serviceable double play ball to George Strickland at short. Strickland, who was known for his exceptional defense, stepped on second base and threw wildly to Wertz at first. Mueller advanced on the play and scored on an RBI single by Mays, giving the Giants a 1–0 lead. The Indians—perhaps reeling from the shocking turn the Series had taken to that point—crumbled in the third as the Giants loaded the bases with one out. Following the prescribed formula, Durocher benched Irvin in favor of Rhodes yet again. The results were hardly surprising as Rhodes drove in a pair of runs with a clutch single. Sloppy defense followed as Davey Williams pushed a bunt to Garcia, whose errant throw allowed another run to score. The Giants padded their lead with runs in the fifth and sixth, moving on to an easy 6–2 win.

The finale was never terribly close. With the Giants holding a three-game advantage, Durocher felt comfortable leaving Rhodes on the bench. Irvin had an excellent game, gathering two hits and a pair of RBIs. Lopez was forced to empty out his bullpen as Lemon was charged with four runs in four-plus innings of work. He left the game with the bases loaded and the Indians trailing 3–0. Summoned from the bullpen, Hall of Famer Hal Newhouser promptly walked in a run and gave up a two-run single. Ray Narleski, Don Mossi, and Garcia closed out the game for Cleveland, which ended in a 7–4 New York win.

Describing what happened to the Indians in the Series, Al Smith remarked, "Rhodes didn't beat us alone. We beat ourselves. We scored only nine runs in four games. We couldn't get any hits. Who would have figured that Rosen and Doby wouldn't drive in any runs and that Avila and Doby would hit well below .200? We didn't think the Giants had a better team, but that our loss was just one of those things."

Celebrating the Giants' first championship since 1933, a cheering throng of supporters greeted players at the airport. A ticker-tape parade followed as the Giants were honored by Mayor Robert F. Wagner Jr. at City Hall. The unlikely Series sweep came to be referred to by some as the "Little Miracle of Coogan's Bluff."

Commenting on the 1954 season in his memoirs, Durocher wrote: "Once again, I was a genius, and just in the nick of time, too, because for two years I'd been just a bum." By the time the Giants' World Series victory celebration was held, word had spread that Durocher intended to sign with NBC as a broadcaster. In the middle of the party, team owner Horace Stoneham reminded Durocher that he still had one year left on his contract. Durocher agreed to delay his departure for at least one season but bluntly remarked to his boss, "Let me tell you something before you get too many drinks in you. This club isn't as good as you think it is. Everything went our way this year. Next year, we're going to have to fill [at least] four big holes." As predicted, the Giants slipped to third place in 1955. They wouldn't win another World Series until 2010. Durocher walked away from managing after the 1955 campaign but returned in 1966 to pilot the Cubs and Astros. He retired for good after the 1973 slate. Sadly, he wasn't alive to witness his Hall of Fame induction in 1994.

The Indians fell to second place in 1955 and began a long descent into non-contention. By the mid-1970s, fans in the Forest City had taken to calling Cleveland Stadium the "Mistake by the Lake." Although the franchise has put some highly respectable squads on the field in recent years, they have also endured the longest championship drought of any current major-league team, having claimed their last World Series title in 1948.

CHAPTER 9

Yankees vs. Dodgers 1955

ALTHOUGH THE YANKEE–DODGER RIVALRY IS AMONG THE MOST CELE-brated in sports, the results have been largely one-sided over the years. The two teams met in October competition five times between 1941 and 1953. On each occasion, the Yankees sent the Brooklynites into the off-season empty handed. Entering the 1955 campaign, the Dodgers were 0-for-7 in World Series play. Fans in Flatbush grew so accustomed to losing that they adopted the saying: "Wait 'til Next Year"—a mantra laced with heartache and unwavering hope.

Reflecting on the epic showdowns of the 1950s, Mickey Mantle wrote in his memoirs, "There was nothing to match the rivalry and mad-ness of facing the Brooklyn Dodgers in the World Series . . . I look at the lineup today and think, what players, what talent, what fans they had. . . . It isn't easy to imagine a team more perfectly suited to a place and time." The 1955 Dodgers appeared to have everything going for them—with the exception of a championship, that is.

But things were about to change.

There were five Hall of Famers in Brooklyn's daily lineup. Having lost a step or two at the age of 36, Jackie Robinson still played with passion and determination. A versatile fielder, he appeared at four dif-ferent defensive stations in 1955. His offensive numbers were deceiving. Although he posted the lowest batting average of his career at .256, his on-base percentage was 50 points above the league average. And he knew how to create havoc on the basepaths, distracting pitchers with feints and footwork that resembled quirky dance steps.

While Robinson was fading in 1955, Duke Snider was in the prime of his career. Hitting almost exclusively out of the third slot in the order, the lefty slugger led the National League with 126 runs scored and 136 RBIs. Although he could be extremely prickly and temperamental at times, fans were more than willing to forgive his trespasses. His 326 homers were the most by any player during the 1950s.

In sharp contrast to Robinson and Snider, who were excitable types, Roy Campanella and Pee Wee Reese were stabilizing forces. Often cited as one of the greatest catchers in history, "Campy" won three MVP Awards in a career abruptly terminated by a car accident in 1958. Short and somewhat pudgy, he was once compared to a Sumo wrestler by sportswriter Roger Kahn. While Robinson sometimes railed against the system and clamored for civil rights, Campanella quietly stuck to the business of baseball. Genial and upbeat, he was referred to by one writer as a "cheerleader, almost childlike in his enthusiasm." Reese is best remembered for helping resolve the internal strife created by the arrival of Robinson in 1947. When other players circulated a petition protesting Robinson's presence, Reese openly defied them by refusing to sign. Over the course of Robinson's turbulent rookie season, Reese offered ongoing encouragement and support. His kind gestures defined him as an honorable, empathetic man worthy of the team captaincy—a title he held from 1949 through 1958.

First baseman Gil Hodges was one of the most reliable two-way players of the era. His smooth fielding and sure hands earned him three Gold Glove Awards. His powerful swing landed him among the NL leaders in home runs and RBIs throughout the 1950s. Marveling at his popularity, teammate Clem Labine once remarked, "Not getting booed at Ebbets Field was an amazing thing. Those fans knew their baseball and Gil was the only player I can remember whom the fans never, I mean *never*, booed."

Another key to the Dodgers' success in 1955 was pitching. Right-hander Don Newcombe—former Rookie of the Year in 1949—enjoyed a spectacular season, posting the highest winning percentage in the NL with a 20–5 record. Swingman Clem Labine won 10 games in relief and three as a starter while saving 11 more. As a collective unit, the

Brooklyn staff paced the NL in strikeouts and saves while posting the lowest earned run average.

On the heels of a disappointing second place finish in 1954, the Dodgers came flying out of the gate, winning their first 10 games. By May 10, they had compiled a 22–2 record. It was smooth sailing from there as they clinched the pennant on September 8—earlier than any club in National League history. *Sport* magazine gave manager Walter Alston a lion's share of the credit, naming him Man of the Year. Although the Hall of Fame skipper was soft-spoken and even-tempered a majority of the time, he was occasionally known to throw chairs, break doors, or invite players to fight with him. "The Dodgers are not the easiest club to handle," a writer from the *Sporting News* asserted. "They are filled with various temperaments, but Alston kept them all in check . . . he knew his men. Those who could got the chance to deliver for him. Those who were reluctant were discarded."

As fate would have it, 1955 was the year the musical *Damn Yankees* became a smash hit on Broadway. The enduring romantic comedy is a modern adaptation of the classic Faust legend. It tells the story of a Washington Senators fan who sells his soul to the devil in exchange for a postseason bid. The play was also based on a book titled *The Year the Yankees Lost the Pennant*, which was released in 1954—a season in which the Bombers did just that. Reminiscing about the 1955 campaign many years later, Mickey Mantle considered the release of the stage adaptation to be a bad omen.

The Yankees had captured so many championships by the mid-1950s, they were literally expected to win every year. "I suppose it's human nature," Mantle explained, "but the Yankees of my era looked on the World Series as a kind of birthright. The front office encouraged you to think of your player's shares as a part of your salary." Elaborating on that statement, pitcher Eddie Lopat described contract negotiations with GM George Weiss as follows: "He'd give you this line that you'd make six or eight thousand in Series money so he could keep your salary down. Once I said, 'What if we don't win? Will you make up the difference?' He said, 'We'll win.' That was the end of it."

The Yankees' failure to qualify for the postseason in 1954 prompted a number of changes in the Bronx. Allie Reynolds—a key member of the starting rotation since 1947—opted for retirement. Pitchers Bob Turley (a Cy Young winner in 1958) and Don Larsen (author of a perfect World Series game in 1956) were acquired from the Orioles in a blockbuster deal involving more than a dozen players. Johnny Kucks—a tall, slender right-hander with an effective sinker—was promoted from the minors. And southpaw Tommy Byrne, who had appeared in just five games for the Yanks during the 1954 campaign, saw his workload increase exponentially.

After a spectacular big-league debut, southpaw Whitey Ford sacrificed two full seasons to military duty. Proving his rookie effort was no fluke, he posted a 34–14 cumulative record in the two seasons following his return. 1955 was one of his most successful campaigns as he led the American League with 18 wins and 18 complete games. Complementing Ford's sensational performance, Turley, Larsen, Kucks, and Byrne combined for 50 wins and a 3.15 ERA.

With a rare combination of raw power and unparalleled speed, Mantle arrived in the majors hailed as the heir to Joe DiMaggio. In the face of unimaginable pressure, he established himself as one of the most productive hitters in the Yankee lineup. But he still had not realized his full potential entering the 1955 campaign. Silencing many of the critics who had been riding him since his 1951 debut, he slugged 37 homers (tops in the AL) while leading the league in several other statistical categories.

Although Mantle still had something left to prove, Yogi Berra had long ago established himself as the top catcher in the AL and perhaps all of baseball. A notorious bad-ball hitter, he was known to make solid contact with pitches that bounced in the dirt. Teammate Hector Lopez remarked of Berra's effect on opposing pitchers: "[He] had the fastest bat I ever saw. He could hit a ball late that was already past him and take it out of the park. The pitchers were afraid of him because he'd hit anything, so they didn't know what to throw. Yogi had them psyched out and he wasn't even trying to psyche them out." Demonstrating his reliability in the clutch, Berra led the Yankees in RBIs for seven consecutive seasons.

His solid all-around play in 1955 earned him his second straight MVP nod. It was the third of his career.

Another major contributor in New York, Moose Skowron enjoyed one of his finest seasons in 1955, posting a .319 batting average—the second-highest mark of his career. He played a number of roles that year, splitting time at first base with Joe Collins and Eddie Robinson. He was also used as a third baseman and pinch-hitter. At least one former teammate cited Skowron as the driving force of the Yankee offense. "Moose, not Mickey, was the guy who won close games for us," relief pitcher Ryne Duren said.

Coming off of their record-setting 1954 campaign (in which they had posted 111 wins), the Indians were still the team to beat in the American League. At the beginning of May, the Yankees were sitting in fourth place with Cleveland on top. But a 16–3 run from May 13 through May 30 put the New Yorkers out in front. They barely held on, sharing the lead for six days in August and one day in September. The return of second baseman Billy Martin, who had been serving in the military for the better part of two seasons, gave the club a boost in the final stretch. A season-high eight-game winning streak enabled the Bombers to build a 3.5-game lead. Cleveland slumped near the finish line, losing six of their last nine games as the Yankees reclaimed the AL title.

Given their performances against the Dodgers in the past, the Yankees were heavily favored to win—even with Mantle nursing a leg injury (which he sustained in mid-September). The Series opened at Yankee Stadium with close to 64,000 fans in attendance. After pitching a scoreless first, Ford gave up a solo homer to Carl Furillo. Robinson followed with a triple and scored on a single by Don Zimmer, putting the Dodgers up, 2–0. But Newcombe couldn't hold the lead, yielding a game-tying homer to Elston Howard in the bottom of the second. Home runs by Duke Snider and Joe Collins followed a bit later. Collins struck twice with a solo shot in the fourth and a two-run blast in the sixth that gave the Yanks a 6–3 advantage. With Ford still on the mound for New York, Furillo led off the top of the eighth with a single. Robinson reached on an error by third baseman Gil McDougald, setting up one of the most iconic plays in Series history.

Zimmer drove Furillo home with a sacrifice fly as Robinson moved to third base. Looking to shake things up, Robinson stole home. Years later, he recalled: "Here we were in our seventh World Series in 50 years and there was hope that this would be the year, but our fans were also ready to shrug their shoulders and say, 'wait 'til next year,' if we lost. The way we were playing in that first game—down 6–4 in the eighth inning—it looked like we might have to wait. . . . It was not the best strategy to steal home with our team two runs behind, but I just took off and did it. I really didn't care whether I made it or not—I was just tired of waiting."

Ford remembered the play vividly, recounting it as follows: "I knew he was going to steal home. I almost dared him to by taking a long windup as he danced off the bag. Sure enough, he took off for the plate and I threw the ball to Yogi and it got there in plenty of time . . . Robinson slid right into the tag. He was out. There was no question about it."

Umpire Bill Summers begged to differ, calling Robinson safe on the play—a decision he defended to the day he died. Berra strenuously argued to the contrary, but his protest fell on deaf ears. After the Yankees held on for a 6–5 victory, Yogi told a writer from the *New York Herald Tribune* (with expletives included) that Robinson's steal was a "lousy showboat strategy." Robinson snapped back: "Tell Berra that any time he wants to give me a run I'll take it." The validity of Summers' call on the play has been endlessly debated over the years.

The pitching matchup for Game 2 featured Tommy Byrne against Billy Loes—a right-hander who had won 10 games for Brooklyn during the regular season. Loes didn't survive the fourth inning as the Yankees staged a two-out rally, tagging him for four runs. It was all they would need as Byrne remained effective throughout, retiring the Dodgers in order five times. The 4–2 New York win put Brooklyn in serious jeopardy as the Series headed to Ebbets Field.

Down but not out, the Dodgers flipped the script in the next two games, beating the Yankees by an aggregate score of 16–8. Campanella and Robinson came up big in the third meeting, combining for five hits, three runs, and three RBIs. "Campy" remained hot in Game 4, gathering three more hits and slamming his second homer of the Series off of Don Larsen.

Figure 9.1 Jackie Robinson is shown here in a photo from the film *The Jackie Robinson Story* in which he plays himself.
PHOTO COURTESY OF THE LIBRARY OF CONGRESS.

It was Duke Snider who stole the show in the fifth game, cracking a pair of long homers off of Yankee starter Bob Grim. His two blasts gave him a total of four for the Series, tying a record set by Babe Ruth. The mark would stand until 1977, when Reggie Jackson went deep five times. The 5–3 Dodger win put the Yankees on the verge of an early exit.

Ford looked more like himself in Game 6, limiting Brooklyn hitters to just one run on four hits while striking out eight. All of the Yankee scoring was attributed to a disastrous first inning by swingman Karl Spooner, who yielded RBI singles to Berra and Hank Bauer before serving up a three-run homer to Skowron. Russ Meyer and Ed Roebuck shut down the Yankees the rest of the way in the 5–1 Brooklyn loss.

Dodger southpaw Johnny Podres entered the Series with a mediocre 29–22 lifetime record (including the postseason). But a win over the Yankees in Game 3 had boosted his confidence considerably. Before the pivotal seventh match, he told teammates that he would carry them to victory if they gave him just one run. Gil Hodges did better than that, driving in two—one in the fourth off of starter Tommy Byrne and another in the sixth off of reliever Bob Grim. Sandy Amoros—a little known Cuban outfielder—became an unlikely hero with a game-saving catch for the Dodgers in the bottom of the sixth.

Billy Martin led off the sixth with a walk and McDougald followed with a bunt single, bringing Berra to the plate. Describing what happened next, Podres recalled, "I had Yogi Berra, two strikes. I threw him a fastball [that] had to be nine [or] ten inches outside. Wasn't even close to being a strike—a little pop fly to left. But it was a slice." Amoros, who had been ordered to position himself toward right field, raced to the left field corner in an all-out sprint and snared the ball, which would likely have dropped for a two-run double had he been late getting there. Just minutes before, Walter Alston had made a brilliant move, shifting Jim Gilliam from left field to second base. The key to the play was Amoros's left-handedness, which allowed him to fully extend his gloved right hand. Gilliam—a right-handed thrower—would have been forced to backhand Berra's drive, making the play extremely difficult. Asked how he came up with the catch, Amoros answered in broken English, "I don't know. I just [ran] like hell."

The Yankees put runners on in the seventh and eighth but failed to score. Closing out a brilliant performance, Podres pitched a 1-2-3 inning in the ninth, giving the Dodgers the first championship in franchise history. "Not even the staunchest American League die-hard could begrudge Brooklyn its finest hour," wrote John Drebinger of the *New York Times*. "Seven times in the past had the Dodgers been thwarted in their efforts to capture baseball's most sought prize—the last five by these same Bombers. When the goal was finally achieved, the lid blew off in Brooklyn while experts, poring into the records, agreed nothing quite so spectacular had been accomplished before. For this was the first time a team had won a seven-game World Series after losing the first two games."

Newcombe, who had gotten extremely angry when beer was dumped on him during Brooklyn's pennant celebration, soaked himself with suds and drank out of his cap. Duke Snider followed suit while pitcher Clem

Labine cried tears of joy. In a gesture of good will, Berra spent a half hour in the Dodger clubhouse congratulating players. Other well-wishers included Casey Stengel and Commissioner Ford Frick.

Confetti—hastily manufactured from assorted office supplies—was dumped from the upper floor of New York's municipal building. In Brooklyn, church bells rang, and factory whistles blew. Celebratory motorcades raced up and down 86th Street and Flatbush Avenue. Jubilant fans lit firecrackers, banged on cowbells, and hung human effigies labeled "Yankees" from lampposts.

Stengel took responsibility for the Game 7 loss, telling reporters, "I played the game wrong. I figured [Podres] wouldn't last, and I had our hitters taking pitches. But he did last, and I was wrong. They should have been up there swinging from the beginning."

The Yankees had their revenge in the 1956 World Series, beating the Dodgers in seven games. It was the last Fall Classic played in Brooklyn. The two clubs would meet on the October stage four more times before the end of the twentieth century. The Yankees won twice, giving them a lifetime 8–3 Series edge against their long-time rivals.

CHAPTER 10

Yankees vs. Pirates 1960

THE 1950S WERE A DECADE BEST REMEMBERED FOR SWEEPING CHANGES in American lifestyles. The Baby Boom, the Cold War, and the growth of suburbia forever altered the cultural landscape. Baseball was evolving, too, as several major-league teams pulled up their roots and established fan bases in new locations. The transformation continued into the 1960s with the dawn of the expansion era.

The 1960 campaign was the last to feature a lineup of eight American League teams. It was also the final year of the 154-game AL schedule. The departure of the Giants and Dodgers to warmer climates had given the Yankees sole possession of the New York market. But after capturing a World Series title in 1958, the Bombers tumbled to third place. It was up to manager Casey Stengel to straighten things out as the new decade arrived.

Nicknamed "the Old Professor," Stengel guided the Yankees to 10 pennants and seven World Series titles in a 12-year span. An avid proponent of the platoon system, he shuffled players in and out of the lineup with little regard for how it affected his relationships with them. "The secret of managing is to keep the guys who hate you away from the guys who are undecided," he famously joked. The loquacious Stengel was immensely popular with sportswriters, who could always count on him for a humorous quote. But his reputation as a clown was deceiving. He was one of the shrewdest managers in the majors. And he maintained tight control over his players. "All that fun stuff was for the press and fans," outfielder Gene Woodling recalled. "You didn't horse around with him."

The star of the show in New York was Mickey Mantle, who had established himself as one of the most powerful sluggers in major-league history. Although methods of measurement weren't terribly scientific in Mantle's day, he was said to have hit at least 10 home runs in excess of 500 feet. His longest shot smashed into the right field façade at Yankee Stadium before bouncing back to the infield. Hampered by chronic knee issues, "the Mick" still managed to club more home runs than any switch hitter in history (536) while capturing three MVP Awards. Healthy all season in 1960, he led the American League with 119 runs scored, 40 homers, and 294 total bases. In spite of his epic performance, he finished second in MVP voting to teammate Roger Maris.

A fine defensive outfielder with a strong throwing arm, Maris started out with Cleveland in 1957 before a trade landed him in Kansas City. When he failed to live up to his potential, he was dealt to the Yankees in a transaction involving seven players. The change of scenery dramatically changed his career trajectory as he captured back-to-back MVP Awards in 1960 and 1961. He is primarily remembered for breaking Babe Ruth's single-season home run record in the latter campaign—an accomplishment that caused him great anxiety while inadvertently souring his relationship with the press and fans. His 112 ribbies and .581 slugging percentage were tops in the American League during the 1960 campaign.

A three-time MVP and 15-time All-Star, Yogi Berra won more World Series that any player in history. After serving as the Yankees' primary backstop for more than a decade, he was no longer able to handle the daily grind of catching at the age of 35. To keep his productive bat in the lineup, Stengel moved him to the outfield part time in 1960. Even on the downside of his career, he was better than a majority of the utility players in the majors, hitting .276 with 15 homers and 62 RBIs. He was virtually unstoppable with the bases loaded, hitting .667 in that scenario while driving in 16 runs.

In Berra's place, Elston Howard was installed as a full-time catcher. Howard maintained first-string status until 1967. Highly skilled defensively, he captured a pair of Gold Gloves in 1963 and 1964. In the former season, he became the first Black player in the American League to win an MVP Award. Many have speculated that Howard might have made it to the Hall of Fame had he not played in Berra's shadow for several years. Explaining the differences in their catching styles, Whitey Ford wrote: "I liked pitching to Howard. At six-foot-two, he was six inches taller than Berra and made a better target. He also set up a foot or more closer to the batter than Berra did. It made me feel like I was right on top of the batter. I threw a curveball that broke down sharply and Howard would catch it a few inches off the ground. With Berra, it might hit the ground and I wouldn't get the strike call."

Ford was the driving force of the Yankee pitching staff throughout the 1950s and early 1960s. He was known for his calmness under fire and ability to deliver clutch performances in key situations. Comfortable on the World Series stage, he set postseason records that still stand for most consecutive scoreless innings and wins. The 1960 season was forgettable for the Hall of Fame southpaw as he struggled with shoulder issues, posting a middling 12–9 record. He entered the Series on a high note, however, having won his last three decisions—one of them a pivotal game that broke a first-place tie with the Orioles.

Ford's mediocre regular season showing placed right-hander Art Ditmar in an unfamiliar role as the ace of the New York staff. His 15 wins and 3.06 earned run average were tops among Yankee starters. In the bullpen, Stengel relied heavily upon Bobby Schantz, Ryne Duren, and Duke Maas to close out games. Schantz—a former AL MVP—was the best of the trio, gathering 11 saves while posting a 2.79 ERA.

The Yankees got off to a sluggish start, entering the month of June in fourth place. The race remained tight until mid-September, when the Bombers closed out the season with a 15-game winning streak. On the heels of that impressive run, a majority of the New York writers favored the Yankees to make quick work of the Pirates, whose last Fall Classic appearance had taken place when Babe Ruth and Lou Gehrig still roamed the basepaths.

The 1960 Pirates were among the most underrated pennant-winning squads in history. Like a dependable domestic car, they weren't flashy, but they completed the journey with maximum efficiency. With the exception of first baseman Dick Stuart (who carried the facetious nickname of "Dr. Strangeglove"), the Bucs were an exceptional defensive ballclub, posting the highest fielding percentage in the National League. Hall of Famers Bill Mazeroski and Roberto Clemente combined for 20 Gold Gloves during their careers. Shortstop Dick Groat, who won the 1960 NL MVP Award, was among the most reliable double play partners in the majors.

Bob Friend and Vern Law carried the bulk of the pitching responsibilities. Law was nicknamed "the Deacon" in reference to his status as an elder of the Mormon Church. A workhorse for the Pirates in 1959 and 1960, he tossed more than 260 innings in both campaigns. His 18 complete games during the 1960 pennant run were tops in the NL. He captured Cy Young honors on the strength of his 20–9 record and 3.08 ERA.

Another durable hurler, Friend reached the 200-inning mark every year from 1955 through 1965. He was described by one researcher as "strong, large, and perhaps a little beefy with a smooth, uncomplicated pitching motion and a demeanor at once quietly intense and unflappable." Friend had superb control, never walking more than 85 batters in any season. He finished with double-digit win totals on nine occasions—a remarkable feat considering that some of the squads he played on finished near the bottom of the standings. The 1960 campaign was one of his finest efforts as he posted an 18–12 record with an earned run average of 3.00.

The Pirates had one of the best closers in the majors at their disposal. A right-hander with a devastating forkball, Roy Face made a name for himself in 1959, when he posted an 18–1 record out of the bullpen—the highest single-season winning percentage of all-time among pitchers with at least 15 victories. In 1960, Face again proved he was a cut above the competition, winning 10 games while saving 24. His numbers were good enough to justify the second of three consecutive All-Star selections.

At the plate, the Pirates had a knack for delivering in the clutch. Smoky Burgess, who was also Pittsburgh's primary catcher, hit .450 with a .500 on-base percentage as a pinch-hitter. He went on to set the all-time record (since broken) for lifetime pinch hits. Burgess wasn't the only player who was reliable when the stakes were high. Clemente compiled a .349 batting average with runners in scoring position. Bob Skinner—a left-hander with a smooth, level swing—was a .333 hitter in "late and close" situations.

With a roster full of uncelebrated heroes, the multidimensional Bucs won 95 games (their highest total in over 30 years) and spent a majority of the season on top of the standings. Although they encountered stiff competition from the Braves and Dodgers, they pulled ahead of the pack by the end of August and maintained a sizeable lead.

Entering the Series, the Yankees had appeared in nine of the previous 11 October showdowns, capturing seven championships. In spite of those numbers, Roy Terrell of *Sports Illustrated* predicted an upset. "The opening line on the 1960 World Series has established the Yankees as five-to-seven favorites—a set of figures which could spread destitution among the nation's bookmakers long before the second week in October has passed," Terrell wrote. "The 1960 World Series is going to be won by singles hit to the opposite field and by tight pitching and the sacrifice bunt and sharp defense and refusal to quit. The Yankees have some of these things, the Pirates have them all. It should be an interesting Series, maybe even a good one, but no one should count on seeing a seventh game. The Pirates will win in six, maybe even five—no matter what the bookmakers said. The Pirates have been ignoring the odds all year."

Terrell's words seemed prophetic after the first game, which was held at Forbes Field in Pittsburgh. Casey Stengel handed the ball to Art Ditmar—a decision that later drew scathing criticism from numerous sources. "When Ditmar was announced as our starter for the opener, we were all buzzing about it," Mantle later recalled. "What about Whitey, who had won more World Series games than any pitcher in history? How could [Casey] not go with Whitey? But he did." Ditmar crumbled under the pressure, retiring just one of the five batters he faced before leaving the game with the Yankees trailing 3–1. The Pirates tacked on three more runs off of Jim Coates and Duke Maas, cruising to a 6–4 win. Stengel's lack of judgment became glaringly obvious when Ford tossed a pair of shutouts, beginning an unprecedented streak of 33.1 consecutive scoreless innings. Had "The Old Professor" selected Ford for the opener, the veteran left-hander would have been available to make three starts.

Game 2 was one of the most lopsided contests in Series history. Mantle smashed a pair of homers and collected five RBIs. Tony Kubek and Bobby Richardson combined for six hits. Half a dozen Pittsburgh hurlers were unable to stop the onslaught as the Yankees scored 16 runs—the highest total by any team since the Bombers massacred the Giants in the second game of the 1936 Fall Classic. The assault on the Pirates continued in the third meeting as Bobby Richardson set a single-game record with six RBIs (tied multiple times since). His 12 RBIs in the Series are also a record that still stands.

The Pirates sent Game 1–winner Vern Law back to the hill in the fourth contest. He fared pretty well, allowing just two runs on eight hits. The Yanks jumped out to a 1–0 lead in the fourth on a solo homer by first baseman Moose Skowron, but the Bucs answered with three runs off of starter Ralph Terry in the top of the fifth. Richardson added another RBI to his totals in the seventh inning before Roy Face slammed the door shut, closing out the game with 2.2 scoreless frames.

There were few highlights for New York in Game 5, which was played in front of more than 62,000 fans at Yankee Stadium. Instead of sending a well-rested Bob Friend back to the mound, Pittsburgh manager Danny Murtaugh turned to Harvey Haddix, a diminutive left-hander who had posted an underwhelming 3.97 ERA during the regular season. Asked by a reporter why the Pirates were taking such a risk, third baseman Don Hoak snapped: "What the hell are you talking about? That little f—er has a heart as big as a f—ing barrel." In his only start of the Series, Haddix held the Yankees to a pair of runs on five hits. Maris hit a towering solo shot in the third, but the Bucs had built a 4–1 lead before then. Mazeroski and Don Hoak drove in two runs apiece. Clemente added another RBI as Pittsburgh pushed the Bombers to the brink of elimination with a 5–2 win.

After a much-needed day off, the Yankees kept their championship hopes alive with a massive 12–0 beatdown at Pittsburgh. Mantle and Berra each drove in a pair of runs. Richardson had another fine offensive showing with three RBIs and two hits—both triples. Ford tossed his second shutout and helped his own cause in the top of the second with an RBI single. After the humbling defeat, Murtaugh reminded his men that the Series would be decided on the number of games won, not the number of runs scored.

The Pirates made a couple of important lineup changes prior to Game 7. Bob Skinner, who had been sidelined since Game 1 with a thumb injury, returned to action in left field. Rocky Nelson, a little-known backup player, replaced Dick Stuart at first base. Although Stuart had hit more homers than any player on the team during the regular season, he was off to a 3-for-20 start in the Series. Nelson—a looming home run threat during his minor-league days—was inserted into the clean-up slot.

The Yankees sent Bob Turley to the mound—a former World Series MVP in 1958. After retiring the first two batters he faced, he walked Skinner and served up a two-run homer to Nelson. Rookie right-hander Bill Stafford took over for the Yanks in the second inning, but was out of his element from the onset, allowing the first two batters he faced to reach safely before yielding a two-run single to Bill Virdon. Schantz gave New York three solid innings of relief as the Bombers came storming back. Skowron's solo homer in the fifth cut the deficit to 4–1. Mantle's RBI single in the sixth was followed by a three-run homer off the bat of Berra. Two more runs in the eighth gave the Yanks a 7–4 lead.

But the game was far from over.

In the bottom of the eighth, Schantz gave up a leadoff single to Gino Cimoli. In the most critical moment of the Series, Virdon followed with a double play ball to shortstop Tony Kubek. The ball took a bad hop and hit Kubek in the throat. Both runners reached safely as Kubek collapsed to the ground in obvious distress. He ended up being transported to the hospital. With a pair of runners aboard and no outs, Groat followed with an RBI single. Skinner moved the runners along with a sacrifice bunt and Nelson flied out, bringing up Clemente, who hit a weak hopper between first base and the pitcher's mound. Having been summoned in relief of Schantz, Jim Coates made a costly mistake when he went for the ball instead of covering first. Virdon scored on the play, making it a 7–6 game. Completing the remarkable comeback, backup catcher Hal Smith blasted a three-run homer, putting the Pirates up by a pair. Ralph Terry promptly took over for Coates, inducing an inning-ending grounder off the bat of Hoak.

In the top of the ninth, Bob Friend was called upon to preserve the 9–7 Pittsburgh lead. He failed to accomplish the task, allowing a pair of singles before being replaced by Haddix. Mantle and Berra each drove in a run, tying the score. With two outs and Haddix still on the mound, Skowron hit a grounder deep in the hole at shortstop. Although an easier play could have been made to first base, Groat bobbled the ball before delivering a hurried throw to second. It sailed wide of the bag, but Mazeroski went into a full stretch to nail a sliding Mantle by a narrow margin. Sportswriter Roger Angell hailed it as the best play of the Series.

Mazeroski followed his sparkling defensive gem with another act of heroism. Describing the most famous at-bat of his career decades later, the Hall of Fame second baseman recalled: "I just went up to the plate saying to myself, 'I gotta hit the ball hard somewhere. I gotta get on base.' The first pitch was high, and I took it for a ball. The next pitch he got down a little bit and I hit it good, but I wasn't sure it was going to go out, so I was busting my tail around first base. When the umpire gave the home run signal, I don't think I touched the ground all the way around second base."

Maz's walk-off homer—the first of its kind in a seven-game Series—gave the Pirates their first championship since 1925. A disconsolate Terry was besieged by a throng of reporters wanting to know what pitch he had thrown to Mazeroski. "I don't know what the pitch was," the hurler responded gloomily. "All I know is it was the wrong one."

Having set Series records for runs (55), hits (91), and team batting average (.338), the Yankees were absolutely stunned. "The Pirates should never beat our club," said Maris to an Associated Press reporter. "I think if we played them all season, we'd beat them real bad. They were real lucky. I think it is impossible for them to get any more breaks than they had in this Series." Mantle, who admitted that he cried in the clubhouse and on the plane ride home to Dallas, agreed with Maris's assessment years later. "The worst disappointment of my baseball career, and the one that hurts to this day was our loss to the Pittsburgh Pirates in the 1960 World Series. The better team lost, the only time I truly felt that way. It wasn't even close."

Figure 10.1 Members of the 1960 Pirates championship squad being honored at PNC Park in Pittsburgh. From left to right: Vern Law, Bill Mazeroski, and Bob Oldis. PHOTO COURTESY OF BROCK FLEEGER ON VISUAL HUNT.

Unaccustomed to losing and intolerant of the experience, Yankee executives replaced Casey Stengel with Ralph Houk before the 1961 campaign. During a subsequent press conference, Stengel insinuated that he had been dismissed due to ageism. "I'll never make the mistake of turning 70 again," he joked bitterly.

The Pirates waited until 1971 to capture their next championship. Clemente and Mazeroski were still in residence by then. The

Yankees made four consecutive World Series appearances following the 1960 debacle. They won twice before experiencing an extensive pennant-drought. As of 2024, Bobby Richardson was still the only second baseman ever to receive World Series MVP honors. He remains the only player from a losing team to claim the award.

Orioles vs. Mets 1969

IN THE EARLY PART OF THE TWENTIETH CENTURY, BASEBALL FANS IN New York were faced with a pleasing dilemma: there were three major-league teams to choose from. It was a magnificent era for the city as the Yankees, Dodgers, and Giants combined for more than 40 pennants and 20 World Series titles from 1900 to 1957. When the Dodgers and Giants moved West in 1958, the Big Apple was left without a National League franchise for the first time in over 70 years. Civic pride ran deep, and fans were justifiably upset. Looking to strengthen his reelection bid, Mayor Robert Wagner Jr. assembled a committee designed to bring an NL club back to the metropolitan area.

Wagner's project came to fruition with the arrival of the Mets in 1962. The earliest rosters were filled with familiar faces such as Gil Hodges, Duke Snider, and Clem Labine (among others). But none of the old hometown heroes helped transform the Mets into contenders as the club lost more than 100 games in four consecutive seasons. Commenting on the woeful state of affairs, Casey Stengel—the team's septuagenarian manager—joked: "[I've] been in this game one-hundred years, but I see new ways to lose 'em I never knew existed before."

In spite of the abominable performances of the early Mets, fans flocked to the ballpark to support their loveable losers. The inaugural squad drew more than 900,000 fans through the turnstiles—a new record for a last-place team. The 1967 club posted the third-highest attendance in the National League despite their wretched 61–101 record. The hapless yet affable Mets provided a welcome distraction from troubling events occurring at home and abroad such as the assassination of John F. Kennedy, the onset of the Vietnam War, and the widespread civil unrest created by racial inequality. Fans who stuck with the Mets throughout the turbulent 1960s would ultimately be rewarded as team owners gradually built a winning squad.

The pitching corps underwent an important modification in 1967 with the addition of Tom Seaver and Jerry Koosman. Nolan Ryan made his full-time debut in 1968 while Tug McGraw worked on control issues in the minors. McGraw's return coincided with the debut of right-hander Gary Gentry. By the end of the decade, the Mets had one of the youngest and most promising staffs in the majors.

A right-hander with a drop-and-drive delivery, Seaver received Rookie of the Year honors in 1967. Over portions of 12 seasons in New York, he lived up to his nickname "Tom Terrific" by capturing three Cy Young Awards. Phillies slugger Mike Schmidt said that Seaver was probably the toughest pitcher he ever faced. "He didn't have a pattern," the Hall of Fame third baseman asserted. "He got me out with whatever he felt like on that night." Seaver turned in one of his finest performances on April 22, 1970, when he set an all-time record with ten consecutive strikeouts against the Padres. He finished the game with 19 strikeouts—another modern era record he shared with two other players until 1986. "I would like to be a great artist," Seaver once told a writer. "I would quit playing if I could paint like Monet or Rousseau. But I can't. What I can do is pitch, and I can do that very well." Few would disagree—especially in June of 1978, when he added a no-hitter to his already impressive Cooperstown resume. During the Mets 1969 pennant run, he reached a personal-high of 25 victories—tops in the majors.

The Mets almost released Koosman from their farm system in the spring of 1966. At the time, the lefty hurler had a good fastball but no breaking ball in his arsenal. With the help of former major leaguer Frank Lary, Koosman mastered the slider. He eventually found a permanent spot in the Mets rotation, finishing second to Johnny Bench in Rookie of the Year voting during the 1968 campaign. Koosman's follow-up effort was sensational as he posted a 17–9 record with a 2.28 ERA.

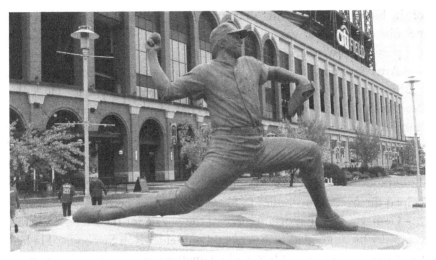

Figure 11.1   This statue of Tom Seaver stands outside Citi Field in New York. Seaver remains the franchise leader in a number of categories, including wins, strikeouts, and complete games.
PHOTO COURTESY OF SLGCKGC ON VISUAL HUNT.

Among the most celebrated pitchers in major-league history, Nolan Ryan set all-time records for strikeouts (5,714), no-hitters (7), and lowest batting average allowed (.204). In his prime, his fastball (measured at 108 miles per hour in a 1974 game against the Tigers) intimidated even the most powerful hitters. "Ryan's the only guy who put fear in me," said slugger Reggie Jackson. "Not because he could get me out, but because he could kill me. You just hoped to mix in a walk so you could have a good night and go 0-for-3." In the early stages of his professional career, Ryan struggled mightily with his control, averaging 6.2 walks per 9 innings over portions of three minor-league seasons. His work ethic also left something to be desired. "That kid had to be the laziest son of a gun I ever saw," recalled Hall of Famer Whitey Herzog—a former minor-league coach in the Mets system. "He was like an old hound on the porch. Nolan Ryan wouldn't roll over to get in the shade. So how the hell could any of us realize he'd come to big-league camp, see Tom Seaver's work ethic and have a conversion? Overnight, he became the hardest-working [pitcher] I ever saw." After a disastrous call-up in September of 1966, Ryan posted a handsome 3.09 ERA during the 1968 campaign. Working primarily out of the bullpen the following year, he averaged more than nine strikeouts per nine innings and won six of nine decisions. His two appearances in the postseason were critical for the Mets.

After spending four years bouncing up and down from the majors to the minors, left-handed relief specialist Tug McGraw finally landed in New York for good in 1969. A colorful character and free spirit, McGraw learned how to throw a screwball under the tutelage of former Yankee star Ralph Terry. It became his bread-and-butter pitch. During the Mets' memorable pennant run in 1969, McGraw won nine games and saved 12 without blowing a single opportunity. By the time he retired, he had helped the Mets and Phillies to four World Series berths.

Gentry was an important piece of the puzzle for the Mets. "His stuff was every bit as good as Seaver's," said outfielder Ron Swoboda. "He had just as live an arm." The 22-year-old flamethrower contributed 13 wins to the Mets' total in 1969 before adding a quality start in the World Series. Misdiagnosed by team physicians, he continued to pitch with arm problems that drove him out of the majors by the mid-1970s.

During the developmental years, Stengel christened his under-achieving ballclub "the Amazing Mets." What was particularly amazing in 1969 was the team's ability to beat opponents in spite of an anemic offense. New York hitters ranked third in strikeouts while compiling one of the worst on-base percentages in the majors. Yet somehow, they generated enough runs to collect 100 regular season victories—a franchise record that stood until 1986. Trailing the Cubs by as many as 10 games in mid-August, the "Amazing Mets" fought their way to the top with an incredible late-season surge. By the end of the year, they had transformed themselves into "the Miracle Mets."

The Baltimore Orioles created their own rags to riches story. Playing as the St. Louis Browns from 1902 to 1953, they finished in fifth place or lower dozens of times. A subsequent move and name change failed to elevate the team's performance as the O's continued to flounder in the standings for more than half a decade. When the 1960s arrived, a much-needed series of upgrades slowly helped the club attain near-dynastic status.

The new and improved version of the Orioles was built around third baseman Brooks Robinson, who became an everyday player in 1958. Nicknamed "the Human Vacuum Cleaner" for his ability to scoop up almost anything hit his way, Robinson won 16 Gold Gloves during his career—more than any infielder in history. A kind-hearted man off the field, he became a hero to fans in Baltimore and a nuisance to opponents. "I'm beginning to see Brooks in my sleep," said Cincinnati skipper Sparky Anderson after Robinson's brilliant defensive performance in the 1970 World Series. Robinson's batting averages were up and down over the years. Although he hit just .234 during the Orioles' pennant-winning effort in 1969, he pounded 23 homers and drove in 84 runs.

A mischievous kid in his younger days, Boog Powell's nickname was derived from the colloquial term "bugger." At 6-foot-4, 230 pounds, he fit the prototypical image of a slugger. After a promising rookie year in 1962, the lefty-swinging first baseman went on to amass more than 80 RBIs for Baltimore during eight seasons, reaching the century mark three times. The pinnacle of his career came in 1970, when he was named American League MVP.

In December of 1965, GM Harry Dalton made one of the smartest moves in franchise history, dealing right-handed fast-baller Milt Pappas to the Reds in exchange for outfielder Frank Robinson. Although Pappas was among an elite group of post-deadball hurlers to win 150 games before the age of 30, he was nowhere close to being on the level of Robinson, who was a 14-time All-Star and two-time MVP. Making an immediate impact in Baltimore, Robinson captured a Triple Crown and led the O's to their first World Series title in 1966. He helped the club return to the Fall Classic in 1969 with a fine offensive showing (32 HRs/100 RBIs/.308 BA). His 586 lifetime homers were fourth on the all-time list when he retired.

While the Orioles were building a solid core of everyday players, they were also taking great strides toward improving their pitching staff. A first-ballot Hall of Famer, Jim Palmer, was added to the Baltimore roster in the spring of 1965. Although he wasn't particularly fast and his breaking balls didn't have exceptional bite, he used his superior intelligence to an advantage. "Palmer is the greatest situation pitcher I've ever seen," said Twins' manager Ray Miller. "He makes them beat him on a single and one run at a time. Most of the homers he gives up are solos because he only works to their power when the bases are empty." While attempting a comeback near the end of his career, Palmer was told by University of Miami coach Lozaro Collazo that he had bad mechanics. Palmer believed that this was true even in his prime. "Looking at films of myself, I felt like maybe I ought to put more into this," he once said. The 6-foot-3 right-hander used a high leg-kick to deliver the ball from an elevated release point. Although he appeared almost nonchalant at times, looks were deceiving as he captured three Cy Young Awards and reached the 20-win threshold eight times. His .800 winning percentage in 1969 was highest in the American League.

A late bloomer, southpaw Dave McNally spent five full seasons in the majors before maximizing his potential. The key to his success was the addition of a slider, which complemented his lively fastball and sharp-breaking curve. With three effective pitches in his cache, he began a run of four consecutive 20-win campaigns. He finished among the top five in Cy Young voting every year from 1969 through 1971. He won 15 consecutive decisions for the O's in 1969.

After toiling in anonymity with the lowly Astros, Mike Cuellar became an overnight sensation in Baltimore, winning no fewer than 18 games in six straight seasons. The Cuban-born southpaw relied on an assortment of screwballs, slow curves, and changeups to keep hitters off balance. Among the most superstitious players in baseball, he adhered to a precise routine on the day of his starts. One teammate recalled that he used the same number of steps to get from the dugout to the mound every time he took the field and wouldn't climb onto the rubber if the rosin bag was lying in front of it. He refused to move the obstruction himself, relying on his infielders to do it for him.

During the mid-1950s, Baltimore GM Paul Richards and farm director Jim McLaughlin initiated a developmental scheme that came to be known as "the Oriole Way." Condensed into a manual that was used by minor-league instructors, the system emphasized fundamentals of the game, such as how to prevent double steals and properly execute cutoffs. When Earl Weaver took over as manager in 1968, he felt that "the Oriole

Way" was being overlooked and brought it back to the forefront. Weaver's *New York Times* obituary described him as a "crusty personality" with "a sandpaper voice, a taste for beer, and a tense, competitive manner." A self-proclaimed "sore loser," he was ejected from 96 games during his career. He currently ranks fourth on the all-time list in that category. Adhering to the Oriole Way, Weaver guided the team to three consecutive pennants beginning in 1969. There was little opposition from rivals that year as the Orioles took over first place on April 16 and remained there for the rest of the year. Their 109 victories put them 19 games in front of the second-place Tigers.

With the addition of four teams in 1969 (including the first major-league franchise to be stationed in Canada), both leagues were split into two rival divisions. A league championship series was added to determine the winners of each circuit. Weaver's platoon squared off against the Twins while the Mets—managed by Hall of Famer Gil Hodges—took on the Braves. Neither matchup was terribly close as both Western Division challengers ended up being swept.

Although the Mets had efficiently eliminated the Braves in the National League Championship Series, most insiders believed that they would be trampled underfoot in the World Series. Game 1—a Saturday matinee played in front of more than 50,000 fans at Baltimore's Memorial Stadium—failed to alter the mindset of odds makers. Seaver had an uncharacteristically rough day on the mound, giving up a solo homer to Don Buford in the first inning before melting down in the fourth. The Mets couldn't do much with Cuellar's slow offerings, scratching out their lone run in the seventh on a pair of singles and a sacrifice fly. In spite of the 4–1 outcome, the Mets remained optimistic. "I swear we came into that clubhouse more confident than we had left it," recalled Seaver. "Somebody—I think it was [Donn] Clendenon—yelled out, 'Damn it, we can beat these guys!' And we believed it. A team knows if they've been badly beaten or outplayed. And we felt we hadn't been. . . . We hadn't been more than a hit or two away from turning it around. It hit us like a ton of bricks."

The Orioles hardly knew what hit them in the next four games, suffering an epic collapse the likes of which have rarely been seen on the

October stage. Koosman stifled the O's through six innings in Game 2, but lost a no-hitter and a shutout in the seventh frame. The Mets generated just enough offense to support Koosman's efforts as Clendenon—a surprise hero for New York—slammed a solo homer in the fourth inning. Infielder Al Weis singled home the deciding run for the Mets in the top of the ninth.

The Series moved to Shea Stadium for the third meeting. Around 56,000 fans turned out to see a career-defining performance by Mets' center fielder Tommie Agee. Agee led off the first with a solo homer then made sure it held up as the winning run with a pair of spectacular catches. The first one came in the fourth inning with two outs and runners on the corners. Orioles catcher Ellie Hendricks drove one of Gentry's offerings to the wall in center field, but Agee made a snow-cone grab on the run to extinguish the threat. With two outs and the bases loaded in the seventh, Paul Blair ripped a Nolan Ryan offering into right-center field, forcing Agee to make a lunging headfirst play. "I thought I might get it without diving, but the wind dropped the ball straight down and I had to hit the dirt," Agee later recalled. In the only World Series appearance of his storied career, Ryan preserved a 5–0 New York win with 2.1 scoreless innings.

The fourth game was a pitching duel between Cuellar and Seaver. Making up for his lackluster performance in the opener, "Tom Terrific" scattered six hits over 10 innings. Cuellar lasted through seven frames, surrendering just one run on Clendenon's second homer of the Series. The Orioles tied the game at one apiece in the top of the ninth on a sacrifice fly by Brooks Robinson. The ball would have dropped for a hit had right fielder Ron Swoboda not made a sensational diving catch. In the bottom of the tenth, Mets catcher Jerry Grote led off with a bloop double that was misjudged by left fielder Don Buford. After Al Weis was intentionally walked, Hodges sent J. C. Martin to the plate to bat for Seaver. A .209 hitter during the regular season, Martin bunted the ball toward relief pitcher Pete Reichert, whose throw to first hit Martin on the wrist. The ball bounced into right field, scoring pinch-runner Rod Gaspar, but the run was controversial. Existing rules prohibit players from interfering with throws to first while running within an allotted distance inside the baseline. Replays strongly suggested that Martin had prevented the throw from reaching infielder Davey Johnson, who was covering first. For whatever reason, umpire Lou DiMuro chose to ignore the infraction, prompting a spirited protest from the Orioles. In the end, the call on the field stood, giving the Mets a 2–1 victory and a 3-games-to-1 Series advantage.

Game 5 featured one of the most unusual sequences in Series history. With the Orioles leading, 3–0, in the bottom of the sixth, Dave McNally—who had allowed just three hits to that point—threw a pitch in the dirt that appeared to clip the foot of leadoff batter Cleon Jones. As home plate umpire Lou DiMuro debated what ruling to make, Hodges improvised a clever strategy. Recounting a similar scenario from the 1957 World Series, the savvy Mets skipper retrieved the ball (which had bounced into the New York dugout) and presented it to DiMuro, drawing the arbiter's attention to a smudge of shoe polish. Swayed by the evidence, DiMuro awarded Jones first base. McNally was clearly rattled by the turn of events, coughing up Clendenon's third homer—a new record for a five-game Series. Jerry Koosman later claimed that Hodges had secretly instructed him to mark the ball by rubbing it on his shoe. DiMuro's decision proved to be the Orioles' undoing as Weis tied the game with a homer in the seventh and Swoboda drove in the deciding run in the eighth. Errors on the same play by Boog Powell and pitcher Eddie Watt gave the Mets an unnecessary insurance run.

After the final out had been made, a wild celebration took place. Describing the scene, *New York Times* reporter William Borders wrote: "To the stock skyscrapers of Wall Street, where a spontaneous tickertape blizzard greeted the World Series victory, to the undistinguished bars of a hundred neighborhoods, where the toasts were in draft beer, the shouted cry was 'We're Number One!' Teachers suspended classes because their transistor equipped students were not paying attention anyway, bosses closed offices early for the same reason, and even policemen shrugged happily as they despaired of keeping order in the streets." There was pandemonium at Shea Stadium, where players were forced to beat a hasty retreat to their clubhouses to avoid the rush of thousands of gleeful fans, who literally tore the field apart, leaving it in a state that resembled the aftermath of a Civil War battle.

On the heels of the stunning defeat, the Orioles won four division titles, two pennants, and one World Series over the next five seasons. The Mets returned to the October Showcase in 1973, losing to the Oakland A's, who were in the midst of a three-year championship run. As of 2024, all three clubs had gone more than 30 years without a World Series title.

CHAPTER 12

Orioles vs. Pirates 1971

SOME WORLD SERIES ARE NOTED FOR THE EVENTS THAT HAPPEN ON the field while others create lasting memories of the people who participate in them. The 1971 Fall Classic was a coming out party for Pirates outfielder Roberto Clemente. Explaining what Clemente's MVP performance did for his legacy, biographer Jon Volkmer wrote: "Baseball fans had always known Roberto was great, but Pittsburgh was not a major market. He was not nearly as famous as he should have been. In the 1971 World Series, Roberto had a stage big enough for his talent, and the entire nation knew he was one of the very best ever to play the game."

A native of Puerto Rico, Clemente was not the first among his fellow countrymen to reach the majors. But his star burned much brighter than those who arrived before him. "He gave the term 'complete' a new meaning," said Commissioner Bowie Kuhn. "He made the word 'superstar' seem inadequate. He had about him the touch of royalty." Clemente unquestionably had a sense of his own importance, believing that he had been chosen by God to play baseball. Yet in spite of all his marvelous skills, he was not an overnight success. Originally a product of the Dodgers farm system, he was acquired by the Pirates in the 1954 Rule 5 draft. Brooklyn VP Buzzie Bavasi later said that the Dodgers' sole reason for signing him was to keep him away from the Giants, who were also interested. Clemente struggled to attain full-time status in the early years, hitting at a pedestrian .275 clip in his first three seasons. He tended to swing wildly at pitches off the plate. Over time, he became more adept at making solid contact, capturing four batting titles between 1961 and 1967.

Passionate and unreserved, Clemente developed a strong social conscience. "Any time you have an opportunity to make a difference in this world and you don't, then you are wasting your time on this Earth," he once said. His sense of pride and justice came to define him as an individual. He spoke out against the racism encountered by many Latin American ballplayers in the United States. On the field, he led by example, always giving 100 percent in spite of chronic back pain that affected him in the wake of a serious car accident. Sadly, his life took a tragic turn on New Year's Eve in 1972, when a plane he had chartered to bring supplies to victims of a massive earthquake in Nicaragua crashed into the Atlantic Ocean with him aboard. The National Baseball Hall of Fame waived the standard five-year waiting period, inducting him in 1973. Recognizing his humanitarian efforts, an award for outstanding sportsmanship and community involvement (formerly known as the Commissioner's Award) was renamed in his honor.

Clemente had a spectacular year in 1971, hitting .341 during the regular season before taking center stage in the playoffs. But his efforts did not single-handedly carry the Pirates to their first championship in more than a decade. The Pittsburgh roster was stacked with talent from top to bottom.

Over the course of his 21-year career, Hall of Famer Willie Stargell endeared himself to fans in the Steel City with his cheerful enthusiasm for the game. "It's supposed to be fun," he once commented. "The man says, 'Play ball,' not 'Work ball,' you know." A power-hitter with a knack for driving in runs when it counted most, the man who came to be affectionately known as "Pops" blasted 475 homers during his career. It has been said that the deep dimensions of Forbes Field and Three Rivers Stadium kept him out of the elite 500–home run club. He reached a statistical peak in 1971, setting personal records for homers (48) and RBIs (125). He finished second in MVP voting to Joe Torre of the Cardinals that year.

Stargell and Clemente were not the only members of the Pittsburgh lineup having their way with opposing pitchers in 1971. Manny Sanguillén's .319 batting average was tops among major-league catchers. Center fielder Al Oliver led the club with 31 doubles and first baseman Bob Robertson cracked 26 homers—second to Stargell.

Figure 12.1   Among the most beloved figures in the history of Pittsburgh sports, Roberto Clemente was MVP of the 1971 World Series. This bronze likeness stands outside PNC Park in Pittsburgh.

In the pitching department, four members of Pittsburgh's starting rotation finished with double-digit win totals. Dock Ellis and Steve Blass were the best of the bunch, combining for a 34–17 record and 2.95 ERA. Blass's story is one of the most puzzling in baseball history. A slender right-hander with a diverse pitch selection, he averaged 16 wins per year from 1968 through 1972. After an All-Star performance in the latter campaign, he lost the ability to consistently throw the ball over the plate. Although he had good control while warming up, he struggled the moment he encountered live action. The condition—which was both physical and psychological—brought about an abrupt end to his career. Other players have fallen victim to "Steve Blass Disease" over the years, most notably Chuck Knoblauch and Steve Sax—neither of whom could be counted on to produce accurate throws from second to first base. Sax recovered but Knoblauch did not, prompting a positional switch to the outfield. Blass, the first player to famously suffer from the peculiar malady (which is sometimes referred to as "the Yips"), was still very much in his prime during the Pirates' 1971 pennant effort, averaging less than three walks per nine innings while striking out 136 batters.

Ellis—an outspoken civil rights activist and habitual antagonist—generated unwanted controversy on multiple occasions during his career. In 1970, he tossed a messy no-hitter while under the influence of LSD (or so he boldly claimed). Four years later, he tried to intimidate the Cincinnati Reds by deliberately throwing at every batter he faced during a game at Three Rivers Stadium. "We gonna get down," he announced before taking the mound that day. "We gonna do the do. I'm gonna hit these motherf—ers." Backing up those words, he plunked Pete Rose, Joe Morgan, and Dan Driessen in succession. He missed the mark with Tony Perez at the plate and was finally removed by manager Danny Murtaugh after aiming a pair of pitches at Johnny Bench's head. The rebellious moundsman managed to get through the 1971 campaign without causing any major problems for the Bucs. In fact, his 19 wins were the most by a Pittsburgh hurler since 1960.

The Pirates got off to a lukewarm start in 1971, but gradually built an 11-game lead over their Eastern rivals. A rough patch in August allowed the Cardinals to gain some ground, but the Bucs eventually recovered, finishing seven games ahead of St. Louis. In the West, the Giants relied on the contributions of four Hall of Famers (Willie McCovey, Willie Mays, Juan Marichal, and Gaylord Perry) to win 90 games—barely enough to hold off their bitter rivals in Los Angeles. The Pirates had little difficulty disposing of the Giants in the NLCS, winning three straight after dropping the opener in San Francisco. Robertson was the offensive star of the series for Pittsburgh along with third baseman Richie Hebner, who launched a pair of homers and drove in five runs.

Meanwhile, in the American League, the Orioles became the first team since the Deadball Era to have four 20-game winners on their staff. Acquired in an offseason trade before the 1971 slate, little-known right-hander Pat Dobson joined a rotation that featured perennial All-Stars Jim Palmer, Mike Cuellar, and Dave McNally. While the other starters enjoyed long-term success, Dobson was destined to become little more than the answer to a trivia question, falling from 20–8 in 1971 to 16–18 the following year.

Collectively, the 1971 Orioles posted the lowest ERA in the majors while allowing the fewest walks in the American League. Only the A's posted a better WHIP average. The Birds were well represented in the bullpen as right-handed closer Eddie Watt compiled a 1.82 ERA while converting 11 save opportunities.

Run production in Baltimore came from the usual sources with Frank Robinson, Boog Powell, and Brooks Robinson each gathering at least 20 homers and 90 RBIs. Davey Johnson, who would later manage the Mets to the best record in franchise history, gathered 72 ribbies and captured a Gold Glove at second base. He wasn't alone as Mark Belanger, Brooks Robinson, and Paul Blair were also honored as the top defensive players at their positions.

Merv Rettenmund was a pleasant surprise for the O's. Known around the majors as a "super-sub," he logged significant time at each outfield station in 1971 while putting up career-high numbers in several offensive categories. His .318 batting average was tops on the club. Rettenmund went on to a highly successful career as a pinch-hitter, compiling the highest on-base percentage of all-time among players with at least 200 appearances in that role.

Things were changing in the AL West as the long-suffering A's were just a year away from capturing their first championship since the 1930s. With Hall of Famers Reggie Jackson, Catfish Hunter, and Rollie Fingers leading the way, the Athletics won 101 games, earning the right to face the Orioles in the ALCS. The series should have been more competitive, but all three of Oakland's starters faltered on the mound. McNally, Cuellar, and Palmer each had quality outings in the Baltimore sweep.

Entering the World Series, the Orioles were riding a 14-game winning streak. The Pirates were expected to crumble against the defending world champions. "When it began, you would have thought the Pittsburgh Pirates were nothing more than the invited guests at the St. Valentine's Day Massacre," Willie Stargell joked. Clemente fell ill with food poisoning on the night before the opening game but refused to be kept out of the lineup. "I don't know if I will ever play in another Word Series, so I must play hard," he had told reporters earlier. "I must not think that my body hurts me all the time."

Game 1 took place at Memorial Stadium in Baltimore with 53,000-plus in attendance. The pitching matchup pitted McNally against Ellis. It was McNally who stumbled first, coughing up three runs in the top of the second inning. But the lead didn't hold up for long as Frank Robinson smashed a solo homer in the bottom of the frame and Rettenmund added a three-run shot an inning later. A homer by Don Buford off of reliever Bob Moose put Baltimore out in front, 5–3. McNally held the Pirates hitless over the final six innings, picking up a complete game victory.

The second meeting was delayed by a day due to rain. Commissioner Bowie Kuhn suggested that the match be played at night, but the Pirates, who were slated to host the first night game in Series history on October 13, issued an emphatic objection. Game 2 was an utter disaster for Pittsburgh as six pitchers collectively yielded 11 runs. All of the Orioles' scoring took place without the benefit of an extra-base hit. The tone for the rest of the Series was set in the top of the eighth, when Hebner ended a 14-inning offensive drought for the Pirates with a three-run homer off of Palmer. With the exception of Games 4 and 6, the Orioles never held another lead.

Steve Blass tossed a three-hitter in the third match, walking just two batters while striking out eight. The Orioles were uncharacteristically sloppy in the field, committing three errors. They ended up with at least one miscue in each of the first five games. The Pirates followed their dominant 5–1 victory with a dramatic come-from-behind win in the fourth meeting, which took place at the newly opened Three Rivers Stadium and was the first World Series game to be played after sundown. There was minor controversy in the third inning when Clemente sent a deep drive down the right field line for an apparent two-run homer. Umpires ruled it a foul ball and replays seemed to validate the call. Backup catcher Milt May drove in the deciding run for Pittsburgh in the seventh with a pinch-hit single off of Watt.

The fifth game was never terribly close as Bucs' hurler Nelson Briles (who had appeared in two prior World Series with the Cardinals) turned in one of the finest performances of his career—a two-hit shutout. The Pirates built a 4–0 lead through five innings, saddling McNally with the loss. Only four Baltimore players reached base that day as Briles yielded a pair of singles and two walks.

After finishing 12 games ahead of the Tigers during the regular season and sweeping Oakland in the ALCS, the Orioles were unaccustomed to win-or-go-home scenarios. The crowd for Game 6 at Memorial Stadium was below capacity at 44,000-plus—an unusual development considering what was at stake. The Pirates jumped out to an early lead with runs in the second and third off of Palmer, one of them coming on a solo homer by Clemente. But the Orioles rallied to tie the score at two apiece in the seventh. A sensational defensive play by Clemente in the bottom of the ninth sent the game into extra innings. With two outs and Belanger on first, Buford drilled a double to the right field corner. Clemente retrieved the ball quickly and fired a one-hop missile to the plate, holding Belanger at third. Reliever Dave Giusti induced a harmless grounder off the bat of Davey Johnson to end the threat. The Orioles got right back to business in the tenth as Frank Robinson drew a one-out walk and moved to third on a single by Rettenmund. Brooks Robinson followed with a sacrifice fly to short-center field. Although Vic Davalillo produced a strong throw to the plate, Frank Robinson—who was slowing up at the age of 36—arrived just ahead of it, forcing a Game 7 showdown.

Anxieties ran high among players before the Series finale. The Orioles had been expected to coast to another championship while the Pirates, who hadn't won anything in over a decade, finally had the prize in their sights. A jittery Blass, who admitted to getting very little sleep the night before, took the mound for Pittsburgh against Cuellar. Baltimore skipper Earl Weaver tried to shake things up in the first inning by lodging a complaint against Blass, who he claimed was not making contact with the rubber. "It's a needling tactic by Earl Weaver," explained NBC broadcaster Curt Gowdy. "If he thought of any way he could upset Blass or the Pirates, he's out there to do it." Blass maintained his composure, holding the Pirates to just one run on four hits. Clemente made a fine running catch on a deep drive by Boog Powell in the first inning then belted a hanging curveball into the left-center field seats with two outs in the fourth. Trailing, 2–1, in the bottom of the ninth, the Orioles sent the heart of their batting order to the plate against Blass, who pitched a 1-2-3 inning.

In addition to a fine defensive performance, Clemente's numbers at the plate were MVP-worthy. He finished the Series with 12 hits—five of them going for extra bases. By the end of the twentieth century, only Lou Brock of the Cardinals and Bobby Richardson of the Yankees had hit safely more times in a seven-game October Classic. Slowed by the effects of injuries and advancing age, Clemente sat out more than 50 games in 1972. He still managed to hit .312 and record the 3,000th hit of his career (a double off of Mets hurler Jon Matlack) in his final regular season at-bat. He added four more hits—one of them a home run—in the NLCS against the Reds.

After the World Series year of 1971, the Pirates made it to the National League Championship Series in three of the next four seasons, losing each time. They returned to the Fall Classic to face the Orioles again in 1979. It was a reboot of the last showdown as the Pirates—with mostly new faces in the lineup—won in seven games. The Orioles added a World Series title to their collection in 1983, but the Pirates have not been as fortunate. At the start of the 2024 campaign, they were in the midst of an extensive championship drought.

CHAPTER 13

Royals vs. Cardinals 1985

ANY DISCUSSION OF THE 1985 WORLD SERIES WOULD BE INCOMPLETE without touching upon the subject of "Whiteyball." The term, which described the managerial strategy of Whitey Herzog, was introduced by sportswriters during the Cardinals' championship season of 1982. With few if any conventional power hitters in the St. Louis lineup, Herzog was forced to utilize speed, defense, and strong pitching to win ballgames. Although the style was perfectly suited to the roomy, artificial turf stadiums of the era, it was not universally admired by the media. "They seemed to think there was something wrong with the way we played baseball," Herzog noted in his memoirs.

Herzog broke into the majors with the lowly Washington Nationals in 1956. After a relatively undistinguished playing career, he scouted and coached for the A's and Mets. In the 1970s, he embarked upon a highly successful managerial stint, guiding the Royals to three successive ALCS appearances. He joined the Cardinals as a manager and GM in 1980. Charismatic and bold with a sharp eye for talent, he steered the club to three pennants and a World Series title during the 1980s. Acknowledging his accomplishments, the Veterans Committee elected him to Cooperstown in 2010.

Willie McGee was the top hitter on Herzog's 1985 squad, capturing the NL batting title with a .353 mark. Tommy Herr was the big run producer, gathering 110 RBIs. Vince Coleman was the sparkplug on the basepaths, swiping 110 bags—a new record for rookies. As a collective unit, the 1985 Cardinals averaged more runs per game than any club in the NL while posting the second-lowest home run total. The only player to reach the 20-homer plateau was first baseman Jack Clark.

Defensively, the Cardinals committed fewer errors than any team in the majors. The most gifted gloveman by far was shortstop Ozzie Smith. Nicknamed the "Wizard of Oz" for his ability to make extraordinary plays look easy, he won 13 Gold Gloves—more than any player at his position. "I think of myself as an artist on the field," he once said. "Every game, I look for a chance to do something that fans have never seen before." One thing that had never been previously witnessed was Smith's gymnastic back flips, which he habitually performed on Opening Day and other special occasions. If there was any weakness in Smith's game, it was his hitting. When he left San Diego to join the Cardinals in 1982, he carried a meager .231 lifetime batting average. But he hit at a respectable .272 clip over the next 15 seasons, raising his cumulative mark by more than 30 points.

Explaining the key to the Cardinals' success in 1985, Smith remarked: "Everybody will say they played above the level they were capable of playing, but I think it was just about everybody contributing and everybody pulling in the same direction and believing we could get it done." Pitching was essential for St. Louis that year as three members of the starting rotation gathered at least 18 wins. Southpaw John Tudor led the league with 10 shutouts and posted the second-best ERA in the majors at 1.93. Dominican-born hurler Joaquin Andujar won 21 games while eating up more than 269 innings. Danny Cox—a big right-hander with an effective fastball/change/slider combo—reached personal-high marks in nearly every statistical category. Closing duties were shared by Jeff Lahti and Ken Dayley, who combined for 30 saves and an aggregate 2.29 ERA.

It took a while for the Cardinals to find their footing. After lagging behind the competition for nearly three months, they finally pulled out in front. The Mets proved to be formidable foes in the second half, stealing the division lead on multiple occasions. But a strong September run (21–9) allowed St. Louis to outpace New York by three games.

The NLCS pitted the Cardinals against the Dodgers, who had posted the lowest collective earned run average in the majors. Los Angeles held a two-game series advantage before dropping four in a row. A freak accident before Game 4 dampened St. Louis's championship hopes.

Coleman had just completed pregame drills and was standing on the field talking to teammate Terry Pendleton. With a light rain falling, the Busch Stadium grounds crew decided to activate the automatic tarp machine. The device had no lights or alarms to indicate that it was in motion and Coleman ended up directly in its path. In spite of Pendleton's valiant efforts to alert groundskeepers and extricate Coleman's leg from beneath the tarp (which weighed half a ton and measured 180-feet in length), the National League's top rookie was sidelined with a fractured bone for the remainder of the postseason. Recounting the incident years later, Cardinals outfielder Andy Van Slyke said candidly: "If Vince Coleman hadn't gotten hurt, we would have won the World Series. It would be like losing Tom Brady for the Super Bowl. That's how much impact Vince Coleman had on our ballclub." Coleman's replacement, Tito Landrum, proved to be a dependable alternative, hitting .378 in the remaining 10 games.

While the Cardinals' 1985 pennant run surprised no one, the Kansas City Royals defied the odds all year long. Among the strongest of the expansion franchises, the Royals had surpassed the .500 mark in just their third season of play. Beaten by the Yankees in three consecutive trips to the ALCS, they found their way to the World Series in 1980, losing to the Phillies. Unsuccessful bids in the 1981 Division Series and 1984 League Championship Series followed. By 1985, many of the Royals' top stars were aging out and the club was not even expected to win the AL West.

Playing in his 12th full season, George Brett was still the premier third baseman in the AL. A fierce competitor with a strong work ethic, he played every game as if the fate of the franchise depended upon it. Utility man Jamie Quirk observed: "[Brett] can't stand to lose. He can't sit down and play a card game that he doesn't want to beat you [at]. That's the way he played baseball. If he had to, he'd take it in his own hands and win the ballgame." A three-time batting champ and AL MVP in 1980, Brett reached a career-high of 30 homers in 1985 while finishing second to Wade Boggs in the America League batting race.

The rest of the heavy hitting was carried out by first baseman Steve Balboni. During his time in the minor leagues, Balboni captured numerous home run crowns. His tremendous power earned him the nickname

Figure 13.1 Over the course of 21 seasons, George Brett established himself as the greatest player in Royals history. After capturing MVP honors in the 1985 ALCS, he hit .370 in the World Series. This statue of Brett is located inside Kauffman Stadium in Kansas City.

PHOTO COURTESY OF BRYCE_EDWARDS ON VISUAL HUNT.

"Bye Bye." An imposing presence at 6-foot-3, 225 pounds, the New England native generated a league-high 166 strikeouts in 1985, averaging one per every 3.6 at-bats. But he also slammed 36 homers and 28 doubles, finishing second on the club to Brett in the latter category.

On the basepaths, Willie Wilson was a looming threat to steal, swiping 30 or more bases in eleven consecutive seasons. He was successful in nearly 80 percent of his attempts during the 1985 campaign, finishing among the league leaders in that category. The deep alleys of Royals Stadium worked to Wilson's advantage as he led the league in triples on five occasions. His 21 three-baggers in 1985 was the most in the majors since the 1940s. Additionally, Wilson's blazing speed allowed him to cover a lot of ground in the outfield. As of 2024, his 2.77 range factor (average number of putouts and assists per nine innings) was still the highest mark of all time among players with at least 500 appearances in left field.

Pitching was one of the Royals' strongest suits during the 1985 pennant race as right-hander Bret Saberhagen captured the first of two Cy Young Awards. Describing his pitching style, one writer observed that he had "nasty, nasty, nasty stuff, maybe the best in the league. He cannot throw a ball straight, yet his control is so good, he almost always has a hitter down in the count." Rail-thin at 6-foot-1, 160 pounds, Saberhagen relied primarily upon his fastball and changeup, mixing in occasional curves and sliders. The combination worked extremely well for him as he won 20 games in 1985 while posting the best strikeout-to-walk ratio in the AL.

Following Saberhagen's lead, every member of the starting rotation finished with double digit win totals. Right-hander Charlie Leibrandt had the heaviest workload (237.2 innings) and lowest ERA among starters at 2.69. Danny Jackson and Mark Gubicza combined for 28 victories and a 1.354 WHIP average, which was better than the league standard.

In the bullpen, the Royals had marquis closer Dan Quisenberry, who relied upon pinpoint control and deceptive mechanics to efficiently dispose of opponents. Originally a side-armer, he switched to a submarine delivery in 1980. His sinking fastball led to a lot of groundball outs, making him the AL saves leader during five seasons.

Kansas City's win over Toronto in the ALCS was just as improbable as the outcome of the pennant race. After clinching the AL West by the slenderest of margins, the Royals stumbled to a 3–1 series deficit against the Blue Jays, who were making the first postseason appearance in franchise history. The depth of the Kansas City pitching staff was on full display in the last three games as Toronto hitters struck out 19 times and stranded 26 runners. Balboni and Brett both delivered game-winning RBIs in the series along with unlikely heroes Jim Sundberg (a veteran catcher known more for his defense) and Buddy Biancalana (a seldom-used utility infielder).

The 1985 Fall Classic was the first all-Missouri matchup since 1944, when the Cardinals faced the St. Louis Browns. Given their checkered postseason past, the Royals entered the Series as underdogs. With nine prior championships to their credit, the Cardinals were the most successful franchise in the majors aside from the Yankees.

Game 1 took place at Royals Stadium with over 41,000 fans on hand. The Cardinals sent Tudor—their staff ace—to the mound against Danny Jackson, who had logged a pair of scoreless appearances in the ALCS. The Royals struck first on an RBI single by Balboni in the second inning, but St. Louis bounced back quickly, tying the game in the top of the third. Cesar Cedeno's double in the fourth proved to be the game-winner for the Cards as Kansas City failed to push another run across against Tudor and Todd Worrell.

It was a frustrating night for Kansas City in Game 2. Charlie Leibrandt came within one out of a shutout before losing it all. After plating a pair of runs in the fourth on consecutive doubles by Brett and Frank White, the Royals were still nursing a 2–0 lead in the top of the ninth. With two outs and Willie McGee in scoring position, Leibrandt gave up an RBI single to Jack Clark and a double to Tito Landrum. After an intentional walk to Cedeno, Terry Pendleton delivered a bases-clearing double. The 4–2 final gave the Cardinals a two-game advantage.

Andy Van Slyke recalled how most insiders were ready to call the Series early. "I can actually remember vividly how the city and the papers and the organization made the mistake of anticipating a World Series championship before it happened. As soon as we heard that, a lot of players reacted very, very negatively because the last thing you want to do is wake up a sleeping bear." The bear was definitely awake in Game 3 as the Royals knocked starter Joaquin Andujar out of the box early, building a 4–0 lead through five innings. The Cardinals managed just one run off of Saberhagen, who scattered six hits and struck out eight. The 6–1 loss was Andujar's fifth consecutive rocky outing dating back to October 2.

Just when things were looking up for the Royals, they encountered a major roadblock, getting shut out by Tudor in Game 4. The match was played in a brisk two hours and 19 minutes as Tudor retired 13 straight batters and allowed only two runners to reach third base. The Cardinals managed just four hits off of starter Bud Black but made them count. Landrum and Willie McGee blasted solo homers. Pendleton tripled and scored on a sacrifice bunt. The 3–0 victory put St. Louis on the verge of their second championship in four years.

With the Series on the line, the Royals remained unfazed. "The pressure was more on the Cardinals," Brett recalled. "They were up three games to one. If they ended up blowing the World Series, they [were] going to remember it for the rest of their lives." Demonstrating the toughness that had come to characterize them all year, the Royals cruised to a 6–1 win in Game 5. Danny Jackson accomplished a rare feat, tossing an "immaculate inning" (three batters, nine pitches, nine strikes) in the bottom of the seventh, victimizing Pendleton, Tom Nieto, and Brian Harper.

Umpire Don Denkinger has often been single-handedly blamed for the outcome of the Series. Although the errant call he made in Game 6 certainly played a role in sealing the Cardinals' fate, it actually took an offensive meltdown, a defensive lapse, and a glaring example of miscommunication to force a Game 7. "I was an umpire for more than 30 years in the major leagues," Denkinger later said. "I know I made a lot of mistakes. That one was just blown out of proportion."

A tense pitching duel between Leibrandt and Cox unfolded in the sixth meeting. After failing to score for 15 straight innings, the Cardinals manufactured a run in the top of the eighth. Taking no chances with the 1–0 lead, Whitey Herzog turned to his bullpen, bringing in southpaw Ken Dayley. The score remained unchanged until the bottom of the ninth, when veteran DH Jorge Orta was summoned to pinch-hit. With Todd Worrell on the mound, Orta hit a seemingly harmless grounder to the right side. First baseman Jack Clark crossed in front of Herr to field the ball as Worrell scrambled to cover the bag. The play was very close and, although game footage later revealed that Orta was out by a narrow margin, Denkinger—observing the action in real time—made the most controversial call of his career.

Safe at first!

Clark and Herr were joined by Herzog in arguing the play, but there was no video review in those days and the call on the field—though clearly mistaken—stood. The game unraveled in a hurry for St. Louis after that. Balboni hit a catchable pop-up in front of the Kansas City dugout. Clark, who was relatively new to his defensive post, allowed it to drop in foul territory as veteran catcher Darrell Porter looked on. Given another opportunity, Balboni singled. With two on and no outs, Sundberg got a good bunt down on his third attempt. Worrell fielded the ball and fired to third base for the out on Orta, but the Royals caught another huge break when Worrell and Porter got their signals crossed with Hal McRae at the plate. Porter was expecting a fastball, but Worrell threw a slider that eluded Porter's glove and allowed the runners to advance. After an intentional walk to McRae, pinch-hitter Dane Iorg delivered the most memorable hit of his major-league career, blooping a game-winning single into right field.

Denkinger didn't realize he had blown the call on Orta until after the game, when Commissioner Peter Ueberroth broke the news. A pair of St. Louis radio broadcasters later gave out Denkinger's phone number and address over the air. Death threats and obscene phone calls promptly followed. Many fans harbored lingering resentment even after the shock of the impending Series loss wore off. Asked about the use of video review to overturn the calls of umpires many years later, Denkinger commented, "The object is to get the call right. That's a good thing. So I'm all for review. And if they had it back then [in 1985], no one would even know my name."

The Royals turned to Saberhagen in Game 7 while the Cardinals countered with Tudor. Brett said he hardly slept the night before and was "scared to death." Saberhagen was in a similar state. "[Game 7] of the World Series was the most nervous I've ever been before," the hurler remarked, "just because of the fact that if we win, we're champions, if we lose, I feel like I let my teammates down, our fans down, the front office down." In the opposing clubhouse, the Cardinals were feeling deflated. "We'd had something taken away from us the night before and we all felt a sense of doom and gloom," said Herzog.

The Series had been close to that point, and no one expected a blowout in the finale. But that's precisely what happened. The Cardinals managed just five hits off of Saberhagen, who had celebrated the arrival of his first child (a son) the night before. The Royals had a banner day at the plate, jumping out to a 5–0 lead through three innings. They poured it on in the bottom of the fifth, adding six more runs on seven hits. Tempers ran high as Andujar—summoned in relief—confronted Denkinger about his strike zone. Herzog, who had been riding the arbiter all night on account of his blown call in Game 6, came out of the dugout to defend Andujar. "We wouldn't even be here if you hadn't missed the f—ing call last night!" spat Herzog. "Well, if you guys weren't hitting .120 in this Series, we wouldn't be here either," Denkinger allegedly retorted.

Herzog was ejected—the first World Series expulsion since Billy Martin was tossed out of Game 4 of the 1976 Fall Classic. Andujar soon followed after arguing with Denkinger a second time. The temperamental hurler had to be restrained by teammates and escorted off the field. He ended up serving a lengthy suspension at the beginning of the 1986 campaign.

The rest of the game was scoreless for both teams. Relief pitcher Ricky Horton described the mood in the St. Louis clubhouse afterward as follows: "We had no hope in that game. It was really just frustration and, in some ways, [we were] glad it was over." Herzog said it was the worst night he ever spent on a ballfield.

The Series set a number of precedents. The Royals were the first team to win a championship after dropping the first two games at home. Their six elimination game wins were the most for a single postseason. The 13 runs surrendered by Kansas City hurlers were the fewest allowed in a seven-game Fall Classic.

The Cardinals returned to the October Showcase in 1987, squaring off against the Twins. As of 2024, they had 23 pennants and 11 World Series titles to their credit. The Royals have not been as successful. After their Series victory in 1985, they remained absent from postseason play for nearly three decades. They ended the dry spell with back-to-back pennants in 2014 and 2015. The latter campaign produced the second championship in franchise history.

CHAPTER 14

Twins vs. Cardinals 1987

THE 1980S ARE LARGELY REMEMBERED FOR WIDESPREAD MATERIALISM and the rise of young, upwardly mobile professionals (popularly known as "yuppies"). Big hair, gaudy colors, and Spandex dominated the fashion scene while New Wave music (popularized by bands such as the Cars, the Talking Heads, and Duran Duran) ruled the music charts. In the world of politics, Republicans held the White House from January of 1981 until the end of the decade. The Cold War dragged on in spite of the concerted efforts of the Reagan Administration to bring it to a satisfactory end. Budding technologies such as personal computers, video game systems, and VCRs became staples in American households. Yet in spite of years of massive consumerism, the global stock market experienced an unexpected crash on "Black Monday" in 1987.

While stocks were falling sharply, offense was on the rise in major-league baseball. More than 4,400 home runs were hit during the 1987 campaign—a new record. Mark McGwire raised the bar for AL rookies with 49 blasts while Yankee icon Don Mattingly set a new single-season mark for grand slams with six. He also homered in eight consecutive games, tying an old record set by Dale Long of the Pirates in 1956. Attempting to explain the offensive outburst, some blamed the scarcity of quality pitching while others claimed that the balls were juiced.

Entering the 1987 slate, the Minnesota Twins had been absent from postseason play for a very long time. Although they assembled some competitive teams in the mid- to late 1960s, there were rough times ahead as the club averaged 89 losses per year from 1980 through 1986 (discounting the strike-shortened season of 1981). A steady infusion of talent in the early part of the decade gradually turned things around.

Born and raised in the Twin City area, hometown favorite Kent Hrbek was among the few bright spots for the Twins in 1982. While the team staggered to a 60–102 record, Hrbek had a spectacular rookie campaign, hitting .301 while driving in 92 runs. He made his only All-Star appearance that year and finished second to Cal Ripken Jr. of the Orioles in Rookie of the Year voting. By the time Hrbek retired after his 14th season with the Twins, he had attained a ranking of second on the all-time franchise list in home runs and RBIs (behind Hall of Famer Harmon Killebrew). Even so, he flew under the radar for most of his career—getting passed over for the All-Star team in 12 consecutive seasons. Irritated by the slight in 1987, he told sportswriters that he would never play in another Midsummer Classic even if he were selected.

A September call-up in 1981, third baseman Gary Gaetti won the starting job the following spring and held onto it for nine full seasons. He was among the club's top RBI men throughout his tenure in Minnesota. Proving he was more than just a one-dimensional player, Gaetti won four straight Gold Gloves beginning in 1986. He had one of his finest offensive showings in 1987, slamming 31 homers while driving in a team-high 109 runs.

Solidly built at 6-foot-4, 210 pounds, right fielder Tom Brunansky came up through the Angels' farm system. Acquired by the Twins in a 1982 trade, he clubbed no fewer than 20 homers in eight consecutive campaigns. He tied a career-high with 32 bombs in 1987. After the poor showings of the early 1980s, Brunansky was ecstatic about the club's turnaround. "It was like having a Triple-A club in the majors," he said. "If they didn't sweep us, they considered it a bad series. We took our lumps and it hurt, but it was a learning experience."

The addition of Cooperstown great Kirby Puckett in 1984 helped guide the Twins to their first .500 finish since the 1970s. Vertically challenged at 5-foot-8, the perpetually smiling Puckett had the build of a professional wrestler. "It was no secret I wasn't going to be tall," he joked with a *Sports Illustrated* writer. "So I figured if I can't be tall, I'll be strong." Puckett's good humor and engaging personality made him universally popular with fans—even outside the Minnesota market. In spite of his relatively brief career (which lasted just 12 seasons), he landed among the franchise leaders in numerous categories. He hit .333 with the bases loaded over the years, blasting seven grand slams. When he left the game in the spring of 1996 on account of blindness caused by acute glaucoma, he carried a lifetime .318 batting average. In honor of the fallen hero, a section of Chicago Avenue was renamed Kirby Puckett Place.

After struggling in his first two years with the Twins, southpaw Frank Viola finally emerged as a dominant presence on the mound. Minnesota coach Johnny Podres said that Viola pitched with more confidence in 1984, going straight after hitters instead of nibbling at the corners, which had been his policy in the previous two campaigns. The new approach worked wonders as he gathered 18 wins and posted a 3.21 ERA—the lowest of his career to that point. Over the next several seasons, Viola remained one of the most successful hurlers in the majors. He came up just short of 200 strikeouts during the Twins' pennant run in 1987 while posting a 17–10 record. He was even better the following year, capturing the AL Cy Young Award.

Among a handful of players born in the Netherlands to reach the majors, Bert Blyleven began his career with the Twins in 1970. He was reacquired in a 1985 trade after several years abroad. In his mid-30s, the veteran right-hander proved to be a valuable asset, winning 17 games in 1986 and 15 more the following season. Blyleven spent most of his career on small market teams and was overshadowed by the higher pro-file pitchers of the era. Durability was one of his strongest assets as he reached the 200-inning mark in 16 campaigns. His 287 career wins and 3,701 strikeouts ultimately led to his enshrinement at Cooperstown after 14 years on the ballot.

The 1987 Twins were vulnerable outside of Minnesota, compiling a 29–52 record on the road—among the worst marks in the majors. But they were unstoppable at the Metrodome, posting the best home record in baseball. Opened in 1982, the stadium featured a fiberglass fabric roof that was self-supported by air pressure (provided by 20 industrial fans). The right field wall had a 7-foot fence with a 16-foot-high plas-tic wall extension—commonly known as "the Baggie" on account of its resemblance to a giant trash bag. The unusual outfield facets coupled with the crowd noise, which was known to reach almost painful levels, provided the Twins with a distinct home-field advantage. During the 1987 World Series, peak decibel levels inside the stadium were found to be comparable to the engine of a jet airliner. "The noise was unbelievable," Puckett later recalled. "Some of the players wore earplugs. It's a good thing our outfield was so used to playing with each other because communication was impossible once the ball was in the air."

The American League West was a relatively weak division in 1987 with only three of seven teams finishing at .500 or above. In sharp contrast, the East was extremely competitive with four clubs posting better overall records than Minnesota. It was an inconsistent year for the Twins as they played glaringly mediocre ball in July and August. The roughest patch occurred in the latter month, when they lost nine of 10 games from August 18 to the 28, squandering a five-game lead over the A's. Both teams faltered down the stretch, but Oakland couldn't capitalize, dropping seven of their last 11. This allowed the Twins to clinch the division with a few games still remaining.

In the National League, the St. Louis Cardinals were still one of the most powerful teams of the era. After the pennant-winning effort of 1985, the club slipped to third place, finishing 28.5 games behind the Mets. Virtually every member of the starting lineup experienced a drop-off in production—most notably Willie McGee, who slumped to .256 at the plate after capturing a batting title the previous year. The 1987 campaign brought about a return to form for most of the Cardinal regulars. McGee raised his batting average significantly while reaching career-high marks in multiple categories. Jack Clark, who sat out more than half of the 1986 slate with an injury, slugged 35 homers and drove in 106 runs. Vince Coleman tore up the basepaths with 109 steals, while Tom Herr, Terry Pendleton, and Ozzie Smith combined for more than 250 RBIs and a .285 batting average.

Pitching was spotty at times, but the Cardinal offense compensated for it, leading the league in walks and stolen bases while posting the highest on-base percentage. Southpaw John Tudor—among the best of the St. Louis starters—was injured on April 19, when Mets catcher Barry

Figure 14.1 The Metrodome in Minnesota was one of the loudest venues in the majors. Noise levels during the 1987 World Series were said to rival those of a jet engine.
PHOTO COURTESY OF ERIC KILBY ON VISUAL HUNT.

Lyons lumbered into the Cardinal dugout in pursuit of a foul ball that ended up in the seats. There was a hard collision and Tudor got the worst of it, sustaining a broken leg. The hurler missed close to four months of action, returning in time to compile a 10–2 overall record. Only three other Cardinal pitchers surpassed Tudor's win total, although they all ended up with moderately inflated ERAs. It was a common problem among NL moundsmen. With batting averages on the rise around the majors, the aggregate National League earned run average was 4.08. The Cardinal staff came in slightly below that at 3.91.

After setting a franchise record with 108 wins in 1986, the Mets "slumped" to 92–70. Taking advantage of the situation, the Cardinals climbed to the top of the division in April and built a commanding lead by the All-Star break. The pennant race heated up in September as the Expos and Mets remained in the hunt. The Cards finished the campaign with back-to-back showdowns against both rivals. In the end, they hung on, winning four of seven games. The season concluded on a sour note as Jack Clark sprained his ankle on September 9 and played sporadically the rest of the way.

In the National League West, the Giants got top-notch performances from first baseman Will Clark and outfielder Chili Davis, leaving the Reds six games behind in the standings. The NLCS was tightly contested as San Francisco jumped out to a 3–2 Series lead. Tudor was the man of the hour in Game 6, shutting out the Giants on six hits. Danny Cox followed with a masterful outing, blanking San Francisco in the finale.

The ALCS was less labor-intensive for the Twins as they eliminated Detroit in five games. Blyleven picked up a pair of wins while Brunansky raked Tiger pitchers for nine RBIs and six extra-base hits. Detroit's collective ERA was 6.70 in the series.

Asked which World Series year was his favorite—1987 or 1991—Hrbek joked, "It's pretty even. . . . Sometimes it's funny—the question I get asked the most is 'Which one was more fun?' or 'Which team was better?' Blah Blah Blah. And I always come back with the smart-aleck answer, saying, 'If you have two kids, which one do you like the most?' They were both unbelievable events in my life."

Handicappers were incredulous when Minnesota clinched the pennant in 1987. The club had begun the campaign with 500-to-1 odds stacked against them. With a minus-20 run differential during the regular season (786 runs scored/806 allowed), the Twins were among the longest of the World Series longshots.

The Series opened in Minneapolis with a boisterous crowd of 55,000-plus on hand. Frank Viola had agreed to be the best man at his brother's wedding, but when the Series opener landed on the same day, he was forced to cancel. While his brother tied the knot, Viola mowed down the opposition, holding the Cardinals to one run in eight innings of work. The Twins had no problems at the plate, chasing starter Joe Magrane and reliever Bob Forsch from the game. Left fielder Dan Gladden enjoyed a moment in the sun, launching a grand slam that gave Minnesota an airtight 7–1 lead.

Noise levels in the Metrodome continued at deafening levels in Game 2 as the Twins battered Cardinal pitchers again, exploding for six runs in the fourth inning. Catcher Tim Laudner, who went 2-for-3 with 3 RBIs, remarked: "Hitting's contagious and we spent all year long picking each other up. One guy's not swinging well, the other guy picks the other up and so forth all the way down the line." The Cardinals countered with four runs of their own off of Blyleven and Juan Berenguer—a right-hander who ended up with a bloated 10.38 ERA in three Series appearances.

In the wake of the two victories, the Twins traveled beyond Minnesota, where they had proved to be beatable all year long. The road curse continued as the Cardinals won three in a row by a combined score of

14–5. Coleman drove in the deciding run in Game 3 with a clutch double off of Berenguer. Third baseman Tom Lawless struck the big blow for St. Louis in the fourth meeting, homering off of Viola. In Game 5, outfielder Curt Ford rose to the occasion with a clutch two-run single off of Blyleven. "I was very much surprised to see him throw as many fastballs as he did in the situation," said Ford after the game. "I was thinking if I was going to beat him, I was going to have to beat him with his best pitch, which is his curveball." Blyleven absorbed the loss in spite of delivering a quality start.

It was bedlam at the Metrodome in Game 6 as fans shouted raucously and waved their "Homer Hankies" throughout. Hrbek and Don Baylor, who was acquired in a late-season trade with the Red Sox, combined for seven RBIs. Puckett reached base in each of his five plate appearances and scored four runs. "I felt sharp today, but they were sharper," Tudor remarked in a postgame interview. "They hit all the bad pitches I made. They hit all the good pitches I made. It was just a bad day all around." The 11–5 blowout moved the Twins one step closer to their first championship since their days in Washington.

The Series finale was much closer as the Cards carried a 2–1 lead into the bottom of the fifth. Puckett tied things up with an RBI double off of Danny Cox. In the sixth, the Twins threatened again, loading the bases with one out. Reliever Todd Worrell retired Gladden on strikes but couldn't prevent Greg Gagne from delivering an infield single that gave the Twins their third run. Gladden capitalized on another opportunity in the eighth, smashing an RBI double to deep right-center field. The 4–2 score held up as the final.

There were three missed calls by umpires in Game 7. In the bottom of the second, Baylor was called out by arbiter Dave Phillips on a close play at the plate. Replays proved conclusively that Coleman's throw from left field arrived late. The Twins got the benefit of an errant ruling in the fifth, when Gagne reached on an infield hit and Puckett doubled him home. Video footage revealed that first base umpire Lee Weyer blew the call on Gagne. The third infraction occurred in the top of the sixth inning, when Tom Herr got caught in a rundown between first and second base. He was ruled out after being tagged by Viola, but there was more than one problem with the call. Not only was Viola's tag late, but Herr's path to the bag was impeded by Hrbek, who should have been called for interference.

After the Twins had completed the shocking upset, St. Louis skipper Whitey Herzog groused: "I still don't know how you win at the Metrodome and I'm not sure I want to know. I do know one week isn't enough for a baseball team to figure it out. The Cardinals could have played there until Easter and never won a game."

The 1987 World Series set a number of precedents. It was the first seven-game Fall Classic in which the home teams won all the games. It was also the only Series (to that point) in which the bottom half of the ninth was never played. A final fact worth noting, the Twins had the worst regular season record of any championship squad in history—a dubious honor that was later claimed by the Cardinals.

In an amusing postscript, players from the championship squad were invited to the White House to receive congratulations from President Ronald Reagan. In late July, the Twins had picked up aging Hall of Famer Steve Carlton from the Indians in a trade. Carlton's poor performance in nine appearances prompted manager Tom Kelly to drop him from the postseason roster. Since he was still a member of the team, Carlton attended the presidential meet and greet. Photos appeared in local newspapers accompanied by the names of each player. Carlton, who was standing in the back wearing dark sunglasses, was mistakenly identified as a secret service agent.

The Twins returned to the World Series with a largely different cast of characters in 1991, beating the Atlanta Braves in seven games. It was their last championship of the twentieth century and the last to date. As of the current era, they have compiled a sub-.500 overall record in regular season play.

Whitey Herzog managed the Cardinals until the 1990 campaign, when he resigned with more than 80 games still remaining. Though many members of the pennant-winning squads were still around at that point, the club had come full circle, dropping to last place in the standings. The Cardinals eventually regrouped and moved on, capturing World Series titles in 2006 and 2011. As of 2024, the team had made 16 postseason appearances in the new millennium.

CHAPTER 15

Athletics vs. Dodgers 1988

AFTER THE OAKLAND A'S WON THREE CONSECUTIVE WORLD SERIES titles beginning in 1972, owner Charles Finley sold off most of his top players. The results were predictable as the team fell on hard times in the latter half of the decade. Taking possession of the franchise in 1980, owner Walter A. Haas Jr. (CEO and proprietor of Levi Strauss & Co.) gradually restored the club to its former glory.

The turnaround began with the addition of outfielder Rickey Henderson in 1979. A fourth-round draft pick, Henderson was the quintessential table-setter, stealing more bases and scoring more runs than any player in history. He had considerable power at the plate, falling just short of 300 lifetime homers. This included 81 leadoff shots—a major-league record. Self-confident to the point of being cocky, Henderson had a peculiar habit of referring to himself in the third person, which he tried to downplay late in his career. According to a myriad of sources, he once left a message on the answering machine of Padres GM Kevin Towers saying: "This is Rickey calling on behalf of Rickey. Rickey wants to play baseball." There were other peculiar Rickey moments—like the time he fell asleep on an ice pack and got frostbite, missing several games as a result—or the multiple times he was spotted by teammates standing naked in front of a full-length mirror admiring his physique while talking out loud to himself. Eccentricities aside, Henderson was an irreplaceable member of the A's for 12 full seasons. He left the club to join the Yankees in 1986 but returned in time for Oakland's stretch run in 1989.

Another key addition to the lineup, third baseman Carney Lansford was acquired in December of 1982. A batting champion with the Red Sox in 1981, Lansford possessed each of the five essential skills with the exception of home run power. Although he finished with double-digit totals on eight occasions, he never went deep more than 19 times in any season. He might have become a household name had his career not coincided with three other marquee third sackers—George Brett, Wade Boggs, and Paul Molitor. Lansford was passed over for the All-Star team in all but one of his prime seasons while his Hall of Fame contemporaries came away with more than 30 combined selections.

In the wake of a surprising ALCS appearance during the strike-shortened 1981 campaign, the A's fell into an extended slump, finishing below .500 for the next five years. The arrival of Jose Canseco and Mark McGwire helped remedy the situation. Colorfully known as the "Bash Brothers," the powerful duo gathered no fewer than 50 homers and 150 RBIs in six consecutive seasons (1987–1992).

Canseco was the first to arrive, making his Oakland debut in September of 1985. Born in Havana, Cuba, he immigrated to the United States with his family when he was very young. He inherited a love of baseball from his father but was a late bloomer, failing to make the Coral Park High School varsity squad until his senior year. He was honored as the AL's top rookie in 1986 and reached the peak of his abilities two years later, when he became the first player in major-league history to hit 40 homers and steal 40 bases in the same season. To date, only five other players have accomplished the feat.

McGwire burst upon the scene in 1987 after making a name for himself with Team USA and the USC Trojans. He smashed 49 home runs in his rookie campaign—a record that stood until 2017. McGwire's star burned brightest in 1998, when he engaged in an epic home run duel with Sammy Sosa of the Cubs. "Big Mac" (as he was widely known) came out on top with 70 blasts—another single-season record that was broken by Barry Bonds in 2001.

Fortune and fame eventually turned to infamy for the Bash Brothers as both players admitted to using performance-enhancing drugs. Canseco gave a detailed account of his indiscretions in his 2005 autobiography,

Juiced: Wild Times, Rampant 'Roids, Smash Hits, and How Baseball Got Big.
McGwire offered a tearful confession during a televised interview with
Bob Costas in 2010.

The Bash Brothers assembled their best slugging numbers in
1987 with a collective total of 80 homers and 231 RBIs. It wasn't enough
to carry the A's to the postseason, however, as the club placed third with
an 81–81 record. The addition of center fielder Dave Henderson and
pitcher Bob Welch in the offseason proved to be the final pieces of the
championship puzzle.

Welch—a slender right-hander—used a variety of pitches to keep
hitters off guard. This included a cut fastball, curve, and changeup. After
a promising debut with the Dodgers in 1978, he developed a sore arm.
He sought treatment for addiction during the 1979 campaign and later
detailed his struggles in an autobiography titled *Five O'Clock Comes
Early: A Young Man's Battle with Alcoholism.* Clean, sober, and healthy,
Welch won at least 14 games for Los Angeles on four occasions between
1982 and 1987. He reached the pinnacle of his career in Oakland, going
73–36 in a four-year span. During the 1988 pennant run, he gathered
17 victories while finishing among the top 10 in shutouts.

After spending the early part of his career with the Mariners, Dave
Henderson (no relation to Rickey) reached his statistical peak while wearing an A's uniform. Known for his gap-toothed grin and light-hearted
enthusiasm, he became a fan favorite in Oakland. "Me having fun takes
nothing away from me doing my job," he once said in reference to his
carefree attitude. "In fact, I'm probably the most concentrated guy out
there." Few would argue with that statement as he averaged more than
20 homers and 80 RBIs per year between 1988 and 1991.

Relief pitching was one of Oakland's strongest suits—especially
during the 1988 campaign, when set-up men Eric Plunk, Greg Cadaret,
and Gene Nelson compiled a 2.99 ERA in 161 combined appearances. In
save situations, manager Tony La Russa routinely turned the ball over to
Dennis Eckersley. Known mainly for his years as a closer, Eckersley was
a starter at the beginning of his career. The Hall of Fame right-hander
tossed a no-hitter for the Indians in 1977 and won 20 games for the
Red Sox the following year. After successfully battling arm problems and

alcohol addiction, he was assigned to the Oakland bullpen in 1987. He wasn't pleased with the arrangement at first, but eventually emerged as one of the top firemen in the AL, gathering 30 or more saves during eight seasons. To date, he remains the only pitcher in history with at least 100 saves and 100 complete games. Eckersley came up with colorful names for his pitches, dubbing them "cheese," "hair," "cookie," and "yakker." He was extremely emotional on the mound, pumping his fist excitedly after key strikeouts.

Eckersley's success out of the bullpen greatly benefited starter Dave Stewart, who estimated that the ultra-reliable reliever preserved more than 40 percent of his victories during their time together with the A's. Stewart, who joined the club in 1986, was among the most effective pitchers on the staff, gathering at least 20 wins in four consecutive seasons.

The A's vanquished their opponents 104 times in 1988 (discounting the playoffs). Nearly 30 percent of those victories were by a margin of five runs or more. With the exception of a few days in April, they maintained sole possession of first place all year. By the end of September, they had built a 14-game lead over the defending world champion Twins.

The ALCS was hardy a contest. Although the Red Sox carried a number of superstars on their roster—including Wade Boggs, Dwight Evans, and Roger Clemens—the A's executed a businesslike sweep. Eckersley—the series MVP—picked up a save in each game while allowing just three runners to reach base by hit or walk. Stewart was equally brilliant on the mound, making a pair of quality starts and compiling a 1.35 ERA. Meanwhile, the Bash Brothers lived up to their billing, clubbing four homers and gathering seven RBIs.

In the National League, the Dodgers defied the odds with a successful pennant run. After finishing below .500 in back-to-back seasons, LA executives let several underachieving ballplayers go and made a handful of key acquisitions before the 1988 campaign. The most important addition to the roster was outfielder Kirk Gibson.

An All-American wide receiver at Michigan State University, Gibson ultimately chose the diamond over the gridiron. It took him a few seasons with the Tigers to establish full-time playing status, but he eventually became one of Detroit's most productive sluggers. In 1984, he built a reputation as a clutch postseason performer, hitting .417 in the ALCS. In the World Series, he drilled a pair of home runs and drove in seven runs, helping the Tigers end a championship drought dating back to the 1960s. Gibson's finest offensive year was 1988 as he led the Dodgers in homers, runs scored, doubles, and slugging percentage. His performance in the postseason made him an October legend.

Offensively, the Dodgers were a middle-of-the-road team in 1988, ranking sixth in runs per game and 11th in on-base percentage. None of that could be blamed on leadoff man Steve Sax. A five-time All-Star, Sax was named Rookie of the Year in 1982. During his seven full seasons in Los Angeles, he hit at a .282 clip while averaging 41 steals per year. In 1983, he developed a sudden inability to accurately throw from second to first base on routine grounders. He eventually conquered the problem, transforming himself into one of the top defensive infielders in the league. During the Dodgers' 1988 pennant bid, he hit .277, swiped 42 bases, and scored 70 runs.

In addition to the efforts of Gibson and Sax, the Dodgers owed a great deal of their success to Orel Hershiser. Hershiser remained undrafted out of high school even after he set a record at Cherry Hill East in New Jersey for most strikeouts in a game. He attended Bowling Green University and caught the eye of scouts after tossing a no-hitter against Kent State. Hershiser became a full-time member of the LA staff in 1984, leading the NL in shutouts. He posted an .864 winning percentage the following year—tops in the majors. Tall and thin with a bookish appearance, he was much tougher than he looked. His aggressive approach and strong work ethic prompted manager Tom Lasorda to nickname him "Bulldog." Using a variety of fastballs and curves, Hershiser hit his peak in 1988, winning 23 games—eight of them by shutout. He finished the campaign with 59 consecutive scoreless innings, breaking a major-league record set by Dodger great Don Drysdale in 1968. He continued his mastery in the postseason, capturing MVP honors in the NLCS and World Series.

Although their contributions seemed small in comparison, the rest of the Dodger pitching staff performed commendably in 1988. Starters Tim

Leary and Tim Belcher combined for a 29–17 record in 71 appearances. Jay Howell and Alejandro Pena won 11 games in relief while saving 33 more. As a collective whole, LA hurlers compiled the second-best ERA in the National League.

The pennant race was close in the NL West, but the Dodgers managed to hang onto first place from May 25 until season's end. Things got dicey in June when the Astros pulled to within a half-game of the division lead. By the third week of September, Houston had fallen to third place and only the Reds remained as legitimate contenders. In spite of a 10–3 run in the final stretch, Cincinnati finished seven games behind LA in the standings.

The NLCS was a classic as the Mets—led by David Cone, Dwight Gooden, and Darryl Strawberry—fell one win short of returning to the World Series for the second time in three years. Game 3 was marred by controversy as Howell—LA's regular-season saves leader—was ejected for having pine tar on his glove. The game was played in cold, damp conditions and Howell admitted to using the sticky substance to get a better grip. Although he offered to get rid of the glove, umpire Harry Wendelstedt felt that an ejection was in order. The hurler ended up being suspended for two days. Gibson came up big for the Dodgers, slamming a game-winning homer in the fourth contest and blasting a three-run shot that helped LA to a 7–4 victory in Game 5. In an unfortunate turn of events, he injured his leg in the sixth game then re-aggravated it in the finale. He could barely walk by the time the World Series opened. With Gibson hobbling and the A's firing on all cylinders, the Dodgers were considered heavy underdogs.

Game 1 was held at Dodger Stadium with 56,000 fans in attendance. Since Hershiser had pitched in Game 7 of the NLCS, he was unavailable for the Series opener. Lasorda was forced to send rookie right-hander Tim Belcher to the mound while La Russa had the luxury of starting a well-rested Dave Stewart. Perhaps feeling the pressure of the moment, Stewart hit Sax with the first pitch he threw, balked him to second base, and served up a two-run homer to Mickey Hatcher. Hatcher got the LA crowd worked up by rounding the bases at full speed. This prompted broadcaster Vin Scully to joke: "He's a *Saturday Evening Post* character."

Regaining his composure, Stewart yielded just one more run over the next seven innings. Belcher had a rough go of it, staking the A's to a 4–2 lead in the top of the second. The big blow was struck by Canseco—a grand slam to deep-center field with two outs. The monster blast reportedly hit an NBC camera, leaving a dent. With the A's nursing a 4–3 lead in the bottom of the ninth, the legend of Kirk Gibson was born.

Eckersley was summoned to close out the game for Oakland. He retired the first two batters before issuing a walk to pinch-hitter Mike Davis. Gibson, who was suffering from a pulled hamstring and strained knee ligaments, had been in street clothes at the start of the game. After a pair of cortisone shots, he was still limping but feeling less pain. With the Dodgers trailing in the late innings, he pulled on his uniform and shuffled to the batting cage beneath the stadium for some practice swings. Summoned to pinch-hit for Alejandro Pena, he worked the count full. By his own admission, he was hoping at best for a blooper over the head of Oakland shortstop Walt Weiss. Essentially swinging on one leg, the ailing slugger did much better than that, pounding a backdoor slider into the right field bleachers for a walk-off homer.

"First of all, it was like almost some kind of foolish thing to go up there and hit because of the shape I was in," Gibson reminisced years later. "I remember when I was rounding the bases, my parents went through my mind. Throughout my career, there were a lot of doubters, a lot of people who directed a lot of criticism at me. People would say things to my dad, and initially, early in my career, they had to defend me. I told them, 'You guys don't have to defend me. I'm going to bust it and I'm going to fail sometimes. But we'll have a laugh some day [and] it will all be worth it.' When I [hit that home run], I thought, 'This is the moment.'" Gibson's moment—which came in his only at-bat of the Series—has appeared in virtually every October highlight anthology ever since. In 2016, Eckersley said he felt honored to be a part of Gibson's achievement. "I've always had a respect for Kirk—the kind of player he was. And for something like that to happen to me, in that moment in baseball, was incredible . . . I can step away from that and appreciate it because I love this game."

Inspired by Gibson's heroics, the Dodgers coasted to a 6–0 victory in Game 2. Hershiser was dazzling on the mound, scattering three hits and striking out eight. While the Bash Brothers went 0-for-7 at the plate, Hershiser raked Oakland pitchers for a pair of doubles and a single. He finished the game with a run scored and another driven in.

During the Dodgers last October visit to Oakland—which took place in 1974—they had dropped three in a row. It was more of the same in Game 3 as they came out on the losing end of a 2–1 pitching duel. Former Cardinal ace John Tudor, acquired in an August trade for fading slugger Pedro Guerrero, was forced to leave the game in the second inning with shoulder tightness. The Dodger bullpen kept the game alive until the bottom of the ninth, when McGwire smashed a homer off of Jay Howell, giving the A's their first (and only) win of the Series.

Before the start of the fourth match, broadcaster Bob Costas provoked the ire of LA skipper Tommy Lasorda when he commented that the club had assembled one of the weakest-hitting lineups in Series history. There was truth in that statement. In addition to Gibson, the Dodgers were playing without outfielder Mike Marshall, who had gathered 20 homers during the regular season. The duo had combined for 45 percent of the club's cumulative home run total. The rest of the players in the Game 4 lineup had managed less than 40 long balls all year. Fortunately for the Dodgers, power proved to be an unnecessary commodity as they capitalized on a walk, a passed ball, and an error in the first inning, jumping out to an early 2–0 lead. Another Oakland miscue in the third frame made it a 3–1 game. The A's brought the winning run to the plate with one out in the bottom of the ninth, but Howell atoned for his Game 3 failure, preserving a 4–3 Dodger victory. In a postgame interview, Lasorda jokingly commented that Costas should be named MVP of the Series.

Hershiser assumed a hero's role in Game 5, allowing just two runs on four hits and going the distance. The punchless Dodgers got a pair of homers from Mickey Hatcher (Gibson's replacement) and Mike Davis, who had compiled a .196 batting average during the regular season. Davis's two-run blast was his only hit of the Series. There was little excitement for the A's until the bottom of the eighth, when Hershiser got

Figure 15.1 During his long stint as Dodgers manager, Tom Lasorda led the team to four pennants and two World Series titles.
PHOTO COURTESY OF DIRK DBQ ON VISUAL HUNT.

into a one-out jam, giving up an RBI single to Stan Javier and walking Dave Henderson. Canseco had a chance to tie the game with one swing of the bat but ended up popping out to first base. With veteran slugger Dave Parker at the plate, Hershiser unleashed a wild pitch that moved the runners up. Just when he seemed to be losing control, he struck out Parker to extinguish the threat. The 5–2 win gave the Dodgers their second championship of the decade. "Nobody thought we would win the division," Lasorda said after the game. "Nobody thought we could beat the mighty Mets. Nobody thought we could beat the team who won 104 games, but we believed it."

Oakland's big three—Canseco, McGwire, and Dave Henderson—combined for a .143 batting average in the Series with just four extra-base hits. The pitchers weren't much better, posting a cumulative 3.92 ERA. Still, La Russa accepted blame for the loss, commenting many years later: "I got out-managed by Tommy [Lasorda], who had his team more prepared. I know it's a long time ago, but it still bothers me and always will. I learned a painful lesson from that." There were better days ahead as La Russa guided the A's and Cardinals to a total of six pennants and three World Series titles. Both he and Lasorda were inducted into the Hall of Fame.

After the Series was over, the A's and Dodgers appeared on the popular TV game show *Family Feud* in what was billed as a World Series rematch. The showdown, which ran for multiple episodes, raised tens of thousands for charity. The A's returned to the World Series in each of the next two seasons but have not been back since. The Dodgers waited until 2017 for a World Series return. After losing back-to-back Fall Classics in 2017 and 2018, they captured the seventh championship in franchise history during the 2020 campaign.

CHAPTER 16

Athletics vs. Reds 1990

THERE WERE DARK CLOUDS HANGING OVER RIVERFRONT STADIUM IN 1990. In August of the previous year, Pete Rose—a beloved member of the fabled "Big Red Machine"—was accused of placing bets on Cincinnati while carrying out his managerial duties. Although he proclaimed his innocence, he was forced to accept a settlement that included a lifetime ban from baseball. In a subsequent press conference, Commissioner A. Bartlett Giamatti announced that Rose's decision to accept the banishment was equivalent to a no-contest plea. Baseball's all-time hits leader ultimately admitted to wagering but claimed that he always bet on the Reds to win.

The 1990 campaign began with a labor dispute that shortened spring training and prompted the postponement of numerous games. In order to complete the schedule, the regular season was extended by a few days. Fay Vincent—who took over for Giamatti in September of 1989—was instrumental in negotiating a settlement between owners and players. It was the seventh work stoppage in major-league history and one of the longest to that point.

Dampening the mood in Cincinnati even further, players and executives were forced to deal with toxic owner Marge Schott, who had a talent for making inappropriate remarks. Schott became popular with fans by keeping the price of tickets and concessions relatively low but tested the patience of her staff regularly with a host of erratic behaviors. At one point, she threatened to fire the entire scouting crew, which she claimed had no benefit to the club. Schott was not opposed to the use of racial slurs and sometimes uttered them in public. In 1991, she was sued by the club's former marketing director for refusing to hire Black employees. She later came under fire for making provocative statements about Adolf Hitler. Her outrageous comments eventually led to her removal from day-to-day operations of the team.

In spite of the troubling undercurrents, the Reds performed exceptionally well in 1990. Pitching was the name of the game as the staff posted the second-lowest ERA in the National League. The bullpen was arguably the best in the majors.

A left-handed closer with a passion for guns, Randy Myers was once described by teammate Jesse Orosco as "crazy." Relying entirely on a fastball/slider combination, Myers worked his way up through the Mets organization and came to Cincinnati in a trade involving three other players. He spent two seasons with the Reds, putting forth his finest effort in 1990, when he saved 31 games and posted a 2.08 ERA in 66 appearances.

Norm Charlton—a southpaw with three effective pitches in his arsenal—served a dual role for the Reds, starting 16 games during the 1990 campaign while making 40 additional relief appearances. In all, he worked more than 154 innings, compiling the third-highest strikeout total on the club. He was actually more effective as a starter, holding opponents to a .222 batting average in that role.

A big man at 6-foot-4, 230 pounds, right-handed flamethrower Rob Dibble was a menacing presence on the mound. "Some say that his fastball doesn't have much movement," one writer remarked. "[But] hell, how much movement do you need when you throw over 100 miles per hour?" Dibble put forth a brilliant effort in 1990, posting the lowest WHIP average on the Cincinnati staff. Intense and hyper-competitive, his temper got the best of him the following year, when he was suspended for injuring a fan with a ball he fired into the stands. It was not his first infraction of the season, nor would it be his last. He was forced to sit out earlier in the year for deliberately throwing a pitch behind the head of a batter. And he was fined a few months later for intentionally hitting a base runner with a relay.

Together, Cincinnati's trio of intimidating relievers came to be known as the "Nasty Boys." Although they posted a collective 2.28 earned run average, they were just wild enough to make batters uncomfortable, plunking eight men and issuing 14 wild pitches. None were opposed to throwing inside to move hitters off the plate.

The ace of the Reds' starting rotation was Tom Browning, a south-paw who made a big splash in his rookie year by winning 20 games—a rare feat for a freshman. He would finish with double-digit win totals in each of the next six seasons, reaching the 15-victory plateau three times. Browning employed a wide variety of offerings, including a screwball, slider, and curve. He attained immortality in September of 1988, when he pitched the 12th perfect game in major-league history. He came close to duplicating the feat a year later, carrying a perfecto into the ninth inning against the Phillies. In 1990, he posted a 15–9 record, leading the league with 35 starts. He could have won a few more games had the Reds not supported him with two runs or less in more than a third of his appearances.

The 1990 Reds were not the most powerful offensive club in the NL (ranking fifth in runs scored and seventh in homers), but they hit for aver-age and demonstrated good speed on the bases. The most accomplished player on the squad was shortstop Barry Larkin. Though he appeared in only 41 games during his big-league debut, Larkin still placed among the top 10 in Rookie of the Year voting. Over the next 18 seasons, he found his way onto 12 All-Star teams, claimed nine Silver Slugger Awards, and won three Gold Gloves in addition to capturing NL MVP honors (in 1995). Larkin was well-suited to the top of the batting order, stealing close to 400 bases during his Hall of Fame career. He also proved to be a capable RBI man when the Reds needed him to be. Larkin hit .301 for the Reds in 1990 and scored 85 runs while gathering 67 ribbies.

Remembered for the trademark goggles he wore on the field, Chris Sabo was a sure-handed third baseman with tremendous drive. Vastly underappreciated defensively, he posted the best fielding percentage among players at his position twice but failed to receive a Gold Glove in either campaign. Sabo had decent power at the plate and demonstrated it during the Reds' 1990 pennant run, slamming a team-high 25 homers. His 38 doubles that year were third most in the league.

Although right fielder Paul O'Neill's best years were spent with the Yankees, he was a key member of the 1990 Reds squad, slashing 44 extra-base hits while driving in 78 runs—second on the club to Eric Davis. O'Neill said that he was pressured by management to swing for the fences during his time in Cincinnati—a practice that lowered his batting averages considerably. Upon joining the Yankees in 1993, he changed his approach to hitting, compiling a .303 mark in nine seasons with New York. By way of comparison, he hit .259 for the Reds over portions of eight seasons. Defensively, O'Neill was one of the best in the majors, regularly appearing among the league leaders in putouts and assists.

Davis—a daring center fielder with extensive range—won three Gold Gloves during the early part of his career. He was also among Cincinnati's most powerful hitters, averaging 30 homers per year between 1986 and 1990. He could have been one of the truly great franchise players had his hard style of play not led to an ongoing series of injuries. In 1990, he hurt his knee and missed more than a month of action. He still managed to smash 24 homers and drive in 86 runs.

Cincinnati skipper Lou Piniella had developed a well-deserved reputation as a hot head during his playing days. Prone to dramatic run-ins with umpires, he kept players under control through intimidation. "I think the players were scared to death of Lou," Reds broadcaster Marty Brennaman recalled. "He told the team in no uncertain terms that he thought it had the talent to go a long way and anything short of their best he would not tolerate. He said it in such a forceful manner that the message got through." Brennaman believed that the key to Cincinnati's success was camaraderie among players. "It was the team that had the greatest chemistry of any team I have been around," the iconic announcer asserted. "Baseball is famous for cliques, understandable when you play 162 games. Guys with like interests will hang out. The team had no cliques . . . all loved one another and all of them had everybody's back. It was just an incredible team to be around. No jealousy, no nitpicking about anything."

Figure 16.1   Lou Piniella's only World Series title as a manager came with the Reds in 1990. He won two championships while playing for the Yankees from 1974 to 1984. He is pictured here in the midst of one of his infamous on-field tantrums.
PHOTO COURTESY OF EMR ON VISUAL HUNT.

The Reds opened the 1990 campaign with nine straight wins and remained in the driver's seat for the rest of the year. They led by as many as 11 games in late July before a 2–11 skid cut the margin to 3 and a half. The division wasn't terribly strong with only three of six teams finishing above .500. The Dodgers had a chance to overtake the Reds in the final days of September but ended up losing five of their last seven games, finishing second. It was Cincinnati's first division title since 1979.

The NLCS pitted the Reds against the Pirates. The series was very close with four of six games being decided by a single run. Cincinnati pitchers effectively stifled Pittsburgh's big bats, holding Barry Bonds and Bobby Bonilla to a collective .179 showing at the plate. O'Neill was the offensive star for the Reds, hitting .471 with four extra-base hits. Myers was lights-out in relief, picking up three saves.

In the American League, the A's capped off a three-year period of dominance with another pennant-winning effort. This time around, it was outfielder Rickey Henderson who stole the show. The Hall of Fame speedster developed a reputation as a "gun for hire" over the years, playing for nine different teams. After a six-year stint with the A's, he spent portions of five seasons in New York. When the Yankees began to flounder in June of 1989, Henderson was dealt back to Oakland. He enjoyed his most successful campaign in 1990, leading the American League in multiple categories while posting a .325 batting average—the highest single-season mark of his career. His efforts earned him AL MVP honors.

In addition to Henderson, the A's got significant contributions from the usual sources as José Canseco and Mark McGwire collectively blasted 76 homers while gathering more than 200 RBIs. In the bullpen, Dennis Eckersley reached the peak of his career as a closer, saving 48 games and posting a microscopic 0.61 ERA—among the lowest single-season marks in history. The veteran hurler surrendered earned runs in just four of his 63 appearances while holding opponents to a feeble .160 batting average. In spite of his sensational performance, he placed fifth in voting for the Cy Young Award. He might have fared better had staff mates Bob Welch and Dave Stewart not combined for 49 wins and 293 strikeouts. Stewart finished third while Welch claimed the award with 15 first-place votes.

Determined to successfully defend their 1989 championship, A's executives went shopping for reinforcements while the season was in progress. On May 13, they acquired former Yankee great Willie Randolph. On August 29, they picked up Hall of Famer Harold Baines and NL batting champion Willie McGee (who logged enough plate appearances before his departure from St. Louis to qualify). All three fared very well during their brief time in Oakland.

The A's ran away with the division title again, accumulating 103 wins and leaving the second-place White Sox nine games behind. The Red Sox, who had barely captured the AL East crown, were completely overwhelmed as Oakland swept the ALCS by an aggregate score of 20–4. Baines was an offensive standout for the A's along with Carney Lansford and Terry Steinbach. The trio collectively compiled a handsome

.415 batting average. Stewart captured MVP honors with a pair of wins and a stingy 1.13 ERA. When the World Series opened in Cincinnati, there was little reason for anyone to believe that the Reds stood half a chance.

There were close to 56,000 fans in attendance at Riverfront Stadium on the night of Game 1. True to form, Marge Schott delivered an unforgettable slip of the tongue, dedicating the World Series "to our wonderful women and men over in the Far East that are serving us." Schott's habit of saying the wrong thing at the wrong time had prompted members of the CBS broadcasting crew to deny her access to live microphones, but she evaded their efforts while the crowd was standing for the national anthem. "I tried to stop her," said Commissioner Fay Vincent, who was with Schott in her private box at the stadium that evening. "But she had a very choice word, then went onto the field and made a fool of herself. . . . I think she was not in control of herself that night." Schott was actually referring to the Middle East, where the Gulf War was in progress. She later stunned First Lady Barbara Bush (who was in attendance) by professing that she hated baseball.

The pitching matchup for Game 1 featured Dave Stewart against José Rijo. Stewart had a six-game postseason winning streak going while Rijo—a big right-hander from the Dominican Republic—had been one of Cincinnati's most reliable hurlers, posting a 14–8 record. Using a combination of fastballs, sliders, and changeups, Rijo pitched seven efficient innings. Lansford and Rickey Henderson went 5-for-9 at the plate, but their efforts were wasted as the A's stranded a total of 11 base runners. Eric Davis launched a two-run homer in the first and added another RBI a few innings later as the Reds put an end to Stewart's streak with a decisive 7–0 victory.

Game 2, which pitted Bob Welch against Danny Jackson, was arguably the most exciting of the Series. Jackson gave up three hits in the first, but got off easy, allowing just one earned run. The Reds answered with two runs in the bottom of the frame, tagging Welch for a pair of doubles. With the score at 2–1 in the top of the third, the A's chased Jackson from the game with a three-run outburst. But the Reds would not be denied, cutting the lead in half in the fourth. In the bottom of the eighth, Billy

Hatcher led off with a triple on a ball that was misplayed by Canseco. Pinch-hitter Glenn Braggs tied the score with an RBI groundout off of reliever Rick Honeycutt.

As the game meandered into the late innings, Piniella told Reds pitching coach Stan Williams that he might need Browning (the projected Game 3 starter) to make an appearance. Anxiety turned to near panic when Browning could not be located. As it turned out, the hurler's pregnant wife (Debbie) had gone into labor during the fifth inning. Browning had left the stadium in haste and forgotten to tell anyone where he was going. Marty Brennaman issued an APB over the radio, which was repeated by TV broadcaster Tim McCarver. Browning heard the announcement but opted to remain at the hospital. "When I heard that, I panicked," he later told a *Sports Illustrated* writer, "but I decided I wouldn't leave Debbie until I knew she and the baby were all right." He was still in his Reds uniform in the delivery room when his son, Tucker, was born.

Meanwhile, back at the stadium, the game stretched into the 10th inning. Piniella, who was down to the last of his reserves at that point, summoned Billy Bates to pinch-hit for Dibble. Bates, whose entire regular-season career with Cincinnati consisted of five hitless at-bats, bounced a pitch from Eckersley off the plate toward third base. Lansford charged the ball but couldn't come up with it. Sabo followed with a single and catcher Joe Oliver drove in the winning run. "The Reds could have had some problems," Brennaman said years later. "Oakland had a damn good team. If they had won that game, they would have accomplished what they set out to do: Go to Oakland even for Games 3, 4, and 5. Game 2 was without a doubt the pivotal game."

A's manager Tony La Russa was inclined to agree. In a postgame interview, he roasted Canseco for his eighth inning defensive gaffe, stating bluntly that the slugger had gotten a "horseshit jump" on the ball hit by Hatcher. "I think that's a play you've got to make if you're going to win the game," he said. La Russa's remark led to some infighting as Canseco fired back: "If he wants to hang the loss on one play, he's totally wrong. And it's totally out of character. Have you ever heard Tony make a statement like that against one of his players? But then again, you always blame the guy making the most money because he's the one who's supposed to be doing the most." With both comments officially on the record, Dave Stewart shared his own thoughts on the topic. "To me, it's gotten to be wait and see with José. Like he hits the home run. For me, it's so what? What are you going to do next? Because so often, he hits a home run and then he doesn't do anything the rest of the game." It was not the last time that Canseco demonstrated deficient skills in the outfield. In May of 1993, he committed the ultimate blunder, allowing a ball hit by Carlos Martinez of the Indians to bounce off of his head and over the fence for a home run.

La Russa and Canseco held a private meeting to smooth things over, but the writing was on the wall. The A's, who had entered the Series with pomp and swagger, were falling apart. Aware of the situation, Rob Dibble boldly declared that Cincinnati pitchers would continue to go right after A's hitters. "I see a lot of teams scared of them," he said. "If you're scared, they bury you."

The Series moved to Oakland for Game 3. As promised, the Reds remained aggressive, building an 8–3 lead through three innings. The A's picked up their runs on a pair of homers by Baines and Henderson. Sabo went deep twice for the Reds and four other Cincinnati players were also credited with RBIs. Neither team scored after the third inning.

With his team mired in a deep hole, Stewart returned to form in Game 4. The Reds lost two players to injury in the first inning as Hatcher was hit by a pitch and Davis ended up with a lacerated kidney after diving for a fly ball hit by Willie McGee. The A's maintained a precarious 1–0 lead until the top of the eighth, when Stewart suddenly lost his command. Larkin and Herm Winningham opened the frame with a pair of singles. O'Neill followed with a bunt that Stewart made a poor throw on. With the bases loaded, Braggs drove in a run on a fielder's choice. Hal Morris then pushed the deciding run across with a sacrifice fly. Rijo—the Series MVP—topped off another brilliant outing by retiring the side in order in the bottom of the eighth. After striking out Dave Henderson in the ninth, he was pulled for Randy Myers, who disposed of Canseco and Lansford to end the game. It was the Reds' first championship since 1976.

Cincinnati's surprising victory marked the second time in World Series history that a team with a win-deficit of at least 10 games had swept a more powerful opponent. The last time it had happened was in 1954, when the Giants made quick work of the Indians. It was not the only major upset in the world of sports during the 1990 calendar year. Back in February, Buster Douglas had shocked the boxing world with a knockout of reigning heavyweight champion Mike Tyson.

The Oakland loss sparked newfound interest in the alleged curse of the Cubs. Before Game 1, *Chicago Tribune* writer Mike Royko had jokingly declared that the A's were "doomed" on account of the ex-Cubs factor. A's hurlers Dennis Eckersley and Scott Sanderson had both pitched for Chicago during the mid-1980s. And the Cubs, who hadn't won a World Series since 1908, were said to be suffering from a curse placed upon them by a local tavern owner in the 1940s. The idea of the A's being jinxed was inherently flawed, however, considering that Cincinnati's left fielder Billy Hatcher had also played for Chicago during his first two seasons in the majors.

In his 2017 memoirs, Lou Piniella wrote, "To this day, all these years later, I still cannot fully describe the elation—and the redemption—I felt sitting in the visiting manager's office of the Oakland Coliseum in the aftermath of winning the World Series." But elation soon turned to aggravation as Schott opted not to buy food for the team's victory party back in San Francisco. Piniella believed that Schott deliberately short-changed players and their families because she was upset about the team having clinched the Series at Oakland. "Only in the insensitive, oblivious, penurious world of Marge Schott could the joy of winning the world championship all but be extinguished within a couple of hours," the former Yankee great asserted.

The depth of Schott's insensitivity became evident when Eric Davis wound up in the hospital for several days and missed the ticker tape parade thrown for the team back in Cincinnati. Not only did Schott refuse to pay for Davis's plane fare home, but she skipped out on the hotel bill his family ran up while staying behind with him. "It left a sour taste in our mouths and left me wondering just how long I was going to be able to put up with Marge's mercurial and crude behavior," Piniella later reflected. The veteran skipper stayed with the Reds until the end of the 1992 campaign, joining the Seattle Mariners the following year.

The "Nasty Boys" were broken up when Myers left the Reds after the 1991 season. Charlton followed at the end of the 1992 slate. In spite of carrying most of the same players from the championship squad, the team staggered to a fifth-place finish in 1991. The Reds returned to the NLCS in 1995 but have not advanced beyond the division series since then.

The A's have suffered a similar fate, making their last trip to the ALCS in 2006 and coming away empty-handed. As of 2024, they had been excluded from World Series play for more than 30 seasons. They lost 112 games in 2023.

CHAPTER 17

Indians vs. Marlins 1997

IN THE LATE 1980S, MAJOR-LEAGUE OFFICIALS APPROVED A PLAN TO ADD a pair of new franchises to the existing National League lineup. After several months of deliberation, a list of possible expansion sites was selected. The top contenders for ownership included a group from Miami headed by H. Wayne Huizenga—co-owner of the Blockbuster Video chain. In 1990, Huizenga purchased a minority share of the Miami Dolphins along with a 50-percent stake in the team's home facility. After closing a deal with big-league executives, Huizenga green-lighted a project to transform Joe Robbie Stadium into a baseball venue.

The Florida Marlins played their inaugural season in 1993 accompanied by the Colorado Rockies, who joined the NL West. Although both teams were colossal flops, combining for 193 losses, neither would wait terribly long to get a taste of the postseason.

From 1969 to 1993, the first-place teams from each division advanced to the league championship playoff with the winners moving on to the World Series. The expansion of the NL in the latter campaign led to a realignment. Both circuits were split into three divisions with a wild card team added to the postseason format. The new divisional playoff was slated to begin in 1994, but a players strike abruptly ended the season in August. Wild card teams officially entered the mix the following year as the Rockies made their first postseason appearance. The Marlins became the second expansion franchise to make the playoffs in 1997.

In spite of the Marlins' appalling 64–98 record in 1993, the rudiments of a winning ballclub were already in place with Gary Sheffield,

Jeff Conine, and Robb Nen making their Florida debuts. Sheffield came up through the Brewers system. He enjoyed a breakout year with the Padres in 1992, winning a batting title with a .330 mark. Traded to the Marlins in June of the following season, he appeared exclusively at third base. In 1994, he was moved to the outfield, which became his primary station from that point forward. A reliable run producer, he reached the century mark in RBIs eight times. He joined the 500–home run club in his final campaign.

Originally property of the Royals, Conine had two separate stints with Florida. He spent a total of eight years with the club and is still among the all-time franchise leaders in more than half a dozen offensive categories. Splitting time at first base and the outfield, he was better suited to the latter position, posting a stellar lifetime fielding percentage.

A right-handed reliever, Nen had a variety of weapons in his arsenal, including a splitter, slider, and curve. After ascending to the majors with the Rangers in 1993, he was traded to Florida around the All-Star break. Nen was wild early in his career, but eventually learned to control his pitches, saving 30 or more games in seven consecutive seasons (1996–2002). He was known for his blazing fastball, which was officially clocked at 102 miles per hour. His slider, which broke sharply down at 92 mph, was nicknamed "the Terminator."

A host of other talented players were welcomed to the fold in the years preceding the Marlins' Cinderella campaign of 1997. After making a few appearances in the spring of 1994, catcher Charles Johnson was sent back to the minors for more conditioning. By the end of the following season, he was a regular in the Marlins lineup. Johnson had sure hands behind the plate and a powerful arm—qualities that earned him four consecutive Gold Gloves beginning in 1995. Though his batting averages typically hovered in the .250 range, he demonstrated abundant power, finishing with double-digit home run totals in nine seasons. He peaked at 31 blasts during the 2000 slate.

In 1996, the Marlins made significant upgrades, promoting Edgar Renteria from the minors and acquiring pitcher Kevin Brown from the Rangers. Renteria was just 19 years old when he arrived in Florida. A native of Colombia, he finished second in Rookie of the Year voting and hung around the majors for 15 more seasons, establishing himself as one of the best all-around shortstops in the game. His performance in the 1997 World Series made him a national hero in his home country.

A right-hander, Brown had half a dozen effective pitches in his repertoire, including a four-seam rising fastball and a splitter. Describing what it was like to work with the five-time Cy Young Award candidate, Paul Lo Duca once said: "He can be hard to catch. I told him sometimes I just go out there and try to knock it down. His fastball moves so much, and he can throw it at 95, 96 mph—just right by you." Brown enjoyed one of his best seasons in his Marlins debut, posting a career-low 1.89 ERA (tops in the majors among starters). He followed with a solid effort in 1997, posting a 16–8 record with 205 strikeouts.

The Marlins used three different managers in 1996. After a disappointing 80–82 finish, team executives hired Jim Leyland to turn things around. A veteran of 11 major-league seasons, Leyland had guided the Pirates to three consecutive division titles beginning in 1990. Other changes would follow as the Marlins splurged on three marquee players: Moises Alou, Bobby Bonilla, and Alex Fernandez.

Alou came from one of the most talented baseball families in major-league history. His father and two of his uncles (all of whom were Dominican born) logged more than 40 years of combined major-league experience. Following in their footsteps, Moises compiled a .303 batting average over 17 major-league seasons, with more than 300 home runs and 1,200 RBIs. He was a six-time All-Star. In 1997, he was Florida's most productive hitter, scoring 88 times and driving in 115 runs.

Acquired as a free agent, Bonilla was among the Pirates' top sluggers in the late 1980s/early 1990s. He spent the 1996 campaign with the Orioles, reaching the 100 RBI plateau for the fourth time in his career. He barely missed with Florida the following year, coming up just four ribbies short. Bonilla grew up in a poor section of New York City. Whenever he failed to meet expectations and was asked if he felt any pressure, he always answered: "This isn't pressure. Pressure is growing up in the South Bronx."

Fernandez made his big-league debut with the White Sox in 1990. It took him a while to find his form, but he eventually blossomed into one of Chicago's top starters, winning a career-high 18 games in 1993. A mainstay in the ChiSox rotation over the next three seasons, the Miami native signed as a free agent with his hometown Marlins before the 1997 campaign. He helped the club capture the NL pennant before a rotator cuff injury put him out of action for the World Series.

Aside from the first two weeks of April, when the Marlins were perched at the top of the division standings, they remained rooted in second place for a majority of the year. A phenomenal 8–1 start benefited them greatly over the long haul. It was a tremendous disadvantage to be sharing a division with the Braves, who carried several Hall of Famers on their roster and made it to the playoffs in 14 consecutive seasons (discounting the strike-shortened 1994 campaign). Atlanta gathered 101 wins in 1997 and finished nine games ahead of the Marlins, who earned a wild card berth.

The feel-good story of the season was the emergence of Cuban-born rookie Livan Hernandez as a pitching ace. A member of the Cuban national team, Hernandez fled the country via Mexico with the help of recruiter Joe Cubas. The Marlins were looking to sign some Latino ballplayers to make the team more marketable to South Florida's sizeable Hispanic community. Hernandez rose quickly through the minors, earning a brief call-up in 1996. He began the 1997 slate in the Eastern and International Leagues before returning to the majors for good in June. An instant sensation, he won each of his first nine decisions and ended the regular season with a stellar 3.18 ERA. With just 21 major-league appearances to his credit, he was the least experienced hurler ever to start Game 1 of the World Series. After some delicate negotiations with the Castro government, Hernandez's mother was allowed to attend Game 7. She had not seen her son in more than two years at that point.

The Braves swept the Astros in the National League Division Series as the Marlins duplicated the feat against the Giants. Bonilla and Conine hit at a combined .348 clip for Florida. The Braves—defending NL champs—were expected to roll over the Marlins in the next round, but the resilient underdog squad pulled off a major upset. Reminiscing about the storybook year of 1997, Jim Leyland told a writer: "The most amazing thing about that season: Just to have the honor to play in the World Series, we had to beat [Greg] Maddux twice, [Tom] Glavine, and

[John] Smoltz just to get there. When you think about [it], that's three guys that just went into the Hall of Fame."

There were interesting developments in the American League as well. Championships were not a regular occurrence in Cleveland during the twentieth century. From 1901 to the arrival of the new millennium, the Indians won just five pennants and two World Series titles. In 1995, they returned to the Fall Classic after a 40-year absence, losing to the Braves. The rise of the Yankees in the AL East created a daunting new challenge, but in 1997, the Indians were poised to make a serious run.

Reflecting on the personnel changes in Cleveland before the 1997 slate, Indians GM John Hart said: "The game is about the players. You need good players to win. You don't always need the best players, but you need good players." Determined to remain in the playoff hunt, Hart acquired outfielders Marquis Grissom and David Justice from the Braves. He signed slugger Matt Williams to play third base and moved Jim Thome to first. Putting the finishing touches on his master plan, Hart hashed out a one-year deal with infielder Tony Fernandez. The results were even better than expected as all five players prospered in their new roles. Thome cracked 40 homers and fielded his position dependably. Williams and Justice (who served as a part-time DH) both reached the 30-homer/100-RBI plateau. Grissom provided speed on the bases and solid defense in the outfield while Fernandez posted his highest batting average in nearly a decade. The rest of the Cleveland roster was a pleasing combination of proven veterans and budding stars.

A native of Venezuela, Omar Vizquel got his big-league start with the Seattle Mariners in 1989. Upon joining the Indians in 1994, he completed a string of nine consecutive seasons with a Gold Glove. He added two more to his collection before he retired, becoming the second most decorated shortstop behind Ozzie Smith. Even Smith couldn't match Vizquel's lifetime fielding percentage, which is the highest of all time among shortstops. In addition to his exceptional fielding, Vizquel had a fine offensive year in 1997, compiling a .280 batting average and leading the AL in sacrifice hits.

Cleveland's pitching corps were anchored by a pair of seasoned right-handers. Though his record for consecutive scoreless innings was long behind him by the time the 1997 campaign arrived, Orel Hershiser continued to be highly effective at the age of 38, winning 14 of 20 decisions. He carried that success into the first two rounds of the playoffs, posting a 2.45 ERA. Hershiser was often preceded in the rotation by Charles Nagy—a 30-year-old breaking-ball specialist with a variety of deceptive offerings. In addition to his signature sinker, Nagy also employed a slurve, which is a peculiar combination of a curve and a slider. The ace of the Cleveland staff in 1997, he won 15 games and fielded his position flawlessly in 34 starts.

Son of a former major leaguer and brother of a Hall of Fame infielder, Sandy Alomar Jr. was a steady presence behind the plate for 11 seasons in Cleveland. He reached his offensive peak in 1997 with career-high marks in nearly every major offensive category. Unofficially recognized as the team's leader, the six-time All-Star and former Rookie of the Year (in 1990) would likely have accomplished much more in his career had he not been sidelined with multiple injuries over the years.

Among the younger stars in the Cleveland lineup, corner outfielders Manny Ramirez and Brian Giles were major components of the 1997 World Series bid. In addition to being one of the most prolific sluggers of the era, Ramirez developed a reputation as an eccentric and non-conformist. His most puzzling moments (including the time he disappeared inside the Green Monster in left field at Fenway Park with a game in progress) were famously explained away as "Manny being Manny." The Indians and Red Sox found him to be largely worth the trouble as he gathered more than 500 homers and 1,600 RBIs while playing for both clubs. Though Giles enjoyed his best slugging years in Pittsburgh, he came of age with Cleveland, logging his first season as a full-time player in 1997. He appeared at every outfield station that year and enjoyed a breakout performance, clubbing 17 homers.

In spite of all the vastly talented players in Cleveland, the Indians got off to a lethargic start in 1997, forging a 12–13 record through April. They spent a majority of June in first place but finished the month just five games above .500. "That group of guys was really close knit," said pitcher Chad Ogea. "You'd go into the locker room before the game and guys are hanging out, playing cards, and having fun. There was a

Figure 17.1   After hitting .324 during the regular season in 1997, Sandy Alomar Jr. slugged five homers and drove in 19 runs during three rounds of the playoffs.
PHOTO COURTESY OF APARDAVILA ON VISUAL HUNT.

moment during the year where we weren't playing up to expectations . . . just kind of not really showing what we could do. We had a players-only meeting and everybody was like 'Hey—let's just do what we're supposed to do—have fun and don't worry about all the other stuff going on. Let's just take care of business.'" The Indians managed affairs quite efficiently in the second half, putting a six-game buffer between themselves and the second-place White Sox.

The division series pitted the Indians against the defending world champion Yankees, who were carrying a roster full of perennial All-Stars. Significant offensive efforts by Derek Jeter and Paul O'Neill were not enough to carry the Yankees back to the ALCS as Cleveland came out on top. Rookie right-hander Jaret Wright won both of his starts while Alomar and Vizquel were the offensive stars for the Tribe.

The ALCS was equally challenging with four games being decided by a single run. Cleveland jumped out to a 3–1 series lead before dropping the fifth meeting at home. Game 6 was a nail-biter that dragged on for 11 innings. In the end, five different Cleveland hurlers held the Baltimore Orioles scoreless. A solo homer by Tony Fernandez sent the Indians back to the World Series for the second time in three years. The Marlins' lack of postseason experience convinced most experts that the Indians would finally end their ponderous championship slump.

Game 1 was held in Florida with more than 67,000 fans on hand. Hernandez got into trouble in the first, giving up a leadoff double to Bip Roberts and an RBI single to Justice. He settled down until the fifth, when Ramirez launched a homer to deep left field. By then, the Marlins had tagged Hershiser for five runs. The most destructive blow came off the bat of Alou, who drove a ball off the left field foul pole for a three-run homer. Johnson immediately followed with a solo shot. The Marlins added a pair in the bottom of the fifth, ending a frustrating day for Hershiser. Meanwhile, the Indians pecked away at Hernandez, scoring a run in the sixth and another in the eighth. With one out and two runners aboard in the ninth, Robb Nen struck out Thome and Alomar to secure a 7–4 win for Florida.

Ogea—a right-hander who had struggled with arm issues during the regular season—was the Game 2 starter for Cleveland. After a bumpy first inning, he settled in nicely, turning in 5.2 scoreless frames. Brown—the Marlins ace—was not nearly as effective, coughing up six runs on 10 hits. A majority of the trouble occurred in the fifth, when Grissom and Roberts delivered RBI singles. Alomar launched a two-run homer an inning later, giving the Indians a 6–1 lead, which held up as the final score.

Close to 45,000 fans saw a messy slugfest in Game 3 at Jacobs Field. Eleven different pitchers took the mound with each allowing at least one runner to reach base. The defense wasn't much better as the teams committed three errors apiece. By the time the game ended at 12:36 a.m., there were 25 runs and 26 hits on the board. Sheffield administered the most damage for Florida, going 3-for-5 with five RBIs. Thome scored three runs for Cleveland and drove in a pair with his second homer of the Series. The final score was 14–11 in favor of the Marlins.

Game 4 was played in hostile weather conditions. There were snow flurries during batting practice and the wind chill was reported at around 15 degrees, making it the coldest game on record. Messy pitching plagued the Marlins again as the Indians scored 10 runs on 15 hits. Jim Eisenreich drove in a run for the Marlins in the fourth and Alou added a two-run homer in the sixth off of Cleveland starter Jaret Wright, but it was as close as Florida would get. The all-around sloppy play in the Series to that point and plodding length of the games drew scathing criticism from multiple sources.

In theory, the clash between Hernandez and Hershiser in Game 5 should have been a pitcher's duel. But the offensive onslaught continued as both clubs combined for 24 hits. Hernandez had trouble spotting his pitches, yielding eight walks. He held on for an ugly win as Hershiser got pounded for six runs in 5.2 innings of work. The game featured a wild ninth inning as the Marlins extended their lead to 8–4 in the top of the frame. The Indians roughed up Nen in their final turn at-bat, plating three runs on a pair of clutch singles by Justice and Thome. With two outs and the tying run on base, Alomar drew a collective gasp from the crowd when he sent a deep drive to right field. It appeared as if it might leave the yard initially, but Sheffield made the catch, giving the Marlins a hard-fought 8–7 victory.

With Cleveland on the brink of elimination, the Series moved back to Florida. The contest drew the largest crowd since Game 5 of the 1959 Fall Classic. In a rematch between Brown and Ogea, it was the latter hurler who got the best of the encounter, scattering four hits and allowing just one run over five-plus innings. Brown was ineffective again, staking the Indians to a 4–1 lead through five frames. The Cleveland bullpen got the job done for a change as closer Jose Mesa picked up his fourth save of the postseason, tying the Series at three games apiece.

On the night before the finale, Cleveland manager Mike Hargrove told Nagy—his projected Game 7 starter—that he would be handing the ball over to Wright instead. "I was disappointed at first," Nagy later recalled. "That's what you live for. I was lined up to pitch that game. I was prepared for it. But then all of a sudden you have to change gears. You can't feel sorry for yourself. You have to do what's best for the team."

Hargrove said it was one of the hardest decisions he ever made. "Charlie is one of my all-time favorite players that I managed," the veteran skipper said. "But I also knew that Charlie would understand my decision, and he wouldn't go off in a corner and sulk."

Wright squared off against veteran southpaw Al Leiter in a tightly pitched game that came down to a battle of the bullpens. Leiter stumbled first, giving up a pair of runs in the third. Wright's only slip came in the bottom of the seventh, when he served up a leadoff homer to Bonilla. According to a popular story, Bonilla got some advice from former Dodger pitcher Joe Black while he was in the on-deck circle. Bonilla was known for chatting up fans before his at-bats and the 1952 Rookie of the Year happened to be sitting in the front row.

The Indians carried a 2–1 lead into the ninth inning and came within two outs of clinching the Series. But Mesa faltered in relief, giving up singles to Alou and Charles Johnson. With runners on the corners, Craig Counsell sent a hard liner down the right field line that was deep enough to push the tying run across. Nen struck out the side in the top of the 10th and Mesa wriggled out of trouble in the bottom of the frame as Nagy was summoned to get the final out with two runners on base. When the Indians failed to break through in the 11th, Hargrove left Nagy on the mound to close out the game. "As a manager, all you can do is put people in positions where their talent can dominate and put them in good positions where they can do their jobs. We felt like we had the people where they needed to be."

He was wrong.

Bonilla led off the 11th with a single through the hole at shortstop. After a failed bunt attempt by Greg Zaun, Tony Fernandez committed a critical error at second base that allowed Counsell to reach safely. Eisenreich was then walked intentionally to set up a play at any base. With the game on the line, Nagy got Devon White to ground into a force-out at home. After a quick strike to Edgar Renteria, Nagy threw a breaking pitch just off the outside corner. Renteria was all over it, lining a solid single into center field. After Counsell crossed the plate with the winning run, Joe Angel (the Marlins radio announcer) proclaimed: "A five-year old child has become king." Counsell remarked years later: "You always want to relive that stuff. . . . To be the guy who got to score that run. Pinch yourself. It's a dream come true."

Reacting to the criticism the Series received, Marlins manager Jim Leyland commented: "I don't think this World Series got the credit it deserved. I truly believe in my heart, had [it] ended the same way that it did against the Yankees or the Dodgers, it might have gone down as the greatest seventh game in the history of the World Series."

In spite of its numerous detractors, the 1997 October Showcase was memorable in many respects. It was one of the highest scoring affairs in history with an average of 11.6 runs per game. The Marlins were the first wild card team to capture a championship. They were also the youngest expansion franchise to come out on top (a short-lived record that stood until 2001). Only three other World Series Game 7s had gone into extra innings.

Just days after their improbable victory, the Marlins staged a fire sale so infamous that it became a running joke. Conine departed for Kansas City. Alou was traded to the Houston Astros. And Leiter was shipped off to New York to play for the Mets. Halfway through the 1998 campaign, Bonilla, Sheffield, Eisenreich, and Johnson were all traded to the Dodgers in exchange for Todd Zeile and Mike Piazza. Piazza wound up being traded to the Mets for several young prospects a few days later.

The Marlins finished the 1998 campaign with a 54–108 record, prompting Leyland's resignation. It was the worst follow-up performance by a championship club ever. In the wake of the debacle, Huizenga sold the Marlins to American businessman John William Henry. The 1997 squad became facetiously known as the first "Rent-a-Team" to win a World Series.

The Indians made three playoff appearances between 1998 and 2001, never advancing beyond the ALCS. They finally returned to the World Series in 2016, losing to the Chicago Cubs. Interestingly, the Cubs had the longest World Series drought to that point, but their seven-game victory over Cleveland flipped the script. At the start of the 2024 campaign, the Indians (renamed the Guardians in 2022) had gone more than 70 years without a championship—the most extensive dry spell in the majors.

CHAPTER 18

Yankees vs. Diamondbacks 2001

AFTER THE "BRONX ZOO" ERA OF THE LATE 1970S AND EARLY 1980S, the Yankees experienced one of the most extensive postseason droughts in franchise history, failing to make the playoffs for more than a decade. Hoping to rebuild a dynasty, petulant owner George Steinbrenner maintained an inflated payroll, importing dozens of established stars and highly touted prospects. As the team continued to slump in the standings, Yankee fans could hardly keep up with all the arrivals and departures. From 1982 through 1993, Steinbrenner went through 10 different managers. Sometimes he even fired and rehired the same people. The results were hardly noticeable as the team never placed higher than second in that span.

A number of positive changes during the 1990s gradually transformed the Yankees into a powerhouse. The addition of center fielder Bernie Williams in 1991 was a step in the right direction. The acquisition of right fielder Paul O'Neill before the 1993 campaign was another major breakthrough. But it was the arrival of the "Core Four"—a quartet of homegrown superstars—that dramatically altered the Yankees' fortunes, bringing four World Series titles in a five-year span.

Mild mannered and unassuming, Williams quietly became one of the best center fielders in Yankee history—quite an accomplishment considering the ones who came before him. Over the course of 16 seasons, he secured a place among the all-time franchise leaders in runs, hits, and total bases while capturing four Gold Glove Awards. He exceeded the

.300 mark at the plate in eight consecutive campaigns, claiming a batting title in 1998 with a .339 mark.

Although he was easygoing off the field, O'Neill had a fiery personality once he stepped between the foul lines. Steinbrenner nicknamed him the "Warrior" for his intensity and determination. O'Neill had an excellent feel for the strike zone, drawing a fair number of walks and running up pitch counts. Typically occupying the third spot in the batting order, he drove in no fewer than 90 runs in six consecutive seasons. Defensively, he was among the best in the majors, posting the highest fielding percentage among players at his position six times.

Andy Pettitte was the first "Core Four" member to earn a permanent roster spot in New York. A big left-hander at 6-foot-5, 235 pounds, he grew up in Texas and was acquired in the 1990 amateur draft. A 14–4 showing in the minors during the 1994 slate prompted an April call-up the following year. He eventually emerged as one of the Yankees most reliable starters. His 219 wins in pinstripes are second only to Whitey Ford. Pettitte was a tough competitor in postseason play, posting a handsome 19–11 record in 44 starts.

For well over a decade at Yankee Stadium, fans were comforted by the popular Metallica song "Enter Sandman." The ominous musical refrain signaled the arrival of Mariano Rivera. Though he only had one primary weapon in his arsenal, it was more than enough to blow away the competition. Describing the movement on Rivera's signature cutter, infielder Tony Womack said: "When he throws it, you think it's straight and the next thing you know, it's on your thumbs." Rivera began his Yankee career as a starter in 1995, but it soon became evident that he was more effective in relief. He spent the 1996 campaign as a set-up man before assuming a role as the team's primary closer. Rivera always felt that his job was simple, describing it with the following words: "I get the ball, I throw the ball, and then I take a shower." But his devastating cutter and unshakable poise on the mound made the job of hitters quite difficult. By the time he retired in 2013, he had piled up an incredible total of 652 saves—an all-time record.

Few players in Yankee history have been as respected and revered as Derek Jeter. It wasn't just about his statistics, which included 14 All-Star appearances, five Gold Gloves, and 3,465 lifetime hits. It was also about his many immeasurable qualities—his engaging personality, his ability to rise to the occasion when he was needed most, and his consummate professionalism on and off the field. Jeter's exceptional play throughout his career not only earned him the prestigious title of team captain but also made him an October legend. He is the all-time postseason leader in more than half a dozen statistical categories. After a brief call-up in 1995, Jeter was demoted to the minors. He was back for good in 1996, earning Rookie of the Year honors. During the Yankees' five-year period of dominance from 1996 through 2000, the iconic shortstop hit well above .300 and scored more than 100 runs every year—numbers ideally suited to the top part of the batting order.

Any discussion about the Yankees' all-time greatest catchers would be incomplete without throwing Jorge Posada's name into the mix. After making short-lived appearances with the team in 1995 and 1996, Posada played backup to veteran catcher Joe Girardi in 1997. He watched, learned, and eventually won the starting job. Posada had decent power at the plate, clubbing at least 20 doubles and 20 homers in the same season on eight occasions. Intimately familiar with the strike zone, he wore pitchers out, averaging 79 walks per year from 2000 to 2007. He peaked at 107 free passes during the former campaign. A five-time All-Star, Posada was known for his lively throwing arm, finishing among the leaders in runners caught stealing in eight consecutive seasons. He might have actually won a Gold Glove had Hall of Famer Ivan Rodriguez not claimed so many of them during Posada's prime years.

The Yankees had a capable supporting cast in 2001 with Tino Martinez at first base, Alfonso Soriano at second, and Scott Brosius at third. Offensively, Martinez was the best of the trio, reaching team-high marks in homers (34) and RBIs (113). Collectively, the Yankees ranked fourth among AL clubs in homers and fifth in runs per game.

Pettitte and Rivera were not the only marquee hurlers on the Yankee staff as Mike Mussina and Roger Clemens combined for 37 wins. Mussina, with his trademark knuckle-curve, and Clemens, with his infamous splitter, struck out over 400 batters. Clemens came close to posting the highest winning percentage in modern history, going 20–1 before losing his last two decisions.

The Yankees spent a majority of the first half in second place before a nine-game winning streak in early July put them out in front for good. By the end of the season, they had built a 13.5-game lead over the Red Sox, who suffered a second half collapse. The BoSox were especially inept against the Yankees, losing 13 of 18 encounters.

The tail end of the 2001 campaign was played in the wake of the infamous terrorist attack on the World Trade Center, which killed more than 2,600 people. In the wake of the calamity, baseball seemed infinitely less important. Many Yankee players went home to their families during a week-long hiatus, but a few others made public appearances to raise the spirits of suffering New Yorkers. Jeter, Williams, and Chuck Knoblauch joined manager Joe Torre on an outing to St. Vincent's Hospital in Manhattan. In his 2009 memoirs, Torre recounted the experience as follows: "We didn't know all these people, who were certainly devastated and huddled around in different groups. You'd look around and see that they had counselors or priests or rabbis in different family settings. They brought out pictures of the family members they were waiting on, pictures of them wearing Yankee hats. Big Yankee fans, which was pretty moving . . . I realized at that point, we had to take a certain perspective for the rest of the season."

In honor of the survivors and the deceased, the Yankees began playing "God Bless America" during the seventh inning stretch. Torre said he got choked up every time he heard it. The Bombers entered the postseason not only as heavy favorites but as symbolic Knights of the Round Table defending the honor of New York City.

The division series against Oakland featured a sensational game-saving play by Jeter. After dropping the first two meetings, the Yankees carried a tenuous one-run lead into the seventh inning of Game 3. Mussina yielded a two-out single to Jeremy Giambi and a double to Terrence Long. With Giambi on the way home, Jeter bolted far beyond his defensive post to snare an offline throw from right fielder Shane Spencer. The hustling Yankee shortstop immediately flipped the ball to the plate in time to nail Giambi by a narrow margin. The Yankees went on to a

1–0 win and eventually took the Series in five games. For years afterward, Jeter's heads-up relay to home was referred to simply as "the flip."

The ALCS was less of a grind for New York as the Bombers won four of five games against a Seattle Mariners squad that had tied a regular season record with 116 wins. Pettitte was in top form, winning both of his starts. Williams, O'Neill, and Soriano were the hitting stars for the Yanks, combining for six homers and 10 RBIs.

In 1998, major-league baseball entered a new phase of expansion with the Tampa Bay Devil Rays joining the AL East and the Arizona Diamondbacks entering the NL Central. To balance out the lineup, the Milwaukee Brewers were shifted from the AL to the NL. Unlike the Rays, who floundered in the divisional basement for several years, the Diamondbacks were competitive early on, making a postseason appearance in their second year of play. After some growing pains in 2000, they emerged as top contenders again.

The 2001 Arizona lineup was full of seasoned veterans. Outfielders Steve Finley, Reggie Sanders, and Luis Gonzalez carried more than 30 years of major-league experience between them. Finley was among the most reliable defensive players in the game, capturing five Gold Gloves. He was pretty handy with a bat as well, averaging 25 homers and 80 RBIs per year during his six seasons with Arizona. Sanders spent just one year with the D'Backs, but it was among the most productive of his career as he set a personal record with 33 homers during the regular season. Gonzalez was a doubles-hitting machine, coming up just shy of 600 two-baggers during his career. From 1999 to 2003, he was one of Arizona's premier run producers, reaching the century mark in RBIs every year. His peak season came in 2001, when he reached career-highs in runs scored (128), homers (57), and on-base percentage (.429) He finished third in MVP voting.

The Diamondbacks' infield was full of thirty-somethings. The club was especially well-represented at the corners with Mark Grace occupying first and Matt Williams stationed at third. Grace had been a model of consistency for the Cubs from 1988 to 2000, winning four Gold Gloves while exceeding the .300 mark at the plate nine times. Williams captured the same number of Gold Gloves and slammed no fewer than 32 homers during six campaigns. He led the NL with 43 blasts in 1994.

The Arizona pitching staff was among the best in the majors with Randy Johnson and Curt Schilling anchoring the rotation. At 6-foot-10, Johnson was one of the tallest pitchers in major-league history. He also had lanky arms, making batters feel like he was right on top of them when he released the ball. An intimidating presence with a perpetual scowl, the "Big Unit's" 97 mph fastball and tendency toward wildness made hitters extremely anxious. He hit 190 batters during his career—fifth on the all-time list. He compensated for it with 4,875 strikeouts—second only to Nolan Ryan.

Schilling, who joined the Diamondbacks midway through the 2000 campaign, was an underachiever early in his career, which began with the Orioles. By the end of the 1990s, he had entered his prime, striking out 300 batters in back-to-back campaigns. Schilling employed a splitter, slider, and 95 mph fastball along with an effective changeup. He led the D'Backs with 22 wins in 2001 and accumulated 293 strike-outs—second on the club to Johnson. Together, the hard-throwing duo combined for more than 660 punch-outs—a rare feat.

The Diamondbacks slumped in July and September, posting a sub-.500 record in both months. The divisional race came down to the wire, but Arizona managed to hold it together in spite of stiff compe-tition from the Giants. Aided tremendously by Barry Bonds's landmark 73 homers, San Francisco wound up just two games out of the running.

The NLDS matched the Diamondbacks against the Cardinals, who had finished in a dead heat with the Astros. It was Schilling who carried Arizona, winning the opener and the finale while going the distance both times. The final game was decided on a walk-off single by second baseman Tony Womack—a veteran speedster who stole 28 bases and hit .266 during the regular season.

In the NLCS against the Braves, it was Johnson's turn to shine as he borrowed a page from Schilling's playbook, becoming the win-ning pitcher in Games 1 and 5. The Hall of Fame southpaw piled up 19 strikeouts in 16 innings and finished with a 1.13 ERA. Craig Coun-sell—known for his odd habit of standing splay-legged at the plate with his arms fully extended skyward—was the Series MVP, gathering eight hits and four RBIs.

Game 1 of the Fall Classic took place at Bank One Ballpark on October 27—the latest opener in Series history. Additional security measures were taken in the wake of the 9/11 attack. According to multiple sources, the manhole covers around the stadium were all welded shut. Schilling was in top form for Arizona, but Mussina was not, lasting just three innings and giving up five runs. Only three of them were earned as David Justice committed a costly error on a fly ball hit by Finley. Reliever Randy Choate had a rough go of it for New York in the fourth inning, allowing four runs of his own—three of which could be attributed to an error by Brosius. An RBI double by Bernie Williams accounted for all the Yankee scoring in a lopsided 9–1 New York loss.

Pitching was the story for Arizona again in Game 2 as Johnson tossed a three-hit shutout, striking out 11 batters. Pettitte was effective through six innings, but the wheels came off in the seventh, when Matt Williams blasted a three-run homer. The convincing 4–0 Arizona victory gave them a commanding Series lead.

The third game was emotional for many as chants of "USA!! USA!!" reverberated throughout Yankee Stadium. George W. Bush became the first sitting US president to throw out a ceremonial World Series pitch since Jimmy Carter. Bush—who was co-owner of the Texas Rangers from 1989 to 1994—insisted on slinging the ball from the pitcher's mound. He delivered a near-perfect strike to New York's backup catcher Todd Greene. Once the game was underway, Clemens was the man of the hour, tossing seven sparkling innings. The only Arizona run came on a sacrifice fly by Matt Williams. Posada put the Yankees on the board in the second inning with a homer off of starter Brian Anderson. Brosius delivered the game-winning run in the bottom of the sixth—a clutch single that chased Bernie Williams across the plate. Rivera picked up a two-inning save—his fifth of the postseason to that point.

Game 4, which was played on Halloween, pitted Schilling against Orlando Hernandez—a Cuban-born right-hander with a high leg-kick and penchant for stalling tactics. "El Duque" (as he was widely known) had established himself as one of New York's most successful postseason hurlers, winning eight consecutive decisions beginning in his 1998 debut. He was excellent in Game 4, allowing just one run in 6.1 innings of work, but relievers Mike Stanton and Ramiro Mendoza did him no favors, staking the Diamondbacks to a 3–1 lead in the top of the eighth. Believing that the game was well in hand, Arizona manager Bob Brenly brought in Byun-Hyun Kim (owner of a 2.94 ERA during the regular season) to close out the game. Kim struck out the side in the eighth but served up a two-run homer to Tino Martinez in the ninth, pushing the match into extra innings. After an uneventful 10th inning for Rivera, Jeter stepped into the batter's box with two outs. It was after midnight by then and a message on the scoreboard read: "Welcome to November Baseball." Rising to the occasion, the Hall of Fame shortstop drilled a game-winning homer that earned him the nickname of "Mr. November."

Game 5 was a sequel to the previous night's miracle on 161st Street. Things remained scoreless until the top of the fifth, when Mussina gave up a pair of solo homers to Finley and Rod Barajas. Arizona starter Miguel Batista polished off 7.2 effective innings before turning the ball over to the bullpen. For the second night in a row, Kim was the goat, serving up a game-tying homer to Brosius with two outs in the bottom of the ninth. The game stretched into the 12th frame, when Soriano delivered the winning blow—a one-out single off of right-hander Albie Lopez.

Commenting on Games 4 and 5, author Tom Verducci dramatically wrote: "Only once before in the 98-year history of the World Series had a team hit a game-saving home run from such a bleak position, and here the Yankees did it two times in a row? It was crazy stuff. It was exactly the kind of stuff a grieving city needed if only to start believing again in something in a suddenly senseless world." Anderson—the pitcher of record in Arizona's Game 3 loss—remarked: "This is beyond nightmare. All I know is that we need to get out of this place—fast."

Outside of Yankee Stadium, the magic was gone. The Diamondbacks had their comeuppance, handing the Bombers a humiliating 15–2 loss in Game 6. As it turned out, Pettitte was tipping his pitches. Arizona hitters were able to identify what offerings were on the way based on the position of Pettitte's hands during his wind-up. He left the game in the bottom of the third with four runs in and a pair of runners aboard. Reliever Jay Witasick had one of the worst outings of any reliever in Series history, allowing eight of the 10 batters he faced to reach safely. Center fielder Danny Bautista was the catalyst for Arizona, gathering three hits and five RBIs on the night.

Game 7 was a battle of the big guns as Clemens squared off against Schilling. The Diamondbacks were the first to draw blood with a run in the bottom of the sixth. But New York answered quickly on an RBI single by Martinez. An eighth-inning solo homer off the bat of Soriano put Arizona in a precarious position. Torre and bench coach Don Zimmer engaged in a spirited debate over who should pitch the bottom of the eighth. Torre was partial to bringing in Mendoza—a reliable set-up man nicknamed "el Brujo" (literally "the Witch Doctor") for the movement on his pitches. Zimmer was in favor of the tried-and-true formula of summoning Rivera. In the end, Torre conceded.

Entering the game, Rivera was unbeaten in 51 career postseason appearances and had converted 23 consecutive save opportunities. He looked strong in the eighth, striking out the side. But in the bottom of the ninth, everything fell apart. Mark Grace led off with a single and David Dellucci was inserted as a pinch-runner. Catcher Damian Miller hit a weak hopper to Rivera, who scooped it up and threw to second. The relay sailed wide as Jeter got tangled up with Dellucci, who slid in hard to break up the double play. With two on and no outs, Brenly called upon infielder Jay Bell to hit for Randy Johnson (who had entered the game in the eighth). Bell laid down a bunt that resulted in a force-out at third base. Erring on the side of caution, Brosius chose to hang onto the ball rather than risk a throw across the diamond to complete a double play. It turned out to be a fateful decision for Arizona. Midre Cummings was summoned to pinch-run for Miller. With one out and the game on the line, Womack doubled down the right field line, tying the score. Rivera, perhaps a bit rattled at that point, hit Craig Counsell with a pitch, bringing Arizona's best regular season hitter—Luis Gonzalez—to the plate. In anticipation of Rivera's signature cutter, Gonzalez choked up on his bat. It was the first time he had done so all year. Looking to just put the ball in play, he fouled off the first pitch then lofted a blooper over the head of Jeter into center field.

Game. Set. Match.

Rivera walked off the field in a daze, later admitting that he had difficulty wrapping his head around what had transpired. In his memoirs, he said that he was in a state resembling mild shock. "There has to be a reason why [that] happened," he lamented. "I just don't know what the answer is." Posada tried to console his good friend, commenting years later: "Mariano had been so good in the Series, in his whole career, but when he blew the save, we got a taste of what we'd been forcing down the throats of a lot of other teams all season. I didn't like the taste of it at all. Adding in the disappointment I felt in having let down the fans and the city, it was even harder to come to terms with not winning the last game of the year."

Figure 18.1   Prior to his appearance in Game 7 of the 2001 World Series, Mariano Rivera had converted more than 20 consecutive postseason save opportunities. He is baseball's all-time regular season saves leader with 652.
PHOTO COURTESY OF CHRISHCONNELLY ON VISUAL HUNT.

Asked about his decision to bring Rivera in for a two-inning save, Torre said: "I didn't lose any sleep over it other than the result. . . . Now, did I do everything right? I don't know. But I know one thing: I wouldn't have done it any differently."

The 2001 Diamondbacks (at four years old) remain the youngest team to win a World Series title. It was the first time a team from a western location (other than California) had claimed the championship. New York's consolidated .183 batting average was the lowest since the 1985 Cardinals.

On an interesting note, the Yankee loss indirectly saved the life of infielder Enrique Wilson. If the Yankees had won, Wilson would have returned to the Dominican Republic on American Airlines Flight 587 after the team's victory parade on November 12. When the Yankees lost, Wilson booked an earlier trip. Tragically, Flight 587 crashed on the Belle Harbor Peninsula in Queens, New York, killing everyone aboard. Mariano Rivera later remarked, "I am glad we lost the World Series because it means that I still have a friend."

The Yankees returned to the Fall Classic in 2003—a story that can be found in the next chapter. The Diamondbacks have made several postseason appearances since their 2001 Series victory. They captured the National League pennant in 2023 but lost to the Texas Rangers in five games.

CHAPTER 19

Yankees vs. Marlins 2003

THE 2003 CAMPAIGN WAS A SEASON OF HIGHS AND LOWS FOR SEVERAL teams. While the Detroit Tigers hit rock bottom, setting an AL record with 119 losses, Kansas City skipper Tony Pena took home the Manager of the Year Award after piloting the Royals to their first winning season in nearly a decade. In the National League, the Florida Marlins came full circle in the wake of a fire sale that had decimated their 1997 World Series lineup.

By the time the curtain opened on the 2003 season, several key players from Florida's championship squad had retired. The rest were scattered to the four winds, performing at peak levels for rival NL clubs. Second baseman Luis Castillo was the only member of the 1997 team to take the field on Opening Day in 2003.

Hailing from the Dominican Republic, Castillo spent four months with the Marlins during their World Series year, finishing the season in the minors. By 1999, he was back for good. A reliable defensive presence, Castillo won three straight Gold Gloves beginning in 2003. In 2007, he completed a string of 143 consecutive games without an error—a short-lived positional record. Many would argue that Castillo was the greatest infielder in Marlins' history. By the time he retired, he was the all-time franchise leader in hits, triples, walks, and stolen bases. His 35-game hitting streak in 2002 is still a record for second basemen (matched by Chase Utley in 2006).

The Marlins were well represented at first base with Derrek Lee swinging a productive bat. A first-round draft pick, Lee made his debut with the Padres in 1997. When San Diego executives learned that the Marlins were dismantling their championship roster, they traded Lee to Florida for pitcher Kevin Brown. Lee had a couple of mediocre seasons before emerging as an eminent power threat. He slugged 31 homers in 2003 while driving in 92 runs—his highest single-season totals to that point.

Lee's corner infield partner, Mike Lowell, was another valuable member of the 2003 squad, leading the team with 105 RBIs. Lowell began his career in the Yankee farm system, but with Scott Brosius entrenched at third base, he wound up being traded for several players of little note. It proved to be a colossal miscalculation on the part of GM Brian Cashman as Lowell remained one of the best third sackers in the majors for a full decade. A four-time All-Star, Lowell averaged 21 homers and 88 RBIs per year from 2000 to 2009.

Catching was one of Florida's strongest suits with Ivan Rodriguez behind the plate. A first ballot Hall of Famer, Rodriguez won more Gold Gloves than any backstop in history, surpassing Johnny Bench in 2004. Offensively, he demonstrated ample power and generated high batting averages. He was dangerous with the bases loaded during his career, hitting at a .314 clip with six grand slams.

There was a wealth of talent in the Marlins' outfield with Juan Pierre in center and Juan Encarnacion in right. Pierre was drafted three times during his amateur days. The Rockies promoted him in 2000 and then shipped him off to Florida in a blockbuster deal before the 2003 slate. With exceptional speed and superior bunting skills, Pierre was well suited to a leadoff role. He averaged 47 stolen bases per year over 13 full seasons while exceeding the .300 mark at the plate five times. In 2003, his 65 steals and 204 hits provided the spark the Marlins needed at the top of the batting order.

Encarnacion was considered a five-tool player and can't-miss prospect at the beginning of his career. Plagued by sporadic injuries throughout his time in the majors, he failed to maximize his full potential. The Marlins acquired him from the Reds midway through the 2002 campaign and retained his services the following year. Healthy all season, Encarnacion reached career highs in nearly every offensive category, including doubles (37) and RBIs (94). He also put on a tremendous defensive display, finishing the year with a perfect fielding percentage. In spite of his exemplary performance, he was overlooked for a Gold Glove.

Wins were evenly distributed among members of the Marlins pitching rotation as Dontrelle Willis, Mark Redman, and Brad Penny each gathered 14 victories. Willis, who was making his major-league debut, captured most of the media attention with his buoyant personality and exaggerated leg-kick. His 3.30 ERA and 142 strikeouts in 27 appearances netted him Rookie of the Year honors. Josh Beckett—a right-hander with a lively fastball—was another reliable starter for Florida, averaging just 3.04 runs per nine frames. He saved his best work for the postseason, walking away with the World Series MVP Award.

If the Marlins had one weakness in 2003, it was their bullpen. Right-hander Braden Looper stumbled in his role as a closer, blowing a total of six saves while running his ERA up to 3.68. Hoping to solve the problem, the Marlins acquired right-hander Ugueth Urbina from the Rangers in July. Urbina finished strong, gathering 11 holds and six saves while posting a 1.41 ERA.

The Marlins began the season with Jeff Torborg at the helm. When the team got off to a 16–22 start, he was fired and replaced by 72-year-old Jack McKeon, whose professional managerial career had begun in the 1950s. "Let's have fun," McKeon said during his first team meeting. "The pressure is on everybody else because we're not supposed to win. Let's show that we can fool the baseball world and show them that we're a hell of a lot better than everybody predicted us to be." McKeon's words seemed to resonate with players. Although the Marlins were unable to catch up with the Braves (who amassed 101 wins), they compiled a 42–25 record in the second half, finishing four games ahead of the Astros in the wild card race.

The divisional playoff pitted Florida against the San Francisco Giants, who had dominated the NL West with a 100–61 record. The Giants won the first game at home but dropped the next three as Marlins' hitters consistently delivered in the clutch. Ivan Rodriguez was among the most productive hitters, compiling a .353 batting average.

In the NLCS, Rodriquez was the driving force yet again, running his postseason RBI total up to 16. The series is best remembered for a wild finish in Game 6 at Wrigley Field. With a 3-games-to-2 advantage and a 3–0 lead in the top of the eighth inning, the Cubs were just five outs away from claiming their first pennant in nearly 60 years. Staff ace Mark Prior was working on a three-hitter when Luis Castillo lifted a pitch into foul territory along the left field line. Moises Alou drifted over and was in the process of making a play when a fan named Steve Bartman reached out and deflected the ball away. Infuriated, Alou slammed his glove on the ground and argued for an interference call. His plea fell on deaf ears. The game went off the rails immediately afterward as Florida sent a total of 12 men to the plate, scoring eight runs on five hits and walking away with a shocking 8–3 victory. In the wake of the foul ball incident, Bartman received multiple death threats and was forced to keep a low profile. A 9–6 Florida victory the following day perpetuated a popularly held belief that the Cubs were "cursed."

In the American League, it was business as usual for the Yankees. They collected 101 wins and finished in first place for the sixth consecutive season (and the eighth time in 10 years). The Bombers had a slightly different look in 2003 with the departure of Tino Martinez, Scott Brosius, and Paul O'Neill—all of whom had left the club after the unsuccessful World Series bid of 2001.

Martinez was replaced by slugger Jason Giambi, whose awesome power inspired the nickname "Giambino"—a variation of Babe Ruth's "Bambino" moniker. Giambi reached the apex of his career with Oakland in 2000, claiming the AL MVP Award with 43 homers, 137 RBIs, and a .476 on-base percentage. He wasn't quite as good in 2003, but he was reasonably close, leading the Yankees in homers, ribbies, and walks.

Brosius's replacement—Robin Ventura—was among the best defensive third basemen in the majors, claiming six Gold Gloves during his career. He made an All-Star appearance in his Yankee debut, but a slow start in 2003 prompted a trade to Los Angeles. When Todd Zeile failed to capably fill the void, Aaron Boone was acquired from Cincinnati. Boone came from a talented baseball family. His grandfather, Ray, had manned the infield for several clubs during the 1950s. His father, Bob, had captured seven Gold Gloves as a catcher in the 1970s and 1980s. His older brother, Bret, was a smooth-fielding, power-hitting second baseman who reached the prime of his career with the Mariners in the early 2000s.

O'Neill's departure led to the signing of Hideki Matsui. A left-handed slugger with formidable power, Matsui was a legend in his homeland, where he had dominated the Japan Central League for nearly a decade. Highly durable, he played in 1,768 consecutive games before fracturing his wrist diving for a ball in 2006. During his 2003 debut, he hit .287 while gathering 59 extra-base hits and 106 RBIs. He finished second in Rookie of the Year voting.

Returning players from New York's dynasty years included Derek Jeter, Bernie Williams, and Jorge Posada. Jeter suffered a major injury on Opening Day when he dislocated his shoulder diving into third. He was out of the lineup until mid-May. Hampered by physical ailments of his own, Williams sat out more than 40 games. Posada was one of the Yankees most reliable hitters, hammering 30 homers and reaching the century mark in RBIs—numbers that earned him his fourth consecutive Silver Slugger Award.

The Yankee pitching staff featured a familiar cast of characters with a rotation comprised of Roger Clemens, Andy Pettitte, Mike Mussina, and David Wells. Pettitte tied a career-high with 21 wins while Clemens and Mussina combined for 34 victories. Wells, who had played on two championship squads in Toronto and New York, was traded back to the Blue Jays before the 1999 slate. He returned via free agency in 2002. A control pitcher with a sweeping curve, the big left-hander was a reliable performer at the back end of the rotation, posting a 34–14 record during his second stint with New York. The Yankee bullpen was rock-solid in 2003 as Mariano Rivera padded his impressive lifetime numbers with 40 saves. The Yankees went 59–5 in his appearances.

The Twins surprised the Yankees with a win in Game 1 of the division series, but the Bombers came storming back, taking the next three meetings by a composite score of 15–3. Alfonso Soriano hit .368 with four RBIs. Jeter accrued a .429 batting average and a .556 OBP. Clemens, Wells, and Pettitte all made quality starts.

The ALCS was an epic clash between the Yankees and Red Sox, who had finished in second place behind New York for the sixth straight season—an exasperating position to be in. Tensions between the two clubs came to a head in Game 3, which was marred by an ugly incident involving Boston pitcher Pedro Martinez and Yankee bench coach Don Zimmer. After yielding a two-run double to Matsui in the fourth inning, Martinez aimed a pitch at outfielder Karim Garcia's head. Garcia retaliated by sliding aggressively into second base to break up a double play. On his way back to the dugout, he taunted Pedro. Angry words were exchanged between several players and umpire Tim McClelland issued a warning to both benches. Things boiled over in the bottom of the frame, when Clemens threw a high pitch to Manny Ramirez. It wasn't even close to being a brushback, but Ramirez started pointing and shouting anyway. The benches cleared and Zimmer made a mad dash for Martinez, who pushed his would-be assailant to the ground. The 72-year-old coach—who had four metal plugs in his skull from a serious 1953 beaning—landed face-first on a discarded bat, sustaining a cut on his forehead. When order was finally restored, the Yankees rallied for a 4–3 victory.

Reminiscing over the dust-up years later, Jorge Posada asserted: "There are a lot of unwritten rules in the game of baseball for how we conduct ourselves as professionals. In all our minds, the ones that have to do with not purposely injuring a player trump all the rest. You don't f—k with a man's career. You don't throw a 72-year-old man to the ground. I'll admit I jumped all over Pedro verbally for what he did that day. I let my emotions get the best of me. If anybody thinks that I crossed a line for doing so or that it in any way, shape, or form compares to what Pedro did in taking the risk of hitting Karim Garcia in the head and seriously injuring him or in tossing Don Zimmer aside, then we don't exist in the same world." Years later, Martinez referred to the incident as the low point of his career. "There hasn't been any other moment where I felt worse in my life—I will tell you, my life—than that moment," the hurler asserted.

The Yankees had a chance to dispose of Boston in Game 6 but couldn't get the job done as Pettitte faltered on the mound. Clemens followed suit in the finale, staking the Red Sox to a 4–0 lead. It didn't hold up as the resilient Bombers rallied to tie the score at five apiece in the bottom of the eighth. Rivera tossed three scoreless frames, carrying the Yanks into the 11th inning. Jeter—who had witnessed some incredible events in New York and believed that Yankee Stadium was inhabited by spirits (a commonly held opinion)—said to Aaron Boone: "The ghosts will show up eventually." Whether or not they actually did can never be definitively proven, but the Red Sox were unquestionably haunted by Boone, who lifted the first pitch he saw from knuckleballer Tim Wake-field into the left field seats for a walk-off home run. The memorable blast made the Yankees appear like a team of destiny.

Game 1 of the World Series was played at Yankee Stadium. The pitching matchup featured Wells versus Brad Penny, who entered the game with a ghastly 10.24 postseason ERA. By way of comparison, Wells had allowed just two runs in two starts. What should have been a slam-dunk for New York went in a completely different direction as the Marlins built a 3–1 lead through five innings. Bernie Williams cut the deficit in half with a solo homer in the bottom of the sixth, but Willis and Urbina provided the Marlins with 3.2 innings of scoreless relief. Things got interesting in the ninth, when the Yankees put two runners on with one out. It was all for naught, however, as Soriano struck out and Nick Johnson flied out to end the game.

The Yankees flexed their muscles in Game 2, chasing starter Mark Redman from the mound in the third inning. Matsui became the first Japanese player to homer in a World Series, launching a three-run shot in the opening frame. Rookie Juan Rivera slammed an RBI double in the second and Soriano added a two-run homer in the fourth, extending the Yankees' lead to 6–0. Andy Pettitte shut out the Marlins through eight innings, scattering five hits and striking out seven along the way. An error by Boone in the ninth led to Florida's only run of the game. It was the last World Series victory for New York at the old Yankee Stadium.

Game 3 started out as a pitchers' duel with Mussina and Beckett battling to a 1–1 tie through seven innings. After a 39-minute rain delay, things fell apart for the Marlins. Jeter slashed a one-out double in the eighth, knocking Beckett from the game. Summoned in relief, Willis walked Giambi and yielded an RBI single to Matsui. He was lifted for veteran right-hander Chad Fox, who struck out Ruben Sierra for the final out of the inning. The Yankees were just getting warmed up, however, as Boone homered off of Fox in the ninth and Bernie Williams added a three-run shot off of Braden Looper. It was Williams's 19th postseason home run—a new record (later broken by multiple players). The 6–1 victory put New York back in the driver's seat.

Game 4 proved to be pivotal to the outcome of the Series. Clemens appeared to be headed for an early exit when he served up a two-run homer to Miguel Cabrera in the first inning followed by three consecutive singles. He eventually settled down, tossing six scoreless frames. The Marlins carried a 3–1 lead into the top of the ninth, but Urbina couldn't hold it as Ruben Sierra tied the game with a timely triple. Looking to subdue the Florida offense, Joe Torre handed the ball to rookie Jose Contreras—a Cuban import acquired back in February. The 31-year-old right-hander got the job done, striking out four batters in two innings of work. Meanwhile, the Yankees wasted a golden opportunity in the top of the 11th as Boone went down swinging and John Flaherty popped out with the bases loaded. The game meandered into the 12th inning, when shortstop Alex Gonzalez launched a 3–2 pitch from Jeff Weaver over the left field wall for a walk-off homer. Asked about the at-bat in a postgame interview, Weaver explained: "It was a sinker than ran back over and I was trying to go down and away. It just didn't go my way there."

Things didn't go the Yankees' way for the rest of the Series.

Prior to Game 5, Giambi told Torre that his knee was causing him great discomfort and that he wouldn't be effective against the top of the Marlins order, which featured Pierre and Castillo (both of whom were accomplished bunters). Torre installed Nick Johnson at first base and benched a slumping Soriano in favor of Enrique Wilson. Another unexpected change took place when starter David Wells left the game early with back spasms. The Marlins teed off on Contreras in the second inning, scoring three runs on two hits and three walks. Pierre added an RBI double in the fourth. Looking uncharacteristically sloppy, the Yankees botched a rundown play in the fifth, which led to two more Florida runs. Trailing, 6–2, in the ninth, the Bombers made things interesting as Giambi blasted a pinch-hit homer and Wilson drove Jeter home with a double. With one out and the tying run at the plate, Urbina retired two of New York's most dangerous hitters—Williams and Matsui. The 6–4 loss put the Yankees on the brink of elimination.

Based on his outstanding work to that point, McKeon decided to start Beckett on short rest in place of Redman in Game 6. Unintimidated by the capacity crowd in New York, Beckett delivered a five-hit shutout. The Yankees struck out nine times and failed to push a runner past second base. Pettitte was cruising for New York until the top of the fifth, when he surrendered a run on three straight singles. The only other Florida run was unearned as Jeff Conine reached on a throwing error by Jeter and scored on a sacrifice fly by Encarnacion. The 2–0 Series-clinching win gave the Marlins their second championship as a wild card entry. It was the second year in a row that a wild card team had emerged victorious.

Evaluating the Yankee loss, sportswriter Tom Verducci asserted: "The Series could have gone either way. A sacrifice fly here, a hit there, a little back and core maintenance training regimen there, and who knows? Maybe it simply was the karmic tariff for those October nights and weeks that had fallen their way, the stuff that made bright, reasonable people believe in the forces of mystique and aura. Maybe the Marlins were a collection agency sent by the baseball gods, or possibly Bud Selig, whose new world order of baseball democracy was just dawning."

Rivera felt that the Yankees were not as powerful as they had been in seasons past, remarking in his memoirs: "As much as it stings to think about, the truth is undeniable: we [were] not the same team we used to be. It [wasn't] even close . . . those teams of ours that won four World Series in five years would've hammered them. They would've found a way and *willed* their way through *as a team*. Because those were guys who cared more about winning than anything else. And it just [wasn't] like that anymore."

Having learned nothing from past mistakes, Florida executives systematically disassembled the 2003 championship squad, piece by piece. By 2006, the Marlins had become also-rans, finishing the season below .500. Aside from one appearance in the 2020 Division Series, they have not made a serious pennant run since.

Figure 19.1   Andy Pettitte deserved much better in 2003. After winning 21 games during the regular season, he went unbeaten in the playoffs until Game 6 of the World Series.
PHOTO COURTESY OF KOWARSKI ON VISUAL HUNT.

In glaring contrast, the Yankees have remained competitive throughout the twenty-first century. In 2009, they captured their 27th championship. It was the last for owner George Steinbrenner, who passed away in 2010. The "Core Four" (Pettitte, Rivera, Jeter, and Posada) had all retired by 2015, leaving a new crop of players to guide the Yankees into the postseason. In spite of a fourth-place finish in 2023, the future was still looking bright for the Bombers at the start of the 2024 campaign. They won the AL pennant (their first in fifteen years) but lost to the Dodgers in the World Series.

CHAPTER 20

Tigers vs. Cardinals 2006

In September of 1999, the Tigers bid farewell to their home of more than 80 years. Although their new stadium—Comerica Park—had many pleasing aesthetic features, its cavernous outfield dimensions greatly hindered run production. Complaints were numerous as the venue took on the facetious moniker of "Comerica National Park."

Looking to improve attendance and build a winning ballclub, owner Mike Ilitch (proprietor of the Little Caesar's Pizza chain) hired Dave Dombrowski to serve as GM. Dombrowski had helped assemble the Marlins' championship squad of 1997 but had also presided over an ill-advised roster purge. One of his first major decisions in Detroit was to shorten the left-center field fence. It didn't help the Tigers much as they lost 119 games in 2003—a new American League record. In the wake of the disaster, Dombrowski began rapidly importing top-level players.

The first important signings included Ivan Rodriguez and Carlos Guillén. Rodriguez—the premier defensive catcher in the majors—brought 13 years of major-league experience to Detroit. Guillén—a staple in the Mariners infield for four seasons—had a breakout year with the Tigers in 2004, clubbing 67 extra-base hits and driving in 97 runs. A knee injury limited his playing time the following year, but he was back in peak condition during Detroit's 2006 pennant bid.

Shoring up the pitching corps, Dombrowski added southpaw Kenny Rogers to the mix. The 41-year-old veteran seemed to get better with age, having averaged 14 wins per year over his previous four campaigns. Rogers joined a pitching staff that had lost a collective total of 91 games in 2005. Improvement was evident all around as Rogers combined with Jeremy Bonderman and Nate Robertson for a 44–29 record. Justin Verlander tied for the team lead with 17 wins, capturing Rookie of the Year honors.

The Detroit offense averaged more than five runs per game, attaining a rank of fifth among AL clubs in that category. Left fielder Craig Monroe cracked 28 homers while Brandon Inge—a former catcher who had been moved to third base to make room for Rodriguez—finished close behind with 27.

The Tigers encountered stiff competition from the White Sox and Twins. Although they finished five games ahead of Chicago in the wild card race, they fell one game shy of the AL Central lead. Detroit and Minnesota were locked in a first-place tie from September 28 through the 30th. Although the Twins lost two of their last three games, the Tigers finished the season on a downswing, going 2–5 in the last week of play.

The ALDS was a surprise to many as the Tigers took three in a row from the Yankees after dropping the first game on the road. Guillén hit .571 and Curtis Granderson (who was playing in his first full season) drove in five runs. Rogers and Bonderman had strong starts, but the Yankees were less fortunate as Hall of Famers Randy Johnson and Mike Mussina both crumbled on the mound. The series victory sent Detroit back to the ALCS for the first time since 1987.

After taking down the Twins in their own division series, the A's offered minimal resistance against the Tigers. Verlander had a rocky outing in Game 2, but the Detroit offense came to his rescue, generating eight runs on 11 hits. Rogers put forth another outstanding effort in the third match, tossing 7.1 scoreless innings. Placido Polanco claimed series MVP honors with nine hits. None of the four meetings were decided by a margin of less than three runs.

The National League pennant race yielded surprising results as the Cardinals captured the NL flag in spite of a mediocre regular season showing. They owed a great deal of their success to Hall of Fame manager Tony La Russa, who had a talent for transforming middling ball clubs into winners. A former infielder with modest abilities, La Russa got his managerial start with the struggling White Sox in the late 1970s. Within a few years, he had transformed the team into division champions. After building a near-dynasty in Oakland during the late 1980s, he arrived in St. Louis. Three pennants and two World Series titles followed.

Entering the 2006 campaign, the Cardinals had won at least 100 games in each of the previous two seasons. The offense was carried by corner infielders Albert Pujols and Scott Rolen. Pujols had burst upon the scene in 2001, capturing Rookie of the Year honors with a spectacular showing at the plate. He went on to set a major-league record for the most consecutive seasons with at least 30 homers from the start of his career (12). Pujols's powerful bat often overshadowed his defensive skills. He posted the highest range factor (average number of putouts and assists per nine innings) among NL first basemen on six occasions.

Rolen's aptitude at the hot corner was universally acknowledged. Only three other third basemen exceeded his lifetime total of eight Gold Gloves. Considered to be a successor to Mike Schmidt, Rolen came up through the Phillies farm system and established himself as a perennial fan favorite, averaging 26 homers and 95 RBIs per year during his five full seasons with the club. A serious shoulder injury hampered his swing in the latter half of his career, but he continued his path to Cooperstown, nevertheless. He had an exceptional year in 2006, gathering 71 extra-base hits and driving in 95 runs.

Elsewhere on the diamond, the Cardinals got significant contributions from Yadier Molina and Jim Edmonds. In his early 20s, Molina was already establishing himself as one of the best defensive catchers in the majors. He led the NL in assists during the 2006 campaign while placing among the top five in fielding percentage and runners caught stealing. Edmonds—an eight-time Gold Glover—was known for his ability to make circus catches on balls that appeared to be out of his reach. He had good power at the plate, launching no fewer than 25 homers during 10 seasons. Entering the final stages of his career, the 36-year-old center fielder went deep 19 times in 2006 and drove in 70 runs.

While the St. Louis offense averaged 4.85 runs per game, pitching was somewhat of an issue as four of the club's primary starters posted ERAs in excess of 5.00. Chris Carpenter was the most reliable member of the rotation, winning 15 games—three of them by shutout. His 3.09 ERA was second in the majors behind Roy Oswalt. Although he was not a high velocity pitcher (typically throwing in the low 90s), Carpenter's offerings had dramatic movement, sinking and tailing sharply away from hitters.

In the St. Louis bullpen, veteran closer Jason Isringhausen saved 33 games but struggled with his control. His 1.457 WHIP average led to 10 blown saves and eight losses. Adam Wainwright was a stabilizing force among the relief corps, posting a 3.14 ERA in 61 appearances while averaging close to a strikeout per inning.

The NL Central was a weak division with only two of six clubs finishing above .500. The Cardinals hit some particularly rough patches, losing eight in a row on two separate occasions. They also experienced a late September swoon, dropping nine of their last 12 games. In spite of their streaky play, they finished a game and a half ahead of the Astros, who had bounced them out of the National League Championship Series the previous year.

For the Cardinals, the 2006 campaign was a tale of two ball clubs. Although they finished the regular season just five games above .500, they took it to another level in October with a .687 winning percentage. The division series wasn't much of a test as they outscored the Padres by a 4–16 margin. Carpenter won both of his starts, allowing just three runs in 13.1 innings of work. Wainwright made three scoreless appearances and picked up a save.

The NLCS was a daunting challenge as the Mets—who tied for the major-league lead with 97 wins—fought tooth and nail to reclaim the National League pennant after a five-year dry spell. It all came down to a critical Game 7 at Shea Stadium. The Mets sent Oliver Perez to the mound while the Cardinals called upon Jeff Suppan, who had delivered a brilliant performance in his previous start. Both hurlers had quality outings and the game remained tied at one through eight frames. In the top of the ninth, Rolen singled and Molina crushed a two-run homer off of reliever Aaron Heilman. Outfielder Preston Wilson later recalled: "It went from deafening noise to where you just couldn't hear anything to a quiet gasp in the stadium." The Mets loaded the bases against

Wainwright in the bottom of the frame, bringing Carlos Beltran—who had already slammed three homers in the series—to the plate. With two outs and a 0–2 count, Wainwright went to his signature pitch. "I said I'm gonna throw the nastiest curveball I've ever thrown and, if he hits it, I'll tip my hat, but if not, we're going to the Series." The pitch landed squarely in the strike zone as Beltran got caught looking to end the game.

With a 12-game differential in the win column, the Tigers entered the World Series as heavy favorites. The showdown was hyped as a rematch of the 1968 October Showcase—a seven-game classic that had been won by the Tigers. It was also billed as a clash between two of the best managers in the game: La Russa versus Leyland. In the end, it was remembered for allegations of trickery, inclement weather, and shoddy defense.

Game 1 was held at Comerica Park. The pitching matchup pitted Verlander against Anthony Reyes, who had posted a substandard 5–8 record during the regular season and stumbled in his only postseason start against the Mets. Reyes looked shaky early on as Craig Monroe doubled in the first inning and Guillén singled him home. But the freshman right-hander settled down after that, retiring 17 straight batters during one remarkable stretch. It was Verlander who faltered, giving up a solo homer to Rolen in the top of the second and a two-run shot to Pujols in the third. The American League Rookie of the Year plodded through five-plus innings, yielding seven runs—one of which was unearned. Both teams played poorly in the field, combining for five errors. Monroe homered off of Reyes in the ninth, but Braden Looper came on to retire the side, preserving a 7–2 St. Louis win.

The Tigers sent Rogers to the mound in Game 2, which was played on a wet, blustery night. Although the veteran southpaw had not allowed a run in either of his previous two starts, he had struggled in prior postseason appearances. "Every player has doubts about what they're capable of at certain given times and I'm no different," he told a journalist. "But it's nice to know that if you're willing to go out there and take the chance and possibly fail again . . . you always have a chance to succeed." He did succeed, extending his scoreless innings streak to 23. But he also touched off a minor scandal when television cameras picked up a dark, shiny smudge at the base of his left thumb. Multiple theories were offered as to what the substance was. Detroit coach Andy Van Slyke believed that it was residue from Tootsie Rolls—the hurler's favorite candy. Cardinals second baseman Aaron Miles speculated that it was pine tar. In a postgame interview, Rogers attempted to set the record straight. "It was a big clump of dirt. I didn't know it was there and they told me, and I took it off, and it wasn't a big deal." But his statement failed to satisfy a number of skeptics as St. Louis batting coach Hal McRae openly accused the hurler of cheating. Downplaying the incident (which was jokingly labeled "Smudgegate" by sportswriters), La Russa went on record saying: "It's not important to talk about. . . . When a guy pitches like that, as a team, we don't take things away from anybody."

On the heels of the 3–1 loss, the Cardinals traveled back to St. Louis, where they had compiled a handsome .612 winning percentage (including the playoffs). Carpenter pitched an absolute gem, holding Tiger hitters to just three hits over eight innings and running his postseason record up to 3–1. The game-winning hit came off the bat of Edmonds—a two-run double in the fourth. The Cardinals tacked on another pair in the seventh on a costly throwing error by relief pitcher Joel Zumaya. Zach Miner uncorked a wild pitch with the bases loaded in the eighth, putting the finishing touches on a 5–0 St. Louis victory.

The fourth meeting was postponed due to heavy rain. Oddly, the Cardinals switched things around so that Game 5 tickets were honored on the night of the fourth match. In turn, the Game 5 crowd was comprised entirely of the Game 4 ticket holders. Fans got their money's worth as both showdowns were very close.

The Tigers jumped out to a 3–0 lead in the fourth game, tagging Jeff Suppan for a solo homer and a pair of RBI singles. But the Cardinals answered with a pair of runs on timely doubles by David Eckstein and Yadier Molina. In the seventh, Eckstein doubled again and came around to score on a throwing error by reliever Fernando Rodney. With two outs and the game knotted at three, Preston Wilson drove So Taguchi home on a single to left field. Pujols, who had been intentionally walked, was thrown out at third base to end the Cardinal rally. The Tigers weren't finished yet as Rodriguez drilled a leadoff double in the eighth and scored

Figure 20.1   Kenny Rogers shut out opponents in all three of his postseason starts in 2006. His World Series appearance generated controversy when a dark smudge was spotted on his pitching hand.
PHOTO COURTESY OF KEVIN.WARD ON VISUAL HUNT.

on another two-bagger by Brandon Inge. In the bottom of the frame, Eckstein—the surprise star of the Series—came through with his third double of the game, sending Aaron Miles across the plate with what held up as the winning run.

With an extra day between Games 3 and 4, Leyland could have picked Rogers as the Game 5 starter. He called upon Verlander instead. Rogers had developed a reputation as a hot head in the wake of an alter-cation with a photographer in 2005. Forced to attend anger management classes, he became an unwelcome presence at a majority of the stadiums he visited afterward. With the "Smudgegate" controversy still simmer-ing, the Tiger skipper decided that St. Louis was not an ideal backdrop for his staff ace. "You know, this is another one of those where it's good for the journalists, because they all have opinions and that's good," said

Leyland before Game 5. "My view is I want to pitch him in Game 2 and 6 . . . I heard one TV personality say he thinks the hostile environment would really motivate Kenny. I don't buy that. I think it would probably work the opposite. I think the environment in Comerica Park motivates Kenny." A writer from the *Baltimore Sun* praised Leyland's decision, remarking: "If we were talking about Roger Clemens, I would have agreed, and I'm pretty sure Leyland would, too, but we're talking about a guy whose emotional stability has been a hot topic of discussion just about everywhere he has played. Leyland knew that would be a force for Rogers at Busch Stadium."

Although it rained most of the day in St. Louis, the downpour stopped in time to complete Game 5. Verlander—who would later establish himself as one of the greatest pitchers of the twenty-first century—was less than adequate in his second World Series start. After wriggling out of a bases loaded jam in the first inning, he coughed up an RBI single to Eckstein in the second. His troubles persisted in the fourth as he committed a critical throwing error that led to two more runs. The Tigers caught a big break in their half of the fourth, when Chris Duncan dropped a one-out popup hit by Magglio Ordonez. Sean Casey deposited the next pitch into the right field seats just inside the foul pole, staking the Tigers to a short-lived 2–1 lead. Jeff Weaver had a strong outing in spite of Casey's blast, scattering four hits over eight innings and striking out nine. Facing elimination in the ninth, the Tigers rallied against Wainwright, putting runners on the corners with two out. Brandon Inge struck out on three pitches, giving the Cardinals their first championship since 1982.

Asked by Fox broadcaster Chris Meyers if he ever imagined that the season would end with a championship, Edmonds said: "No, I don't think anybody did either. I think we shocked the world. I think this is an unbelievable experience. . . . We just played together as a team. We had a bunch of guys—young guys from the minor leagues, couple guys from other organizations, couple of core guys, and everybody just played together at the right time." Following up on those remarks, Meyers proposed that manager Tony La Russa had been faced with his biggest challenge yet. "Most challenging by far with these idiots we've got," Edmonds joked. "I won't use that term because Boston used that term, but we got a bunch of wild men on our team."

With 12 errors committed in five games, the Series was far from a classic. But the Cardinals' improbable postseason run remains one of the most surprising turns in baseball history. Their 83–78 regular season record was the worst ever for a championship club. By the same token, the Tigers' transformation from 119-game losers in 2003 to pennant-winners three years later was equally astonishing. Of all the teams that have lost at least 110 games during the modern era, none have been able to reverse their fortunes as quickly as Detroit (to date).

In the afterglow of their 10th world championship, the Cardinals missed the playoffs in three of the next four seasons. They returned to the Fall Classic in 2011, facing a Rangers team that looked much stronger on paper. The Tigers encountered a similar scenario, slumping in the standings for four consecutive campaigns before advancing to the league championship series in 2011. They captured a pennant the following year but ended up being swept by the Giants in the World Series.

CHAPTER 21

Rangers vs. Cardinals 2011

THE RELOCATION OF THE GIANTS AND DODGERS IN THE LATE 1950S inspired the American League to expand its horizons. In 1961, the Senators moved to Minnesota and became the Twins. Two teams were added to the AL lineup—the Los Angeles Angels and the "new" Washington Senators. The old Senators (who were also known as the "Nationals" for many years) had been a star-crossed club. The 1960s incarnation was equally hapless, averaging 94 losses per year during the first decade of play. Hoping to stay afloat, owner Bob Short moved the struggling franchise to Texas in 1972 and renamed it. By the late 1970s, the Rangers had become a consistently competitive presence in the AL West. A first-place finish in 1994 was nullified by a labor dispute, but the club went on to make three division series appearances over the next five campaigns. In 2010, fans in the Lone Star State finally got what they had been waiting for—a World Series berth. Though the Giants were the team of destiny that year, the Rangers returned for another serious bid the following season.

The Texas lineup was fully stocked with capable sluggers. The most gifted by far was Adrián Beltré. As a kid growing up in the Dominican Republic, Beltré focused a majority of his attention on basketball and tennis. It wasn't until his early teen years that he began to excel at the sport that would make him famous. Signed by the Dodgers at the age of 15, Beltré landed the organization in hot water over a forged birth certificate. He made his big-league debut four years later, gradually emerging as one of the top third basemen in the majors. His best year with LA came in 2004, when he smashed a league-high 48 homers and finished second in MVP voting. His contract changed hands twice before he landed in Texas for the 2011 campaign. Endearing himself to fans, he led the team with 32 long balls while capturing a Gold Glove—the third of his career to that point.

Beltré wasn't the only Texas player hammering pitches out of the park on a consistent basis. Four other members of the lineup blasted at least 25 home runs. One of the most popular of the bunch was left fielder Josh Hamilton. Hamilton's ascent to the majors was inspiring to many. Plagued by alcohol and opiate addiction, his career nearly went off the rails before it even started. With the help of a "support partner," he was able to curb his problem drug use and attain stardom. In 2001, Hamilton was ranked number one among big-league prospects. But his debut in the majors was delayed until 2007. Traded by the Reds in the offseason, he entered the prime of his career with Texas, making five consecutive All-Star appearances and winning an MVP Award. A shoulder injury during the spring of 2011 kept him out of action for over a month, but he returned in late May, slamming 31 doubles and 25 homers in 121 games.

Rounding out a talented cast, Michael Young, Ian Kinsler, and Nelson Cruz punished opposing pitchers all year. A "super-utility" man appearing at four different infield stations, Young compiled a .338 batting average—the highest single-season mark of his career. Kinsler provided a pleasing combination of power and speed with 32 homers and 30 stolen bases. He also finished among the league leaders in multiple defensive categories at second base. Cruz—among the most industrious hitters to come from the Dominican Republic—missed a significant chunk of playing time but still managed to collect 58 extra-base hits and 87 RBIs in 124 games. He and Kinsler became the first teammates in major-league history to homer in each of the first three games of the season.

Collectively, the Rangers' offense ranked second in hits and second in homers while averaging more than five runs per game. It was a bountiful harvest for Texas pitchers as every member of the starting rotation gathered at least 13 wins. C. J. Wilson and Derek Holland tied for the team lead with 16 victories, but Wilson's ERA was a full point lower. A sturdily built southpaw with a number of effective pitches in his arsenal, Wilson made an All-Star appearance and finished among the top 10 in strikeouts. In the Rangers' bullpen, closer Neftali Feliz saved 32 games while set-up man Darren Oliver—playing in his 18th season—compiled a 2.29 ERA in 61 appearances.

The Rangers held onto first place through most of the first half in spite of a lackluster performance in May. A 12-game winning streak in July broke a tie with the Angels. It was a rough month as a horrifying accident occurred at the Ballpark in Arlington. During a game against the Oakland A's on July 7, Josh Hamilton tossed a souvenir ball to a spectator named Shannon Stone. Stone, who was sitting in an upper tier, slipped through a gap in the railing and fell 20 feet onto a concrete surface. He was rushed to the hospital but died en route. It was the second incident of its kind at a major-league park that year. In May, a fan named Robert Seamons sustained fatal injuries in a fall at Coors Field.

The Rangers finished strong, winning 10 of their last 11 games and broadening their lead over the Angels. Game 1 of the American League Division Series was a surprise to many as the Tampa Bay Rays pummeled C. J. Wilson in a 9–0 blowout. The rest of the games were close, but the Rangers won all three. Kinsler, Beltré, and Mike Napoli (a backup catcher who had slugged 30 homers during the regular season) all delivered game-winning hits.

In the American League Championship Series, it was the Nelson Cruz show. The hard-hitting outfielder homered in five of six games while driving in 13 runs. Doug Fister of the Tigers was the only pitcher to tame the series MVP, holding Cruz to a pair of infield pop-ups and a strikeout in Game 3. Cruz's six home runs were a new ALCS record. His 11th inning homer in Game 2 was the first walk-off grand slam in postseason history. His three-run shot in the 11th inning of Game 4 made him the first player to hit multiple extra-inning homers in the same postseason series. The Rangers clinched in six games, earning a World Series encore.

Five years removed from their championship season of 2006, the St. Louis Cardinals still had a few familiar faces. In spite of a wrist injury that kept him out of several games, Albert Pujols led the team in homers and RBIs for the seventh straight year. Yadier Molina had one of his best seasons ever, posting a .305 batting average—the highest mark among NL catchers. Tony La Russa began the season in third place on the all-time list for managerial wins. He would attain a ranking of second before retiring for good in 2022.

Acquired as a free agent, Lance Berkman joined the Cardinals shortly before spring training. A veteran of 12 seasons and an accomplished postseason hitter, he finished second on the club to Pujols in homers and RBIs. Berkman, who swung from both sides of the plate, had far more power from the left side. Defensively, he was fairly versatile, appearing at four different positions during his career.

The St. Louis pitching staff was solid yet unspectacular. Seven NL clubs posted better collective ERAs and 12 accumulated more strikeouts. Kyle Lohse was the winningest pitcher on the team with 14 victories. Chris Carpenter—another holdover from the 2006 World Series squad—deserved much better as St. Louis hitters supplied him with two runs or less in 12 of his appearances. He ended up with 14 no-decisions, finishing the season with an 11–9 record. Fernando Salas and Jason Motte were the stars of the bullpen, but they were unreliable at times, absorbing eight losses and blowing 10 saves.

The year began on a positive note as Cardinal great Stan Musial received the Presidential Medal of Freedom. The team had lobbied for the prestigious honor throughout the 2010 slate, labeling the campaign "Stand for Stan." Things took a dark turn on February 20, when Cardinals co-owner and treasurer Drew Bauer died unexpectedly in his home at the age of 66. Bauer, who also served on the board of directors, had held a major stake in the club for 15 years. Less than a week after Bauer's passing, staff ace Adam Wainwright—a 20-game winner in 2010—was flown back to St. Louis to have his right elbow examined. He ended up being lost for the entire season to Tommy John surgery.

The misery continued during the month of May, when third baseman David Freese sustained a broken hand after being hit by a pitch. He was out of action for two months. A few days later, La Russa came down with a case of shingles and missed six games. Adding insult to injury, outfielder Matt Holliday underwent an emergency appendectomy. The well-traveled slugger, who had made stops in Colorado and Oakland before arriving in St. Louis, was sidelined for over a week.

In spite of their various woes, the Cardinals hovered near the top of the NL Central standings for most of the year. They played mediocre ball in July and August, allowing the Brewers to build a comfortable division lead. A September resurgence kept St. Louis alive in the wild card hunt. The race was close, but in the end, the Cardinals outpaced the Braves by a single game.

St. Louis appeared to be overmatched in the NLDS against the Phillies, who had won 102 games and were heavily favored to capture the pennant. The Philadelphia lineup featured some of the best of the era, including Hall of Fame pitcher Roy Halladay, shortstop Jimmy Rollins, and second baseman Chase Utley. All three delivered sensational performances, but the Cardinals came out on the winning end of three close ballgames, derailing the Phillies' shot at making their third World Series appearance in a four-year span.

Incensed by the calls of home plate umpire Jerry Meals during Game 2, La Russa griped to a TBS broadcaster: "They're pitching to two different strike zones and, against a good club or any club, that's not an advantage you want to give." Fined for the remark, which he delivered during a televised interview, La Russa accepted the punishment without protest. "I'm embarrassed that I crossed the line," he said apologetically. "I know where the line is. I got upset and I crossed it." The series finale featured a memorable pitching duel between Halladay and Carpenter. Halladay surrendered the only run of the game in the first inning and followed with seven brilliant frames. Carpenter tossed a three-hit shutout, completing a stunning upset. Utility-men Skip Schumaker and Ryan Theriot were unlikely heroes for the Cardinals in the series, combining for 12 hits in 20 at-bats.

There was no love lost between St. Louis and Milwaukee in the NLCS. Carpenter's use of intimidation tactics got under the skin of multiple Brewers hitters. "He yells at people," said pitcher Zack Greinke. "He just stares people down and stuff. Most pitchers don't do that. And when guys do, I guess some hitters get mad. . . . There's other pitchers in the league that do it, but I don't know, a lot of guys on our team don't like Carpenter." On the flip side, the Brewers had a habit of staging theatrical celebrations on the field, which irritated various members of the

Cardinals. "Sometimes, the exuberance can spill over into a realm that I don't feel is appropriate," Berkman remarked.

The Brewers offense was driven by NL MVP Ryan Braun and All-Star first baseman Prince Fielder. The power-hitting duo combined for more than 70 homers and 200 RBIs during the regular season. Although they padded those totals significantly in the NLCS, it wasn't enough as the Cardinals had an offensive explosion of their own, battering Milwaukee pitchers for 43 runs in six games. Freese was the MVP of the series, hitting at a torrid .545 pace. Pujols and Holliday collectively gathered 14 ribbies as St. Louis completed a highly improbable pennant run. Their penchant for staging late rallies and overcoming adversity led to the nickname of the "Cardiac Birds."

When the 2002 All-Star Game ended in a controversial tie, commissioner Bud Selig adopted a new policy. From 2003 to 2016, the result of the Midsummer Classic determined home field advantage in the World Series. Prince Fielder's game-winning homer in 2011 proved to be a very important moment for the Cardinals as they ended up hosting the last two postseason games at Busch Stadium, where they had habitually dominated opponents. The Cardinals and Rangers had not played each other since 2004, when they were paired in a regular season matchup.

The 2011 NLDS had been marked by multiple appearances of a gray squirrel—most notably in the fifth inning of Game 4, when the animal ran across home plate while Roy Oswalt was in the process of delivering a pitch. After the Cardinals won the series, St. Louis fans adopted the squirrel as a mascot. They began wearing "Rally Squirrel" T-shirts to games and waving towels with a squirrel motif. The towels were out in full force during Game 1 of the World Series, which took place at Busch Stadium and featured a showdown between Wilson and Carpenter. Wilson was the first to stumble, hitting Pujols with a pitch in the bottom of the fourth and serving up a double to Holliday. Both runners scored on a single by Berkman. The 2–0 St. Louis lead evaporated quickly, however, as Napoli crushed a two-run homer in the top of the fifth. Unable to hold down the fort, Wilson got into another jam in the sixth, giving up a double to Freese and a two-out walk to Nick Punto. Rangers manager Ron Washington made a questionable choice when he summoned right-hander Alexi

Ogando to stifle the rally. Ogando—a second-year player who had made just two relief appearances all year—promptly surrendered an RBI single to pinch-hitter Allen Craig. Neither team scored another run, making Craig's clutch hit the game winner. The contest was marred by controversy in the ninth, when Beltré grounded to third for the second out of the inning. Replays showed that he had fouled the ball off of his foot.

Game 2 was the most tightly pitched contest of the Series as the teams combined for just three runs on 11 hits. Both managers relied heavily on their bullpens with Washington sending four hurlers to the mound and La Russa making a total of five pitching changes. The game was scoreless until the bottom of the seventh, when Rangers starter Colby Lewis put runners on the corners with two outs. Believing that lightning would not strike twice, Washington brought Ogando in to face Craig. In the words of iconic Yankee great Yogi Berra, it was déjà-vu all over again as Craig came through with another RBI single, putting the Cardinals up, 1–0. The battle of the bullpens ended in favor of Texas as Jason Motte, Arthur Rhodes, and Lance Lynn failed to prevent the Rangers from taking a 2–1 lead in the top of the ninth. Neftali Feliz shut down the Cards in the bottom of the frame, picking up his fifth save of the postseason.

Effective pitching was nonexistent in Game 3 at Arlington as 21 runs were scored in a five-inning span. The night belonged to Pujols, who put on an unprecedented offensive display. Senior ESPN writer Jayson Stark gushed: "Three home runs in a World Series game? Five hits in a World Series game? Six RBIs and 14 total bases in a World Series game? Who does this? That's what we ask ourselves. Well, nobody does this. That would be the correct answer. Or at least no one else ever has. Not all in one night at least. . . . And now this night gets to reverberate through history, floating on a cloud where only the most fabled World Series game ever staged gets to float." Reflecting on Pujols's performance, teammate Skip Schumaker commented: "I really do believe that, at the end of his career, [Pujols] should be mentioned for the greatest player of all-time—right-handed or left-handed." The Cardinal slugger's massive night at the plate overshadowed a number of other fine performances as Molina drove in four runs and Beltré pounded out four hits. The 16–7 win put St. Louis back in charge of the Series.

But the advantage would be short lived.

In the wake of their 16-run explosion (the second highest total in a World Series game to that point), the Cardinals fell into a funk, scoring just two runs in the next two meetings. Derek Holland was sensational for the Rangers in the fourth match, allowing two hits in 8.1 innings. The Texas bullpen stepped up again in Game 5, holding the Redbirds scoreless from the sixth inning on. There was a costly managerial mix-up in the bottom of the eighth, when St. Louis pitching coach Derek Lilliquist misinterpreted a request from La Russa to warm-up Motte and Marc Rzepczynski. Rzepczynski was the only one throwing when La Russa made a second call to the pen, instructing Lilliquist to get Motte—the St. Louis closer—ready. In a peculiar turn of events, Lilliquist mistakenly thought the Cardinal skipper had called for Lance Lynn. Unable to get their signals straight, the Cards sent Rzepczynski to the mound with one out and two runners on base. David Murphy singled and Napoli followed with a two-run double, giving the Rangers a 4–2 lead. Since Motte was not yet ready, Rzepczynski remained in the game for one more batter, striking out Mitch Moreland. Lynn was summoned to face Kinsler while Motte continued to warm up. He issued an intentional walk, giving La Russa's pitcher of choice enough time to prepare. Elvis Andrus struck out to end the inning, but the damage had already been done. The timely rally gave the Rangers a 3-games-to-2 Series edge.

Game 6 was pushed back a day due to rain. Both managers sent their Game 2 starters to the mound. Unlike the previous showdown, it was a sloppy slugfest. Five errors were committed, and 28 hits were allowed. Seven pitchers had been used by the end of the seventh inning. The Rangers came close to clinching the first championship in franchise history, carrying a 7–5 lead into the bottom of the ninth. Defying the odds, the Cards dug deep and staged a remarkable rally, tying the score on a double by Pujols, a walk to Berkman, and a triple by Freese. It was a heart-breaking turn of events for Feliz, who had entered the game with six saves and a 0.87 postseason ERA.

The Rangers got back to work in the top of the 10th. Andrus singled with one out and Hamilton blasted the first pitch he saw from Motte into the right-center field stands. Many other teams would have folded,

Figure 21.1   Albert Pujols is one of only four players to hit at least 700 home runs in his career. One of those blasts is pictured here.
PHOTO COURTESY OF DIRK DBQ ON VISUAL HUNT.

but the irrepressible Cardinals staved off elimination with another late-inning rally. Berkman and Theriot were both credited with RBIs as the game continued into the 11th frame. After the Rangers failed to score in their half of the inning, Freese ended things quickly with a lead-off homer. In a postgame interview, Berkman said: "If we lose tomorrow night, then this just becomes a nice footnote in history. If we win tomorrow night, this becomes a pretty big deal."

It already was a pretty big deal.

The Cardinals were the first team to overcome deficits in the ninth and 10th innings of a World Series game and the first to score runs from the eighth inning on in an 11-inning October contest. *Houston Chronicle* correspondent Richard Justice recalled the scene in the St. Louis dressing room afterward. "Freese told his story with emotion and eloquence as we gathered around his locker the night he became a World Series hero for his hometown team. How he was so burned out that he quit baseball after High School, and only then did he begin to understand how much he loved it. How he would never forget the people who had his back along the way (and those that hadn't). How injuries threatened to derail his major-league career almost before it began. He was 28 years old the night a legend was born."

Another chapter was added to the legend in Game 7 as Freese came through yet again with a two-run double that tied the score in the bottom of the first. He finished the Series with five extra-base hits, seven RBIs, and a .348 batting average—numbers that made him an obvious choice for MVP. After a rocky first inning, Carpenter pitched five efficient frames, running his postseason record up to 4–0. Allen Craig—an unsung hero for St. Louis—drilled his third homer of the Series off of Matt Harrison in the bottom of the third. It proved to be the game-winning blast in the 6–2 Series-clincher. Asked what the mood was like in the clubhouse before the game, Motte told Ken Rosenthal of FOX Sports: "We're a loose bunch of guys. We were in there hanging out, dancing around, had music playing. That's how we play the best and we came out and we were able to do it today and it's just amazing."

In defeat, the Rangers had the dubious distinction of being the first club to lose back-to-back World Series since the Braves in 1991 and 1992. They returned to the playoffs in 2012 as a wild card team. It was the first year that the postseason included an independent wild card round. After losing to the Orioles, the Rangers earned consecutive Division Series berths in 2015 and 2016. In 2023, they finally captured the first World Series title in franchise history, beating the Arizona Diamondbacks.

The year 2011 was the final World Series title of La Russa's storied career. He temporarily retired at season's end, returning in 2021 to lead the White Sox to a first-place finish in the AL Central. He stepped down the following year due to health issues. The Cardinals returned to the World Series without him in 2013, losing to the Red Sox in six games. Freese was unable to rekindle his postseason magic, going 3-for-19 at the plate. Pujols left St. Louis after the 2011 campaign, signing a blockbuster deal with the Angels. He entered the exclusive 700 home run club in 2022.

CHAPTER 22

Astros vs. Nationals 2019

ANYONE NEW TO THE GAME MIGHT FIND IT HARD TO BELIEVE, BUT THE
Houston Astros were once underdogs. Long before they captured four
American League pennants in a six-year span, the Astros went 18 consecutive seasons without a playoff berth. They waited more than 40 years
to make their first World Series appearance, entering the postseason as
a wild card team and getting swept by the long-suffering White Sox in
2005. The moment fans had dreamed of finally arrived in 2017, when the
Astros ended a long championship drought with a dramatic seven-game
victory over the Dodgers. What should have been a triumphant moment
for the club ended up being tarnished by allegations of foul play.

Sign-stealing has been intrinsic to baseball throughout its extensive
history. Many players and coaches have enhanced their reputations by
studying and interpreting the gestures of opponents. But the use of tech-
nology to steal signs has traditionally been frowned upon. In September
of 2017, the Red Sox were fined for using a smartwatch in an attempted
sign-stealing scheme. Around the same time, a number of players began
noticing peculiar activity during games against the Astros. White Sox
reliever Danny Farquhar was among the first to voice concerns. "There
was a banging from the dugout almost like a bat hitting the bat rack every
time the change-up signal got put down," he later recalled. In August
of 2018, members of the Oakland A's noted that Houston players were
clapping in the dugout before particular pitches. The A's filed an official
grievance, prompting the Cleveland Indians to join the growing list of
plaintiffs.

The Astros' sign-stealing operation became a matter of public record in 2019, when *The Athletic* published a detailed report. In it, Mike Fiers—a pitcher who had played on the 2017 World Series squad—openly admitted that a camera stationed in the center field seats had been used to detect the signs of opposing catchers. Players or staffers watching the camera feed from behind the Houston dugout were able to alert batters in advance as to what pitches were coming. An official investigation confirmed widespread accusations that the Astros had cheated during their championship season of 2017. Harsh punishments were handed out as Houston quickly became the most despised team in the majors.

Their reputation as "bad guys" didn't stop the Astros from winning. They followed up their World Series run with another trip to the ALCS. Although they fell three victories short of a pennant, they came back even stronger the following year.

Around the horn, the Astros had one of the most gifted infield platoons in the majors. After fifteen spectacular seasons in the Cuban National Series, first baseman Yuli Gurriel defected to the United States and signed with Houston. He posted his best major-league numbers in 2019, slugging 31 homers and driving in 104 runs. He finished second on the club to third baseman Alex Bregman, who went deep 41 times and gathered 112 ribbies. The Astros' middle infield combination of Jose Altuve and Carlos Correa made other teams envious. Altuve entered the 2019 campaign as a three-time batting champion and six-time All-Star. Correa—the 2015 AL Rookie of the Year—was on pace for a 40-homer/120-RBI season before injuries limited him to 75 regular season games.

The Astros got additional contributions from outfielders Michael Brantley and George Springer, who combined for 126 extra-base hits and a .303 batting average. As a collective unit, Houston hitters posted the highest on-base percentage in the majors while generating the fewest strikeouts. Home runs were evenly distributed with seven players slamming at least 20.

The Houston pitching corps were equally impressive in 2019, collecting the most strikeouts in the American League while allowing the fewest runs per game. Justin Verlander was the ace of the staff with 21 wins.

His 300 strikeouts and 0.803 WHIP average (tops in the majors) gave him a slight edge over teammate Gerrit Cole in balloting for the Cy Young Award. Cole had one of his finest all-around seasons, leading the league with 326 strikeouts and a 2.50 ERA.

Anticipating a deep postseason run, the Astros bolstered their starting rotation with the addition of Zack Greinke, who arrived in late July via a trade with the Diamondbacks. A six-time All-Star and former Cy Young Award winner, Greinke had established himself as one of the most versatile pitchers in the majors with more than half a dozen effective pitches in his repertoire. The right-handed junk-baller baffled opponents with offerings ranging from 60 to 90 miles per hour. He forged an 8–1 record for Houston down the stretch and followed with several successful outings during the playoffs.

In spite of a tepid start in the early spring, the Astros won 107 games—a new franchise record. They climbed into first place on April 28 and stayed there for the rest of the season, leaving the A's 10 games behind in the standings. It was a forgettable year for the American League overall as eight clubs finished below .500 and three ended up with more than 100 losses.

The American League Division Series proved to be evenly matched as the Tampa Bay Rays—winners of the wild card showdown against Oakland—rallied from a two-game deficit to force a pivotal fifth meeting at Houston. After tossing a gem in the second game, Cole was up to the challenge in the finale, holding the Rays to one run over eight frames while striking out 10 batters. Brantley and Altuve both homered for Houston in the 6–1 win.

The regular season series between the Yankees and Astros was very close with Houston taking four of seven games. After sweeping the Twins in their own divisional playoff, the Yankees were hoping to avenge their loss to Houston in the 2017 ALCS. On the heels of a 7–0 win in the opener, the Bombers dropped four of the next five games, extending their championship slump to 10 seasons (an eternity in the eyes of Yankee fans and executives).

Following a pattern similar to the Astros, the Nationals waited a very long time to make a World Series appearance. After 36 years of futility in Montreal, the team moved to Washington and scrapped the old Expos moniker. The changes proved to be superficial as the Nationals wallowed near the bottom of the standings in six consecutive campaigns. Over the next decade, GM Mike Rizzo made gradual improvements to the lineup. By 2019, he had finally assembled the right combination of players.

Originally drafted by the Pirates, Trea Turner opted to play for North Carolina State University instead of signing a big-league contract. He played several years of college ball before starting his professional career in the Padres' farm system. He ended up being acquired by the Nationals in a deal involving three clubs. Turner made his Washington debut in 2015, appearing primarily at second base. After a trial in the outfield the following year, he returned to his natural position of shortstop. His exceptional speed and ability to put the ball in play made him a good fit for the leadoff spot. During Washington's 2019 pennant run, he stole 35 bases and scored 96 runs.

Born and raised in Houston, Anthony Rendon enrolled at Rice University, where he won several prestigious awards for his stellar play on the diamond. Selected by the Nationals in the first round, he began his minor-league career in 2012. He was ranked among the top 20 prospects at the time of his pro debut. A right-handed slugger with solid power, Rendon picked up the nickname "Tony Two Bags" for his ability to hit doubles. In 2019, he led the league in that category for the second straight year. He also blasted 34 homers and drove in a league-high 126 runs, capturing a Silver Slugger Award. A multidimensional player, Rendon posted the highest fielding percentage among NL third basemen for three straight seasons (2016–2018).

Born in Santo Domingo, outfielder Juan Soto was just 17 years old when he began his professional career. He ascended quickly through the minors and was the first teenager to play for Washington since Bryce Harper (in 2012). Soto's 22 circuit blasts in his 2018 debut made him the third teenager in major-league history to reach the 20-homer mark. He finished second in Rookie of the Year voting. His follow-up was even better as he tied for the team lead with 34 long balls. He also drew 108 walks, running his on-base percentage up to .401. He would go on to lead the league in both categories on multiple occasions.

A versatile defensive player who appeared at six different stations during his career, Howie Kendrick was in his 12th season when he was acquired from the Phillies in July of 2017. An Achilles tendon injury put him out of action for most of the following year, but he returned to health in 2019, hitting .344 with 17 homers and 62 RBIs. He was an integral part of the Nationals' postseason run.

In recent years, statisticians have employed a mathematical formula to determine which major-league stadiums are friendliest to hitters. Although the ballpark in Washington made pitching somewhat challenging, the Nationals' staff performed exceptionally well in 2019, finishing among the top three in team shutouts and strikeouts per nine innings.

A right-handed flame thrower who routinely hit 100 mph on the radar gun, Stephen Strasburg arrived in the majors with high expectations. At the time of his professional debut, he was considered to be the number one prospect in baseball. Called to Washington in June of 2010, he struck out 14 batters in his first game, falling just short of a record. By August, he had sustained a torn collateral ligament in his right elbow, which forced him to undergo Tommy John surgery. The Nationals handled Strasburg carefully over the next few seasons, limiting him to a pitch count. He reached the 200-inning mark for just the second time in his career during the 2019 slate, winning 18 games—more than any other hurler in the NL.

A three-time Cy Young Award winner, Max Scherzer arrived in Washington via free agency in 2015. He averaged 16 victories and 274 strikeouts per year during his first five seasons with the club. In addition to a four-seam fastball and cutter, Scherzer also employed a curve and a changeup. A questionable umpiring decision deprived him of a perfect game in 2015, but he ended up with a no-hitter—the first of two that season. In 2016, he tied a single-game record with 20 strikeouts against the Tigers. Hampered by shoulder and back issues during the 2019 slate, he missed several starts in July and August. He still managed to win 11 of 18 decisions while posting the lowest ERA on the staff at 2.92.

Another essential member of the starting rotation, southpaw Patrick Corbin had somewhat of a checkered past. After posting an unwieldy 5.15 ERA for the Diamondbacks in 2016, he was temporarily demoted

Figure 22.1   Right-hander Stephen Strasburg hit his stride in 2019, leading the NL with 18 wins. He won two more games in the World Series, walking away with MVP honors.
PHOTO COURTESY OF DBKING ON VISUAL HUNT.

to the bullpen. He returned to form over the next two seasons, reaching a personal high of 246 strikeouts in 2018. Acquired by the Nationals during the offseason, he posted a 14–7 record in his Washington premiere with a 3.25 earned run average—among the top ten marks in the National League.

With the exception of the West, where the Dodgers ran away with the division lead, the NL races were tight. The Nationals got off to a horrific 19–31 start but accrued a .660 winning percentage from that point forward, earning the right to face the Brewers in the winner-take-all wild card game. A capacity crowd in Washington celebrated wildly after the Nationals rallied from a 3–1 deficit in their final at-bat. Soto delivered the game-winning hit with the bases loaded, ending Milwaukee's playoff run.

With 106 wins and a roster packed with All-Stars, the Dodgers were expected to breeze through the NLDS against Washington. But things didn't go as planned. Atoning for four prior postseason failures, the Nationals overcame a pair of blowout losses, taking the series in five games. The pivotal moment came in the eighth inning of the finale, when Rendon and Soto homered on consecutive pitches from Dodger ace Clayton Kershaw, knotting the score at 3. The game was still tied in the 10th, when Kendrick launched a game-winning grand slam off of reliever Joe Kelly. "It was electric," Kendrick said afterward. "Probably the best moment of my career. We never gave up. The city had faith in us. We believed in ourselves. Everybody came through for us."

Fig 22.2 Slugger Howie Kendrick came alive in the 2019 NLDS and NLCS, carrying the Nationals' offense.
PHOTO COURTESY OF ALL-PRO REELS ON VISUAL HUNT.

The NLCS was anticlimactic in comparison as Washington bowled over St. Louis in four games. Kendrick earned series MVP honors with four doubles, four RBIs, and a .333 batting average. Although the sweep afforded the Nationals several days of rest, it also put them in a precarious position. With the exception of the 1995 Atlanta Braves, every team that had entered the Series after a long layoff had fared poorly. Most insiders figured that Washington's luck would finally run out against the Astros.

Entering Game 1, Houston starter Gerrit Cole had not been charged with a loss in more than four months. He had won 16 consecutive decisions during that span. On the night of the Series opener, however, Nationals starter Max Scherzer was just a little bit better at his job. The Astros opened the scoring in the bottom of the first as Gurriel slammed a two-run double. Scherzer settled down after that, tossing four effective innings. Vulnerable to the home run throughout his career, Cole gave up solo shots to Soto and Ryan Zimmerman. Soto's two-out double in the top of the fifth gave Washington a 5–2 lead. Springer homered for the Astros in the seventh and doubled in another run an inning later to keep the game close. But Sean Doolittle pitched a 1-2-3 ninth, securing the victory for the Nationals. It was the first World Series win for a Washington team since the 1933 squad. Reflecting on Cole's performance, Springer told a writer: "He's human. He was bound to lose one eventually. They got the hits when they needed them, but he's our guy and when he gets the ball again, I'm sure he'll be ready to go." Right fielder Adam Eaton, who tagged Cole for an RBI single in the fifth, was optimistic about his club's chances. "You can have the best season in the world," he said, "but if you don't perform on the stage in seven games, I don't think it really matters."

Game 2 was an utter disaster for the Astros bullpen. More than 43,000 fans at Minute Maid Park saw a promising pitcher's duel end with a sloppy late-inning meltdown. Verlander and Strasburg were shaky in the first, each allowing a pair of early runs. But things quieted down after that until the top of the seventh, when Kurt Suzuki homered and Victor Robles followed with a walk, ending Verlander's day on the mound. Reliever Ryan Pressly, who had compiled a highly serviceable 2.32 ERA during the regular season, had one of the worst outings of his career, issuing two walks, three singles, and a wild pitch. Alex Bregman added a critical error at third base, helping the Nationals' cause. By the time Josh James came in to mop up, the Nats had built an 8–2 lead. Eaton drilled a two-run homer off of James in the eighth and Michael A. Taylor followed with a solo shot off Chris Devenski in the final frame, extending the Washington lead. "We have a really good team," said Astros manager A. J. Hinch after the staggering 12–3 loss. "Clearly, the Nats have outplayed us—bottom line. They came into our building and played two really good games. We're going to have to try to sleep off the latter third of this game."

It was the Nationals who fell asleep in the next three games, stranding a total of 25 base runners while hitting at a collective .175 clip. The Houston bullpen really stepped up, providing 10 innings of scoreless relief. Michael Brantley drove in the game-winner for the Astros in the third meeting and Yuli Gurriel delivered the deciding blow the following night. Completing the sweep at Nationals Park, Houston breezed to a 7–1 victory in Game 5. Scherzer was scheduled to start for the Nationals but ended up being shelved due to neck and back spasms. Right-hander Joe Ross, who had begun the season in the bullpen, got the start for Washington, serving up a pair of two-run homers. Cole was sensational on the mound, striking out nine batters in seven innings of work. He got the benefit of multiple borderline calls from home plate umpire Lance Barksdale, whose performance prompted a number of journalists to strongly advocate for the implementation of computerized strike zones. Controversy aside, the Astros executed one of the most dominant road performances in World Series history. "The Astros have established themselves as baseball's best team over the last six months for a reason," asserted a writer from *Sports Illustrated*, "and that's been on full display over the last three days, in terms of pitching and offense and defense alike. They've simply been the better team. That leaves the Nationals with everything they've done wrong—and the ghosts of all the *what-if* turning points that could have gone the other way. . . . To exit with a list of *what-if* moments is a letdown in and of itself, naturally, at once a collection of adjustments to make and frustrations to move on from."

The Nationals most definitely moved on—especially in Game 6, when they cruised to a 7–2 victory. Rendon was the offensive star for Washington with five RBIs. Eaton and Soto both homered off of Verlander, whose mediocre five-inning start dropped his record to 1–4 in the 2019 postseason. There was more umpiring controversy in the top of the seventh, when Trea Turner was called out at first base by home plate arbiter Sam Holbrook. Turner pushed a bunt to the third base side of the mound then interfered with a throw from Astros reliever Brad Peacock. Although the call was not reviewable according to MLB guidelines, Nats manager Dave Martinez argued anyway. He ended up being ejected during the seventh inning stretch after taking up the debate with Holbrook again.

Scherzer got the start for Washington in the finale against Greinke. It was the first Game 7 to feature a matchup between former Cy Young Award winners. The Astros jumped out to a 2–0 lead on a home run by Gurriel and an RBI single by Correa. But the Nats would not go quietly. Adhering to their adopted postseason mantra—"Stay in the fight!"—they rallied in the top of the seventh. A solo homer by Rendon and a one-out walk to Soto ended Greinke's day on the mound. He was replaced by Will Harris, who had logged 20 consecutive scoreless appearances (including the regular season) before coughing up a run in Game 6. For the second day in a row, Harris was ineffective, serving up a two-run bomb to Kendrick. The Nationals tacked on more runs in the eighth and ninth before handing the closing assignment to Daniel Hudson. Hudson, who had fared poorly in Game 5, redeemed himself by retiring three of Houston's most dangerous hitters (Springer, Altuve, and Brantley) in order. The 6–2 win made the Nationals the second team in history to win a World Series after falling 12 games below .500 in the standings (the Braves had pulled it off in 1914).

Dave Martinez offered glowing praise to Rendon and Kendrick in a postgame interview. "There's guys that in a big moment you want up there. They've come through all year long for us in big ways. They have a knack [for staying] calm and [doing] what they need to do." In the opposing clubhouse, A. J. Hinch gave full credit to the Nationals for their uplifting Series victory. "This isn't about not performing at home or anything we didn't do," he told a reporter. "I come away incredibly impressed by the team that we played and got beat by."

The World Series loss in 2019 did not deter the Astros from maintaining their status as one of the most powerful teams in baseball. After dropping the ALCS to the Tampa Bay Rays in 2020, they made two consecutive Fall Classic appearances. They brought home their second championship in 2022.

The Nationals have been far less successful, following their triumphant October run with a last place finish the following year. By 2022, most of their key players had departed, leaving them with a punchless lineup. Their 107 losses that year were the most since 1976.

Appendix 1

Series Trivia

1906

- The 1906 World Series brought out the worst in some Chicago fans. Two teenagers held up a local grocery store to raise money for tickets. And a city councilman named Charles Martin was arrested after a drunken altercation with a rival Cubs fan.

- Cubs hurler Ed Reulbach's one-hitter in Game 2 of the Series was the first of its kind. But even with a single hit, the White Sox (known as the "Hitless Wonders") found a way to score a run, capitalizing on a walk, a wild pitch, and an error by Hall of Fame shortstop Joe Tinker.

- Pitcher Ed Walsh struck out at least one batter in all nine innings of Game 3—a feat that remained unmatched until 1968, when Cardinals hurler Bob Gibson turned the trick.

1914

- This was the first real sweep in World Series history. The Cubs had taken four games in a row from the Tigers in 1907, but the first meeting had ended in a tie.

- Braves pitcher Dick Rudolph pitched 18 innings—a new record for a four-game Series. His workload represented nearly half of the pitching staff's combined total (39 innings).

- At least one author has suggested that some members of the A's might have conspired to throw the Series although there is no verifiable proof of it. Heavy bets were placed against the A's through bookmaker Sport Sullivan, who was later implicated in the 1919 World Series scandal.

1919

- Several days before the Series, the White Sox were listed as 3-to-1 favorites. But as rumors of a fix circulated, and substantial amounts of money were placed on Cincinnati to win, the Reds carried 8-to-5 betting odds.
- Hall of Fame catcher Ray Schalk, who was not in on the fix, did his best to undermine the conspirators, throwing out 10 would-be base-stealers—a new record.
- The 1919 Fall Classic signaled the end of the Deadball Era. Only one home run was hit during the Series. During the 1920s, there was an average of seven homers per year.

1923

- The Yankees got permission from Commissioner Landis to allow Lou Gehrig to play in the Series, but existing rules prohibited teams from making late-season roster changes without approval from the opposing manager. Hoping to give his team an edge, Giants skipper John McGraw vetoed the addition of Gehrig, who had been called up from Hartford of the Eastern League.
- It was the third straight Series to feature the same opponents— the only time this has ever happened.
- It was the last time during the twentieth century that a team with a new stadium won a championship. Interestingly, the Yankees won again in 2009—the year Yankee Stadium III opened. They won the American League pennant in 1976—the inaugural year of Yankee Stadium II.

1924

- This was the first Series to use the 2-3-2 home game pattern. The format was officially adopted the following year.

- The Nationals hit just 22 home runs as a team during the 1924 regular season (less than half of Babe Ruth's total that year). But they managed to slug five during the Series.

- At 27 years old, Bucky Harris was the youngest manager to win a Series.

1926

- The Yankees followed this Series loss with sweeps in 1927, 1928, and 1932. They didn't lose another postseason game until 1936.

- The World Series MVP Award was still a long way off, but it would have been a tall order to determine who was most deserving in 1926. Pete Alexander was brilliant in all three appearances, but four players tied for the Series lead with 10 hits.

- Alexander's drinking problems persisted, and he was never able to hold a steady job after retiring from baseball. He worked for carnivals, flea circuses, and was even hired as a security guard at the National Baseball Hall of Fame.

1942

- Entering the Series, the Yankees had won each of the previous eight Fall Classics they appeared in.

- Every player on the 1942 Cardinals roster (with the exception of one) had come up through the Cardinals' farm system, which had been put in place by Hall of Fame executive Branch Rickey.

- After the St. Louis victory, Rickey left the Cardinals to serve as president of the Brooklyn Dodgers. His crowning achievement came in 1946, when he facilitated the breaking of baseball's color barrier by signing Jackie Robinson to play for the Montreal Royals of the International League. As most reasonably informed fans know, Robinson was promoted to the Dodgers the following year.

1955

- The Series loss—the first for a Yankee squad led by Casey Stengel—ended a long run of dominance for the club. The Yanks would lose again in 1957, 1960, 1963, 1964, and 1976.

- This was the first Series in which an MVP was selected. The award went to Dodger hurler Johnny Podres.

- The Dodger victory was later referenced in the popular Billy Joel song "We Didn't Start the Fire."

1960

- The Series included seven past, present, or future MVPs: Dick Groat, Roberto Clemente, Yogi Berra, Bobby Shantz, Mickey Mantle, Elston Howard, and Roger Maris. Berra, Mantle, and Maris each won the award multiple times.

- Television networks made a habit of taping over their sports broadcasts prior to the 1970s. The only complete game footage of the 1960 World Series known to exist was discovered in the basement of a California home that once belonged to Bing Crosby. The black-and-white recording features Game 7 in its entirety.

- The Series set more than 50 new statistical records.

1969

- Prior to the 1969 campaign, the Mets had never won more than 73 games in a season.

- The Mets' pennant-winning effort extended a ponderous postseason drought for the Cubs, who led the NL East at the end of August then dropped 11 of their next 13 games, allowing the Mets to overtake them in the standings.

- The Mets' Series victory was the second big upset for a New York team over a Baltimore opponent. Earlier in the year, the Jets had defeated the Colts in Super Bowl III.

1971

- Roberto Clemente was the first Spanish-speaking player to win a World Series MVP Award.

- The victorious Pirates were outscored in the Series. The trend would continue in 1972 and 1973—both of which were also seven-game affairs.

- After hitting safely in all seven games of the 1960 Series, Clemente hit safely in every game of the 1971 Fall Classic, finishing his career with a perfect track record in the World Series.

1985

- This was the first Series in which all of the games were played at night.

- It was the last Series in which a designated hitter was not used in an American League ballpark. In 1986, the designated hitter became a permanent October fixture in American League parks.

- Don Denkinger's infamous blown call was not the only flawed decision made by officials in Game 6. The game was scoreless in the fourth inning, when Frank White was called out by umpire Bill Williams on an attempted steal of second base. Replays showed that White was safe. Had the correct call been made, he would likely have scored on a subsequent single by Pat Sheridan.

1987

- This was the first World Series featuring games indoors.

- In 2003, a superintendent from the Metrodome, Dick Ericson, admitted to adjusting the ventilation system inside the stadium in the hope of making balls hit by the Twins travel farther. When the Twins were batting in the late innings of close games, Ericson would activate additional fans blowing toward the outfield. He claimed that the fans were fully activated when Kirby Puckett hit a dramatic game-winning homer in Game 6 of the 1991 World Series. "I don't feel guilty," he told a reporter. "It's your home field advantage. Every stadium has one." There is no concrete evidence to support the fact that Ericson's ruse actually worked.

- In 2015, broadcaster Al Michaels claimed that the Twins added artificial crowd noise at the Metrodome to distract and intimidate opponents. Twins president Dave St. Peter adamantly denied the accusation.

1988

- Although Oakland's "Bash Brothers" had just two hits in the Series, both were home runs. Canseco launched a grand slam in Game 1 and McGwire slugged a walk-off shot in Game 3.

- The Los Angeles bench players picked up the nickname "Stuntmen" for their ability to reliably perform in place of higher-profile Dodger stars. Mickey Hatcher—who subbed for an injured Kirk Gibson—was the best of the Stuntmen, hitting .368 in the Series with a pair of homers.

- Orel Hershiser's record-breaking 59-game consecutive scoreless innings streak in 1988 would not have been possible without the help of umpire Paul Runge, who erased a run scored by the Giants with a controversial interference call. After completing the memorable streak (which is still an all-time record), Hershiser tossed eight more scoreless innings in the NLCS against the Mets.

1990

- This was the third Series sweep in Cincinnati history. After being victimized by the Yankees in 1939, the Reds made quick work of the Yankees in 1976.

- The four major Ohio-based sports teams failed to capture another championship until 2016, when the Cleveland Cavaliers won the NBA Finals.

- Another abominable offensive performance by Mark McGwire and Jose Canseco in the 1990 Fall Classic dropped the Oakland slugging duo's collective World Series batting average to .172.

1997

- The Series featured the first Fall Classic games played in the state of Florida.
- This was the only World Series that did not include the New York Yankees from 1996 through 2001.
- Cleveland Reliever Jose Mesa's inability to save Game 7 sparked a bitter feud with teammate Omar Vizquel, who referred to Mesa as a "choker" in his autobiography. After being traded from Cleveland, Mesa vowed to hit Vizquel every time he faced him. But the jilted hurler failed to fulfill that promise.

2001

- The Diamondbacks' championship was the first ever won by one of the four major men's sports teams stationed in Arizona.
- It was the first time the home teams won every game in a Series that did not include the Minnesota Twins.
- It was the first time the MVP Award was shared by two players (Randy Johnson and Curt Schilling).

2003

- This was the second consecutive World Series victory for a wild card team. (The Angels had won in 2002.)
- Although it was billed as the 100th Anniversary of the World Series, it was not the 100th ever played. There were no Series games in 1904 or 1994.
- The Series featured the last Fall Classic games to take place at Pro Player Stadium and Yankee Stadium II.

2006

- There were five errors committed by Detroit pitchers in this Series—a new record.

- Tony La Russa became the second manager to lead teams from both leagues to World Series titles. He joined Sparky Anderson, who won championships with the Reds and Tigers.

- The Cardinals were the fourth team to win a World Series in their home stadium's inaugural season. Busch Stadium III had opened in April. Other first-year stadiums to have a championship squad in residence included Forbes Field (1909), Fenway Park (1912), Yankee Stadium I (1923), and Yankee Stadium III (2009).

2011

- Rangers' pitchers walked 41 St. Louis hitters, surpassing a dubious record set by the Marlins in 1997.

- The Cardinals came within one strike of being eliminated twice in Game 6. They were the second team in history to win the World Series after being put in that position.

- Each game played in St. Louis reportedly generated enough tax revenue for the city to avoid laying off municipal workers in the wake of budget cuts.

2019

- This was the first World Series in which the visiting teams won all seven games and the sixth time in a row that the Series winners clinched on the road.

- The Nationals (originally the Expos) were the last team from the 1969 expansion class to make a World Series appearance. Other teams making their debuts in 1969 included the Royals, Padres, and Brewers (originally the Seattle Pilots).

- A number of Nationals players refused to attend the traditional White House visit in a show of opposition to President Donald Trump.

Appendix 2

Team/Player Stats

1906
CHICAGO WHITE SOX OVER
CHICAGO CUBS (4–2)

Top Performers
White Sox

2B	Frank Isbell	.308	4 R	4 2B	4 RBI			
3B	George Rohe	.333	2 R	1 2B	2 3B	4 RBI	3 BB	
P	Nick Altrock	W 1	L 1	18 IP	11 H	2 ER	5 SO	1.00 ERA
P	Ed Walsh	W 2	L 0	15 IP	7 H	1 ER	17 SO	0.60 ERA
P	Doc White	W 1	L 1	15 IP	12 H	3 ER	4 SO	1.80 ERA

Cubs

CF	Solly Hofman	.304	3 R	1 2B	2 RBI	3 BB		
RF	Frank Schulte	.269	1 R	3 2B	3 RBI			
P	Ed Ruelbach	W 1	L 0	11 IP	6 H	3 ER	4 SO	2.45 ERA

MVP: none chosen
Hypothetical MVP: Ed Walsh
Winning Player's Share: $1,874
Losing Player's Share: $440

1914
BOSTON BRAVES OVER
PHILADELPHIA A's (4–0)

Top Performers
Braves

C	Hank Gowdy	.545 BA	3 R	3 2B	1 3B	1 HR	3 RBI	5 BB
2B	Johnny Evers	.438 BA	2 R	2 RBI				
P	Bill James	W 2	L 0	11 IP	2 H	0 ER	9 SO	0.00 ERA
P	Dick Rudolph	W 2	L 0	18 IP	12 H	1 ER	15 SO	0.50 ERA

A's

P	Eddie Plank	W 0	L 1	9 IP	7 H	1 ER	6 SO	1.00 ERA
3B	Frank Baker	.250 BA	2 2B	2 RBI				

MVP: none chosen
Hypothetical MVP: Hank Gowdy
Winning Player's Share: $3,910
Losing Player's Share: $2,835

1919
CINCINNATI REDS OVER
CHICAGO WHITE SOX (5–3)

Top Performers

Reds

LF	Pat Duncan	.269 BA	3 R	2 2B	8 RBI			
RF	Greasy Neale	.357 BA	3 R	1 3B	4 RBI			
CF	Edd Roush	.214 BA	6 R	1 3B	7 RBI	3 BB		
P	Hod Eller	W 2	L 0	18 IP	13 H	4 ER	15 SO	2.00 ERA
P	Jimmy Ring	W 1	L 1	14 IP	7 H	1 ER	4 SO	0.64 ERA
P	Dutch Ruether	W 1	L 0	14 IP	12 H	4 ER	1 SO	2.57 ERA
P	Slim Sallee	W 1	L 1	13.1 IP	19 H	2 ER	2 SO	1.35 ERA

White Sox

LF	Joe Jackson	.375 BA	5 R	3 2B	1 HR	6 RBI		
RF	Buck Weaver	.324 BA	4 R	4 2B	1 3B			
C	Ray Schalk	.304 BA	1 R	2 RBI	4 BB			
P	Dickey Kerr	W 2	L 0	19 IP	14 H	3 ER	6 SO	1.42 ERA

MVP: none chosen
Hypothetical MVP: Hod Eller
Winning Player's Share: $5,207
Losing Player's Share: $3,254

1923
NEW YORK YANKEES OVER
NEW YORK GIANTS (4–2)

Top Performers
Yankees

RF	Babe Ruth	.368	8 R	1 2B	1 3B	3 HR	3 RBI	8 BB
3B	Joe Dugan	.280	5 R	2 2B	1 3B	1 HR	5 RBI	3 BB
LF	Bob Meusel	.269	1 R	1 2B	2 3B	8 RBI		
2B	Aaron Ward	.417	4 R	1 HR	2 RBI			
P	Bullet Joe Bush	W 1	L 1	16.2 IP	7 H	2 ER	5 SO	1.08 ERA
P	Sad Sam Jones	W 0	L 1	1 SV	10 IP	5 H	1 ER	3 SO	0.90 ERA

Giants

2B	Frankie Frisch	.400	2 R	1 3B	1 RBI			
LF	Irish Meusel	.280	3 R	1 2B	1 3B	1 HR	2 RBI	
RF	Ross Youngs	.348	2 R	1 HR	3 RBI			
P	Art Nehf	W 1	L 1	16.1 IP	10 H	5 ER	7 SO	2.76 ERA

MVP: none chosen
Hypothetical MVP: Babe Ruth
Winning Player's Share: $6,143
Losing Player's Share: $4,113

1924
WASHINGTON SENATORS OVER
NEW YORK GIANTS (4–3)

Top Performers
Senators

OF	Goose Goslin	.344	4 R	1 2B	3 HR	7 RBI		
2B	Bucky Harris	.333	5 R	2 HR	7 RBI			
P	Tom Zachary	W 2	L 0	17.2 IP	13 H	4 ER	3 SO	2.04 ERA
P	Firpo Marberry	SV 2	8 IP	9 H	1 ER	10 SO	1.13 ERA	

Giants

2B	Frankie Frisch	.333	1 R	4 2B	1 3B	4 BB		
3B	Freddie Lindstrom	.333	1 R	2 2B	4 RBI	3 BB		
1B	Bill Terry	.429	3 R	1 3B	1 HR	1 RBI		
P	Art Nehf	W 1	L 1	19.2 IP	15 H	4 ER	7 SO	1.83 ERA

MVP: none chosen
Hypothetical MVP: Bucky Harris
Winning Player's Share: $5,960
Losing Player's Share: $3,820

1926
ST. LOUIS CARDINALS OVER NEW YORK YANKEES
(4–3)

Top Performers
Cardinals

1B	Jim Bottomley	.345	4 R	3 2B	5 RBI				
RF	Billy Southworth	.345	6 R	1 2B	1 3B	1 HR	4 RBI		
SS	Tommy Thevenow	.417	5 R	1 2B	1 HR	4 RBI			
P	Grover Alexander	W 2	L 0	1 SV	20.1 IP	12 H	3 ER	17 SO	1.33 ERA
P	Jesse Haines	W 2	L 0	16.2 IP	13 H	2 ER	5 SO	1.08 ERA	

Yankees

CF	Earle Combs	.357	3 R	2 2B	2 RBI	5 BB			
1B	Lou Gehrig	.348	1 R	2 2B	4 RBI	5 BB			
RF	Babe Ruth	.300	6 R	4 HR	5 RBI	11 BB			
P	Herb Pennock	W 2	L 0	22 IP	13 H	3 ER	8 SO	1.23 ERA	
P	Waite Hoyt	W 1	L 1	15 IP	19 H	2 ER	10 SO	1.20 ERA	

MVP: none chosen
Hypothetical MVP: Grover Alexander
Winning Player's Share: $5,585
Losing Player's Share: $3,418

1942
ST. LOUIS CARDINALS OVER
NEW YORK YANKEES (4–1)

Top Performers
Cardinals

C	Walker Cooper	.286	3 R	1 2B	4 RBI			
3B	Whitey Kurowski	.267	3 R	1 3B	1 HR	5 RBI		
RF	Enos Slaughter	.263	3 R	1 2B	1 HR	2 RBI	3 BB	
P	Johnny Beazley	W 2	L 0	18 IP	17 H	5 ER	6 SO	2.50 ERA
P	Ernie White	W 1	L 0	9 IP	6 H	0 ER	6 SO	0.00 ERA

Yankees

CF	Joe DiMaggio	.333	3 R	3 RBI	
SS	Phil Rizzuto	.381	2 R	1 HR	1 RBI
3B	Red Rolfe	.353	5 R	2 2B	

MVP: none chosen
Hypothetical MVP: Johnny Beazley
Winning Player's Share: $6,193
Losing Player's Share: $3,352

1954
NEW YORK GIANTS OVER
CLEVELAND INDIANS (4–0)

Top Performers
Giants

PH/OF	Dusty Rhodes	.667	2 R	2 HR	7 RBI				
3B	Hank Thompson	.364	6 R	1 2B	2 RBI	7 BB			
CF	Willie Mays	.286	4 R	1 2B	3 RBI	4 BB			
P	Johnny Antonelli	W 1	L 0	1 SV	10.2 IP	8 H	1 ER	12 SO	0.84 ERA

Indians

1B	Vic Wertz	.500	2 R	2 2B	1 3B	1 HR	3 RBI

MVP: none chosen
Hypothetical MVP: Dusty Rhodes
Winning Player's Share: $11,118
Losing Player's Share: $6,713

1955
BROOKLYN DODGERS OVER
NEW YORK YANKEES (4–3)

Top Performers

Dodgers

CF	Duke Snider	.320	5 R	1 2B	4 HR	7 RBI		
1B	Gil Hodges	.292	2 R	1 HR	5 RBI			
C	Roy Campanella	.259	4 R	3 2B	2 HR	4 RBI		
P	Johnny Podres	W 2	L 0	18 IP	15 H	2 ER	10 SO	1.00 ERA

Yankees

C	Yogi Berra	.417	5 R	1 2B	1 HR	2 RBI		
2B	Billy Martin	.320	2 R	1 2B	1 3B	4 RBI		
P	Whitey Ford	W 2	L 0	17 IP	13 H	4 ER	10 SO	2.12 ERA

MVP: Johnny Podres
Winning Player's Share: $9,768
Losing Player's Share: $5,559

1960
PITTSBURGH PIRATES OVER
NEW YORK YANKEES (4–3)

Top Performers
Pirates

RF	Roberto Clemente	.310	1 R	3 RBI				
2B	Bill Mazeroski	.320	4 R	2 2B	2 HR	5 RBI		
P	Vern Law	W 2	L 0	18.1 IP	22 H	7 ER	8 SO	3.44 ERA
P	Harvey Haddix	W 2	L 0	7.1 IP	6 H	2 ER	6 SO	2.45 ERA

Yankees

2B	Bobby Richardson	.367	8 R	2 2B	2 3B	1 HR	12 RBI	
1B	Moose Skowron	.375	7 R	2 2B	2 HR	6 RBI		
C	Elston Howard	.462	4 R	1 2B	1 3B	1 HR	4 RBI	
CF	Mickey Mantle	.400	8 R	1 2B	3 HR	11 RBI	8 BB	
P	Whitey Ford	W 2	L 0	18 IP	11 H	0 ER	8 SO	0.00 ERA

MVP: Bobby Richardson
Winning Player's Share: $8,418
Losing Player's Share: $5,125

1969
NEW YORK METS OVER
BALTIMORE ORIOLES (4–1)

Top Performers

Mets

1B	Donn Clendenon	.357	4 R	1 2B	3 HR	4 RBI		
2B	Al Weis	.455	1 R	1 HR	3 RBI	4 BB		
P	Jerry Koosman	W 2	L 0	17.2 IP	7 H	4 ER	9 SO	2.04 ERA
P	Tom Seaver	W 1	L 1	15 IP	12 H	5 ER	9 SO	3.00 ERA

Orioles

P	Mike Cuellar	W 1	L 0	16 IP	13 H	2 ER	13 SO	1.13 ERA
P	Dave McNally	W 0	L 1	16 IP	11 H	5 ER	13 SO	2.81 ERA

MVP: Donn Clendenon
Winning Player's Share: $18,338
Losing Player's Share: $14,904

1971
PITTSBURGH PIRATES OVER
BALTIMORE ORIOLES (4–3)

Top Performers
Pirates

RF	Roberto Clemente	.414	3 R	2 2B	1 3B	2 HR	4 RBI
C	Manny Sanguillén	.379	3 R	1 2B			
P	Steve Blass	W 2	L 0	18 IP	7 H	2 ER	13 SO	1.00 ERA
P	Nelson Briles	W 1	L 0	9 IP	2 H	0 ER	2 SO	0.00 ERA

Orioles

3B	Brooks Robinson	.318	2 R	5 RBI	3 BB		
RF	Frank Robinson	.280	5 R	2 HR	2 RBI		
LF	Don Buford	.261	1 2B	2 HR	4 RBI	3 BB	
P	Jim Palmer	W 1	L 0	17 IP	15 H	5 ER	15 SO	2.65 ERA
P	Dave McNally	W 2	L 1	13.2 IP	10 H	3 ER	12 SO	1.98 ERA

MVP: Roberto Clemente
Winning Player's Share: $18,165
Losing Player's Share: $13,906

1985
KANSAS CITY ROYALS OVER
ST. LOUIS CARDINALS (4–3)

Top Performers

Royals

3B	George Brett	.370	5 R	1 2B	1 RBI	4 BB		
LF	Lonnie Smith	.333	4 R	3 2B	4 RBI	3 BB		
CF	Willie Wilson	.367	2 R	1 3B	3 RBI			
P	Bret Saberhagen	W 2	L 0	18 IP	11 H	1 ER	10 SO	0.50 ERA
P	Danny Jackson	W 1	L 1	16 IP	9 H	3 ER	12 SO	1.69 ERA

Cardinals

LF	Tito Landrum	.360	3 R	2 2B	1 HR	1 RBI		
1B	Jack Clark	.240	1 R	2 2B	4 RBI	3 BB		
P	Danny Cox	W 0	L 0	14 IP	14 H	2 ER	13 SO	1.29 ERA
P	John Tudor	W 2	L 1	18 IP	15 H	6 ER	14 SO	3.00 ERA

MVP: Bret Saberhagen
Winning Player's Share: $76,342
Losing Player's Share: $54,922

1987
MINNESOTA TWINS OVER
ST. LOUIS CARDINALS (4–3)

Top Performers

Twins

CF	Kirby Puckett	.357	5 R	1 2B	1 3B	3 RBI			
2B	Steve Lombardozzi	.412	3 R	1 2B	1 HR	4 RBI			
LF	Dan Gladden	.290	3 R	2 2B	1 3B	1 HR	7 RBI	3 BB	
C	Tim Laudner	.318	4 R	1 2B	1 HR	4 RBI	5 BB		
P	Frank Viola	W 2	L 1	19.1 IP	17 H	8 ER	16 SO	3.72 ERA	
P	Bert Blyleven	W 1	L 1	13 IP	13 H	4 ER	12 SO	2.77 ERA	

Cardinals

CF	Willie McGee	.370	2 R	2 2B	4 RBI				
C	Tony Pena	.409	2 R	1 2B	4 RBI	3 BB			
P	Todd Worrell	W 0	L 0	2 SV	7 IP	6 H	1 ER	3 SO	1.29 ERA

MVP: Frank Viola
Winning Player's Share: $85,581
Losing Player's Share: $56,053

1988
LOS ANGELES DODGERS OVER
OAKLAND A's (4–1)

Top Performers
Dodgers

LF	Mickey Hatcher	.368	5 R	1 2B	2 HR	5 RBI		
RF	Mike Marshall	.231	2 R	1 3B	1 HR	3 RBI		
P	Orel Hershiser	W 2	L 0	18 IP	7 H	2 ER	17 SO	1.00 ERA

A's

CF	Dave Henderson	.300	1 R	2 2B	1 RBI		
P	Dave Stewart	W 0	L 1	14.1 IP	12 H	5 ER	5 SO	3.14 ERA

MVP: Orel Hershiser
Winning Player's Share: $108,665
Losing Player's Share: $86,223

1990
CINCINNATI REDS OVER
OAKLAND ATHLETICS (4–0)

Top Performers
Reds

3B	Chris Sabo	.563	2 R	1 2B	2 HR	5 RBI		
SS	Barry Larkin	.353	3 R	1 2B	1 3B	1 RBI		
C	Joe Oliver	.333	2 R	3 2B	2 RBI			
LF	Eric Davis	.286	3 R	1 HR	5 RBI			
P	José Rijo	W 2	L 0	15.1 IP	9 H	1 ER	14 SO	0.59 ERA
P	Rob Dibble	W 0	L 0	4.2 IP	3 H	0 ER	4 SO	0.00 ERA

A's

LF	Rickey Henderson	.333	2 R	2 2B	1 HR	1 RBI	3 BB	
P	Dave Stewart	W 0	L 2	13 IP	10 H	5 ER	5 SO	3.46 ERA

MVP: José Rijo
Winning Player's Share: $112,534
Losing Player's Share: $86,961

1997
FLORIDA MARLINS OVER
NEW YORK YANKEES (4–3)

Top Performers

Marlins

1B	Darren Daulton	.389	7 R	2 2B	1 HR	2 RBI	3 BB		
C	Charles Johnson	.357	4 R	1 HR	3 RBI				
LF	Moises Alou	.321	6 R	2 2B	3 HR	9 RBI	3 BB		
RF	Gary Sheffield	.292	4 R	1 2B	1 HR	5 RBI	8 BB		
P	Livan Hernandez	W 2	L 0	13.2 IP	15 H	8 ER	7 SO	5.27 ERA	

Indians

2B	Tony Fernandez	.471	1 R	1 2B	4 RBI				
3B	Matt Williams	.385	1 2B	1 HR	3 RBI	7 BB			
C	Sandy Alomar Jr.	.367	5 R	1 2B	2 HR	10 RBI			
1B	Jim Thome	.286	8 R	1 3B	2 HR	4 RBI	5 BB		
P	Chad Ogea	W 2	L 0	11.2 IP	11 H	2 ER	5 SO	1.54 ERA	
P	Jaret Wright	W 1	L 0	12.1 IP	7 H	4 ER	12 SO	2.92 ERA	

MVP: Livan Hernandez
Winning Player's Share: $279,260
Losing Player's Share: $201,014

2001
ARIZONA DIAMONDBACKS OVER
NEW YORK YANKEES (4–3)

Top Performers
Diamondbacks

OF/DH	Danny Bautista	.583	1 R	2 2B		7 RBI		
CF	Steve Finley	.368	5R		1 HR	2 RBI	4 BB	
3B	Matt Williams	.269	3 R	2 2B	1 HR	7 RBI		
LF	Luis Gonzalez	.259	4 R	2 2B	1 HR	5 RBI		
P	Randy Johnson	W 3	L 0	17.1 IP	9 H	2 ER	19 SO	1.04 ERA
P	Curt Schilling	W 1	L 0	21.1 IP	12 H	4 ER	26 SO	1.69 ERA

Yankees

RF	Paul O'Neill	.333	1 R	1 2B				
P	Roger Clemens	W 1	L 0	13.1 IP	10 H	2 ER	19 SO	1.35 ERA
P	Mariano Rivera	W 1	L 1	SV 1	6.1 IP	6 H	1 ER	7 SO	1.42 ERA

MVP: Randy Johnson and Curt Schilling
Winning Player's Share: $188,468
Losing Player's Share: $113,226

2003
FLORIDA MARLINS OVER
NEW YORK YANKEES (4–2)

Top Performers
Marlins

LF	Jeff Conine	.333	4 R	1 2B	3 BB			
CF	Juan Pierre	.333	2 R	2 2B	3 RBI	5 BB		
P	Josh Beckett	W 1	L 1	16.1 IP	8 H	2 ER	19 SO	1.10 ERA
P	Brad Penny	W 2	L 0	12.1 IP	15 H	3 ER	7 SO	2.19 ERA

Yankees

SS	Derek Jeter	.346	5 R	3 2B	2 RBI			
CF	Bernie Williams	.400	5 R	2 2B	2 HR	5 RBI		
P	Andy Pettitte	W 1	L 1	15.2 IP	12 H	1 ER	14 SO	0.57 ERA
P	Mike Mussina	W 1	L 0	7 IP	7 H	1 ER	9 SO	1.29 ERA

MVP: Josh Beckett
Winning Player's Share: $306,150
Losing Player's Share: $180,890

2006
ST. LOUIS CARDINALS
OVER DETROIT TIGERS (4–1)

Top Performers
Cardinals

3B	Scott Rolen	.421	5 R	3 2B	1 HR	2 RBI		
SS	David Eckstein	.364	3 R	3 2B	4 RBI			
C	Yadier Molina	.412	3 R	2 2B	1 RBI	3 BB		
P	Chris Carpenter	W 1	L 0	8 IP	3 H	6 SO	0 ER	0.00 ERA
P	Jeff Weaver	W 1	L 1	13 IP	13 H	4 ER	14 SO	2.77 ERA

Tigers

1B/DH	Sean Casey	.529	2 R	2 2B	2 HR	5 RBI	
SS	Carlos Guillén	.353	2 R	1 2B	2 RBI	3 BB	
3B	Brandon Inge	.353	2 2B	1 RBI			
P	Kenny Rogers	W 1	L 0	8 IP	2 H	0 ER	5 SO	0.00 ERA

MVP: David Eckstein
Winning Player's Share: $362,173
Losing Player's Share: $291,668

2011
ST. LOUIS CARDINALS OVER
TEXAS RANGERS (4–3)

Top Performers

Cardinals

3B	David Freese	.348	4 R	3 2B	1 3B	1 HR	7 RBI	5 BB	
C	Yadier Molina	.333	1 R	2 2B	9 RBI	4 BB			
RF	Lance Berkman	.423	9 R	1 2B	5 RBI	5 BB			
P	Chris Carpenter	W 2	L 0	19 IP	17 H	6 ER	13 SO	2.84 ERA	
P	Jaime Garcia	W 0	L 0	10 IP	8 H	2 ER	10 SO	1.80 ERA	

Rangers

3B	Adrián Beltré	.300	5 R	2 2B	2 HR	3 RBI		
2B	Ian Kinsler	.360	2 R	1 2B	2 RBI	7 BB		
C/1B	Mike Napoli	.350	2 R	1 2B	2 HR	10 RBI	6 BB	
P	Derek Holland	W 1	L 0	10.1 IP	4 H	1 ER	7 SO	0.87 ERA

MVP: David Freese
Winning Player's Share: $323,170
Losing Player's Share: $251,516

2019
WASHINGTON NATIONALS
OVER ASTROS (4–3)

Top Performers
Nationals

LF	Juan Soto	.333	6 R	2 2B	3 HR	7 RBI	5 BB	
RF	Adam Eaton	.320	5 R	2 HR		6 RBI	4 BB	
3B	Anthony Rendon	.276	3 R	3 2B	2 HR	8 RBI	3 BB	
P	Stephen Strasburg	W 2	L 0	14.1 IP	12 H	4 ER	14 SO	2.51 ERA
P	Patrick Corbin	W 1	L 1	10 IP	10 H	4 ER	10 SO	3.60 ERA

Astros

DH	Yordan Álvarez	.412	2 R	1 HR	2 RBI	4 BB		
1B	Yuli Gurriel	.310	3 R	2 2B	1 HR	5 RBI		
OF	George Springer	.296	6 R	4 2B	2 HR	4 RBI	7 BB	
2B	Jose Altuve	.303	4 R	3 2B	1 RBI			
P	Zack Greinke	W 0	L 0	11 IP	9 H	3 ER	9 SO	2.45 ERA

MVP: Stephen Strasburg
Winning Player's Share: $382,358
Losing Player's Share: $256,030

Bibliography

"1903: The First World Series." *This Great Game: The Online Book of Baseball.* https:// thisgreatgame.com/1903-baseball-history/.

"1906: The Hitless Wonders." *This Great Game: The Online Book of Baseball.* https:// thisgreatgame.com/1906-baseball-history/.

"1919 World Series." *Baseball Almanac.* https://www.baseball-almanac.com/ws/yr1919ws .shtml.

"1926 World Series." *Baseball-Reference Bullpen.* https://www.baseball-reference.com/ bullpen/1926_World_Series.

"1927: The Yankee Juggernaut." *This Great Game: The Online Book of Baseball.* https:// thisgreatgame.com/1927-baseball-history/.

"1960 Pirates Remember History-Making World Series 60 Years Later." WPXI News, October 13, 2020.

"1960 World Series." *Baseball-Reference Bullpen.* https://www.baseball-reference.com/ bullpen/1960_World_Series.

"1971 World Series | Game 7, Pirates at Orioles." Posted by Pittsburgh Pirates. Streamed live on May 19, 2020. YouTube video. https://www.youtube.com/watch ?v=phQ7wUGOawo.

"1971 World Series." *Baseball Almanac.* https://www.baseball-almanac.com/ws/yr1971ws .shtml.

"1985 World Series." *Baseball Almanac.* https://www.baseball-almanac.com/ws/yr1985was .shtml.

"1985 World Series: The Wild and Crazy Complete Story of the Kansas City Royals Unlikely Win." FOX Sports, October 29, 2015.

"1988 World Series." *Baseball-Reference Bullpen.* https://www.baseball-reference.com/ bullpen/1988_World_Series.

"2006 World Series Film-Full." YouTube video. https://www.youtube.com/watch?v =IONnVuWnNsM.

"2006 World Series, Game 5: Tigers @ Cardinals." YouTube video. https://www.youtube .com/watch?v=nhl_cl4tp2k.

"Aaron Boone Is Poised to Produce More Yankee Miracles." *New York Post*, December 6, 2017.

Almasy, Steve. "World Series Game 7: Washington Nationals Defeat Houston Astros to Clinch First World Series." CNN, October 31, 2019.

Baccellieri, Emma. "Nationals' World Series Run on the Brink After Game of Close—and Missed—Calls." *Sports Illustrated*, October 28, 2019.

Balazs, Rick. "Jim Hegan." Society for American Research Biography Project. https://sabr.org/bioproj/person/Jim-Hegan/.

Bernstein, Dan. "Astros Cheating Scandal Timeline, from the First Sign-Stealing Allegations to a Controversial Punishment." *The Sporting News*, July 24, 2020.

Borders, William. "Paper Blizzard Wraps City in Blanket of Joy." *New York Times*, October 17, 1969.

"Boston Takes Third Game 5–4, in 12th Inning." *New York Times*, October 13, 1914.

"Braves Victory Crowning Upset of Athletic Year." *Philadelphia Evening Ledger*, October 14, 1914.

"Casey Stengel Quotes." *Baseball Almanac*. https://www.baseball-almanac.com/quotes/quosteng/shtml.

"Connie Mack." National Baseball Hall of Fame. https://baseballhall.org/hall-of-famers/mack-connie.

Corbett, Warren. "Dusty Rhodes." Society for American Baseball Research Biography Project. https://sabr.org/bioproj/person/Dusty-Rhodes/.

Crane, Andrew. "Pedro Martinez Reveals Story of Infamous Don Zimmer Brawl." *New York Post*, October 15, 2021.

Daley, Arthur. "Sports of the Times: The Psychic Durocher Clicks." *New York Times*, September 30, 1954.

DeGregorio, George. *Joe DiMaggio: An Informal Biography*. New York: Scarborough Books, 1983.

Drebinger, John. "Dodgers Capture First World Series, Podres Wins, 2–0." *New York Times*, October 5, 1955.

———. "Pirates Win, 10–9, Capturing Series on Homer in Ninth." *New York Times*, October 14, 1960.

Durocher, Leo, with Ed Linn. *Nice Guys Finish Last*. Chicago: University of Chicago Press, 2009.

Enders, Eric. *The Fall Classic: The Definitive History of the World Series*. New York: Sterling Publishing, 2007.

"Ericson Admits to Adjusting Ventilation System." ESPN, July 26, 2003.

Evers, John J. "Four Straight Evers Predicts." *New York Times*, October 13, 1914.

Faber, Charles F. "Freddie Lindstrom." Society for American Baseball Research Biography Project. https://sabr.org/bioproj/person/Freddie-Lindstrom.

Fay, John. "Billy Bates Only Had a Moment with the Reds—But, Oh, What a Moment." *Cincinnati Enquirer*, May 15, 2020.

Fletcher, David. "Buck Weaver." Society for American Baseball Research Biography Project. https://sabr.org/bioproj/person/buck-weaver/.

Ford, Whitey, with Phil Pepe. *Few and Chosen: Defining Yankee Greatness Across the Eras*. Chicago: Triumph Books, 2001.

Frisaro, Joe. "1997 Marlins: Wild Card to World Series Champs." MLB, June 26, 2017.

———. "Remembering Marlins' 1997 World Series Championship." *Palm Beach Post*, May 14, 2022.

"George Brett Quotes." *Baseball Almanac*. https://www.baseball-almanac.com/quotes/quobrett/shtml.

Gonzales, Richard, and Mark Katlov. "Nationals Beat the Astros 12–3 in Game 2 of the 2019 World Series." NPR, October 23, 2019.

Gonzalez, Alden. "Gibson, Eck Recall Famous Home Run at Torre's Event." MLB, April 29, 2016.

Hensler, Paul. "Dave Henderson." Society for American Baseball Research Biography Project. https://www.sabr.org/bioproj/person/Dave-Henderson/.

Herzog, Whitey, and Keven Harrigan. *White Rat: A Life in Baseball*. New York: Harper & Row, 1987.

Hirsch, James S. *Willie Mays: The Life, the Legend*. New York: Scribner & Sons, 2010.

Honig, Donald. *The New York Mets: The First Quarter Century*. New York: Crown Publishing Group, 1987.

"Howie Kendrick Crushes 10th Inning Grand Slam as Nationals Win First Postseason Series, Advance to NLCS." *Sports Illustrated*, October 10, 2019.

Hruby, Patrick. "The Long, Strange Trip of Dock Ellis." ESPN, August 24, 2012.

James, Bill, and Rob Neyer. *The Neyer James Guide to Pitchers: An Historical Compendium of Pitching, Pitchers, and Pitches*. New York: Fireside Books, 2004.

James, Bill. *The New Historical Baseball Abstract*. New York: Free Press, 2003.

"Jim Palmer Quotes." *Baseball Almanac*. https://www.baseball-almanac.com/quotes/quopalm.shtml.

"Joe DiMaggio Quotes." Official Joe DiMaggio Fan Site. https://www.joedimaggio.com/the-legacy/quotes-about-joe/.

Keraghosian, Greg. "This World Series Game 30 Years Ago Marked the Beginning of the End for the A's Dynasty." *San Francisco Chronicle*, October 24, 2020.

Krell, David. "Johnny Podres." Society for American Baseball Research Biography Project. https://sabr.org/bioproj/person/Johnny-Podres/.

Levitt, Daniel R. "Pat Moran." Society for American Baseball Research Biography Project. https://sabr.org/bioproj/person/Pat-Moran.

Lindner, Dan. "Kid Gleason." Society for American Baseball Research Biography Project. https://sabr.og/bioproj/person/kid-gleason/.

Macht, Norman. "Jack Barry." Society for American Baseball Research Biography Project. https://sabr.org/bioproj/person/Jack-Barry/.

Madden, Bill. "Tony LaRussa Still Reminisces on 1988 World Series; Rangers' Mike Adams Underwent Culture Shock." *New York Daily News*, October 21, 2011.

Mantle, Mickey, with Mickey Herskowitz. *All My Octobers: My Memories of 12 World Series When the Yankees Ruled Baseball*. New York: HarperCollins, 1994.

"Mariano Rivera Quotes." *Baseball Almanac*. https://www.baseball-almanac.com/quotes/mariano_rivera_quotes.shtml.

McCann, Dick. "Cards Win, 4–2, Take Series." *New York Daily News*, December 6, 1942.

McDonald, Anna. "Postseason Highlight and Heartache: 1997 Cleveland Indians." ESPN, October 7, 2016.

McGowen, Roscoe. "Stars' Play Fails to Surprise Pilot." *New York Times*, September 30, 1954.

Miller, Doug. "Denkinger Cool with Reminders of Mistaken Call in '85 World Series." MLB, October 20, 2014. Retrieved January 1, 2023.

"Miller Huggins." National Baseball Hall of Fame. https://basebalhall.org/hall-of-famer /huggins-miller.

Mitchell, Houston. "Greatest Moment in Dodger History No. 1: Kirk Gibson's World Series Home Run." *Los Angeles Times*, April 30, 2016.

"MLB 1987 World Series Highlights." Posted by Luigi Aguilera on April 21, 2016. YouTube video. www.youtube.com/watch?v=byj9d31Ic_w.

Montville, Leigh. *The Big Bam: The Life and Times of Babe Ruth*. New York: Doubleday, 2006.

"Mordecai Brown." *Baseball-Reference Bullpen*. https://www.baseball-reference.com/ bullpen/Mordecai_Brown.

Mulder, Craig. "President Roosevelt Gives 'Green Light' to Baseball." National Baseball Hall of Fame. https://baseballhall.org/discover/inside-pitch/roosevelt-sendsgreen -light-letter.

National Baseball Hall of Fame and Museum. *The Hall: A Celebration of Baseball's Greats*. New York: Little, Brown and Company, 2014.

Nelson, Amy R. "Tony LaRussa Argues, Wins." ESPN, October 2, 2011.

Nemec, David, and Saul Wisnia. *100 Years of Major League Baseball: American and National Leagues 1901–2000*. Lincolnwood, IL: Publications International Ltd., 2000.

"Nolan Ryan." *Baseball-Reference Bullpen*. https://www.baseball-reference.com/bullpen/ Nolan_Ryan.

Nowlin, Bill. "Tom Brunansky." Society for American Baseball Research Biography Project. https://sabr.org/bioproj/person/tom-brunansky/.

Olney, Buster. "Epilogue: The Last Night of the Yankee Dynasty." ESPN, May 3, 2005.

"Ozzie Smith." National Baseball Hall of Fame and Museum. https://baseballhall.org/ hall-of-famers/smith-ozzie.

Perry, Danny. *We Played the Game: Memories of Baseball's Greatest Era*. New York: Black Do & Leventhal Publishers, 1994.

Peterson, Lindsey. "Twins Win 1987 World Series: Remembering That Day 35 Years Later with Kent Hrbek." WCCO Radio Indianapolis, October 25, 2022.

Peterson, Richard. *The St. Louis Baseball Reader*. Columbia, MO: University of Missouri Press, 2006.

Pietrusza, David, Matthew Silverman, and Michael Gershman. *Baseball: The Biographical Encyclopedia*. Toronto, Canada: Sport Publishing, 2003.

Piniella, Lou, and Bill Madden. *Lou: Fifty Years of Kicking Dirt, Playing Hard, and Winning Big in the Sweet Spot of Baseball*. New York: HarperCollins, 2017.

Posada, Jorge, with Gary Brozek. *The Journey Home: My Life in Pinstripes*. New York: HarperCollins, 2015.

"Rabbit Maranville." National Baseball Hall of Fame. https://baseballhall.org/hall-of -famers/maranville-rabbit.

Rappaport, Ken. *Bobby Bonilla*. New York: Walker and Company, 1993.

"Remember the 'David Freese Game'? We Do." MLB, October 27, 2021.

Richter, Francis C. "Philadelphia News." *Sporting Life*, August 5, 1905.

Ritter, Lawrence. *The Glory of Their Times: The Story of Early Days of Baseball Told by the Men Who Played It.* New York: MacMillan Co., 1966.

Rivera, Mariano, with Wayne Coffey. *The Closer: My Story.* New York: Little, Brown and Company, 2014.

"Roberto Clemente Quotes." *Baseball Almanac.* https://www.baseball-almanac.com/quotes/Roberto_clemente_quotes.shtml.

Robinson, Jackie, with Alfred Duckett. *I Never Had It Made: An Autobiography of Jackie Robinson.* New York: HarperCollins, 1995.

"Rogers Hornsby Quotes." *Baseball Almanac.* https://www.baseball-alamanc.com/quotes/quohorn.shtml.

"Ross Youngs." National Baseball Hall of Fame. https://baseballhall.org/hall-of-fame/youngs-ross.

Saccoman, John. "Gil Hodges." Society for American Baseball Research Biography Project. https://sabr.org/bioproj/person/Gil-Hodges/.

"Sandy Amoros Gives Simple Explanation." *New York Times,* October 5, 1955.

Schmuck, Peter. "Leyland Makes Rogers Call Without a Smudge of Doubt." *Baltimore Sun,* October 28, 2006.

Sheldon, Mark. "Brennaman Recalls 'Unimaginable' 1990 Reds." MLB, April 29, 2020.

———. "Classic Seasons." MLB, February 7, 2022.

Shyer, Brent. "1955 Dodger World Championship Is One for the Ages." Walter O'Malley biographical website. https://www.walteromalley.com/en/features/1955-dodger-world-championship-one-for-the-ages/introduction/. Retrieved December 11, 2022.

"Smudgegate Verdict Is In." *Sarasota Herald-Tribune,* October 24, 2006.

Stark, Jayson. "Albert Pujols Messes with Texas." ESPN, October 22, 2011.

"St. Louis Cardinals Win 2011 World Series." Posted by Luke. October 29, 2011, YouTube video. 12:54. https://youtube.com/watch?v=fNEWmrcpmBY.

Stout, Glenn. *Yankees Century: 100 Years of New York Yankees Baseball.* New York: Houghton Mifflin, 2002.

Swaine, Rick. "Roy Campanella." Society for American Baseball Research Biography Project. https://sabr.org/bioproj/person/roycampanella/.

Terrell, Roy. "Beat 'Em Bucs." *Sports Illustrated,* October 3, 1960.

"Tinker to Evers to Chance. Baseball's Sad Lexicon by Franklin Pierce Adams." *Baseball Almanac.* https://www.baseball-almanac.com/poetry/po_sad.shtml.

"Tom Seaver Stats." *Baseball Almanac.* https://www.baseball-almanac.com/players/player.php?p=seaveto01.

"Tony La Russa Fined for TV Comments." ESPN, October 4, 2011.

Torre, Joe, with Tom Verducci. *The Yankee Years.* New York: Doubleday, 2009.

"Ty Cobb Quote." *Baseball Almanac.* https://www.baseball-alamanc.com/quotes/quocobb.shtml.

Vorperian, John. "Tommie Agee." Society for American Baseball Research Biography Project. https://www.sabr.org/bioproj/person/tommie-agee/.

Waldo, Ronald T. *Baseball's Roaring Twenties.* Lanham, MD: Rowman & Littlefield, 2017.

Waldstein, David, and Bernie Hoffman. "How the Nationals Won Game 1 of the World Series." *New York Times*, October 22, 2019.

"Walter Johnson Quotes." *Baseball Almanac*. https://www.baseball-almanac.com/quotes /quojhns.shtml.

Wancho, Joseph. "Ossie Bluege." Society for American Baseball Research Biography Project. https://sabr.org/bioproj/person/Ossie-Bluege/.

Weber, Bruce. "Earl Weaver, a Volatile, Visionary Manager, Dies at 82." *New York Times*, January 19, 2013.

Wheeler, Lonnie. "Schott Just Kept Shooting Herself in the Foot." ESPN, September 17, 1999.

"Why the Washington Nationals Were Once Known as the Senators." United States Senate. https://www.senate.gov/artandhistory/minute/Washington_Nationals _Once_Known_as_Senators.htm.

"Willie Mays Quotes." *Baseball Almanac*. https://www.baseball-almanac.com/quotes/ quomays.shtml.

"Willie Stargell." National Baseball Hall of Fame and Museum. https://baseballhall.org/ hall-of-famers/stargell-willie.

"Yanks Win Title; 6–4 Victory Ends $1,063, 815 Series." *New York Times*, October 16, 1923.

"Yogi Berra Quotes." *Baseball Almanac*. https://www.baseball-almanac.com/quotes/ quoberra.shtml.

"Zack Greinke Calls Out Chris Carpenter." ESPN, October 8, 2011.